Crimes of Colour

Crimes of Colour:
Racialization and the Criminal
Justice System in Canada

EDITED BY
Wendy Chan and
Kiran Mirchandani

broadview press

NATIONAL LIBRARY OF CANADA CATALOGUING IN PUBLICATION DATA

Main entry under title:
   Crimes of colour : racialization and the criminal justice system in Canada

Includes bibliographical references and index
ISBN 1-55111-303-1

1. Crime and race — Canada.
2. Discrimination in criminal justice administration — Canada.
I. Mirchandani, Kiran, 1968-   II. Chan, Wendy, 1966-

HV9960.C2C72 2001   364'.089'00971   C2001-901569-0

BROADVIEW PRESS, LTD.
is an independent, international publishing house, incorporated in 1985.

North America
Post Office Box 1243,
Peterborough, Ontario,
Canada K9J 7H5
Tel: (705) 743-8990
Fax: (705) 743-8353

3576 California Road,
Orchard Park, New York
USA 14127

customerservice@broadviewpress.com
www.broadviewpress.com

United Kingdom
Thomas Lyster, Ltd.
Unit 9, Ormskirk Industrial Park
Old Boundary Way, Burscough Rd.
Ormskirk, Lancashire L39 2YW
Tel: (01695) 575112
Fax: (01695) 570120
books@tlyster.co.uk

Australia
St. Clair Press
P.O. Box 287, Rozelle, NSW 2039
Tel: (612) 818-1942
Fax: (612) 418-1923

Broadview Press gratefully acknowledges the financial support
of the Book Publishing Industry Development Program,
Ministry of Canadian Heritage, Government of Canada.

Cover design by Zack Taylor. Typeset by Zack Taylor.

Printed in Canada

Contents

Preface

This volume originated out of a shared interest in critical rather than descriptive approaches to understanding how racial identities are constructed in the criminal justice system. We were frustrated with assumptions of neutrality and felt that there had been a failure to consider processes of racialization in discussions of crime and of the function and operations of the criminal justice system in Canada. And so we embarked on the search for alternatives, and developed alliances and working relationships with the authors whose work appears in this collection. Through their work, and our interactions with one another, we have learned not only about our topic, but also about cross-disciplinary communication, collegiality, trust, and friendship. This has been a truly equal collaboration; the names of the editors appear in alphabetical order.

We would like to thank our research assistants at OISE/UT, Janice Cripps Picheca and Gurpreet Singh Gohal, who contributed greatly to the final production of this manuscript. We are also indebted to the reviewers who provided us with critical feedback, the editors at Broadview Press, and each of the authors whose work appears in this collection.

WENDY CHAN
School of Criminology, Simon Fraser University.

KIRAN MIRCHANDANI
Ontario Institute for Studies in Education,
University of Toronto (OISE/UT).

1

From Race and Crime to Racialization and Criminalization

KIRAN MIRCHANDANI AND WENDY CHAN

Introduction

In the fall of 1999, a decision by the Supreme Court of Canada to enforce an Aboriginal treaty right to catch fish out of season for subsistence and to earn a "moderate income" gave rise to what was widely reported as an "East Coast Fish War." In the midst of the controversy, a letter by Michelle Hill (of the Tyendinaga Mohawk Territory, Deseronto) was published in the *Toronto Star* (9 Oct. 1999). She wrote: "Once again, The Star reports with a slant an incident involving the aboriginal community of this country. It is a shame when newsworthy events are printed with a subliminal message." That "subliminal message" is the topic of this collection. We are concerned with questioning and challenging "subliminal messages" found in the justice system. While there has been increasing interest in race and crime in Canada, most discussions so far have not focused on the dynamics through which individuals and groups are racialized, and the ways in which the racialization of specific groups is implicit in processes of criminalization. The essays in this book explore the merging of racialization with criminalization within the context of Canada's economic, social, and cultural landscape.

A brief review follows of attempts that have been made to link race and crime in the Canadian literature. We argue that much of this literature has viewed the category of "race" as unproblematical, allowing debate to focus on the assumed propensity of members of certain groups to commit crime. The utility of the systematic collection of statistics on the racial origins of offenders is therefore assumed. We then draw on the work of Robert Miles, Floya Anthias, Stephen Small, and others to discuss the need for a shift from an analysis of "race" to an analysis of "racialization." Similarly, we argue for the need to examine the processes of "criminalization" through an exploration of the connections between crime, the state, and criminalization. We suggest how such shifts would create the space for new ways of looking at the connections between race and crime in Canada. Finally, we provide an overview of the chapters in this collection that consider various connections between the processes of racialization and criminalization.

Race and Crime Research in Canada

A review of the literature on race and crime in Canada suggests that much of it offers empirical, quantitative discussions about the relationship between race and crime.

The events during the late 1980s and early 1990s at Oka, Quebec, and in Ontario involving the use of provincial police to quell Aboriginal protest has sparked a lively discussion about the way in which racialized groups are policed in Canada, with the mounting evidence that certain groups are "over-policed" or heavily surveilled and, hence, tend to find themselves more frequently caught up in the criminal justice system (Anderson, 1990; Jackson, 1994; Mosher, 1996; O'Reilly-Fleming, 1994; Ungerleider, 1994). Police relations with Aboriginal groups and other racialized groups are seen to be saddled with conflict, distrust, and bias. These sentiments have been further exacerbated by police shootings of suspects in jurisdictions across the country. Attempts to improve police-community relations through various task forces and public inquiries often serve merely to further highlight the negative sentiments many communities hold towards the police force (Ontario, 1989).

Another prominent theme in current Canadian debates is the focus on the extent of crime committed by racialized groups, particularly "Black" people, and their treatment in the criminal justice system. Henry, Hastings, and Freer's (1996) study of public perceptions of race and criminality highlights how criminal activities are racialized and the effects of these perceptions on the treatment of Black offenders in the justice system. Other writers have attempted to unpack a race-crime relationship by focusing on various types of crimes, such as homicide (Moyer, 1992); exploring and explaining differences in crime rates among racialized groups (Cheung, 1980; Hagan, 1985; Gordon and Nelson, 1996); and examining the treatment of black offenders in the justice system (Doob, 1994;

Mosher, 1996). All these studies use quantitative data primarily or exclusively to elaborate their discussions and many conclude that the relevance of "race" is significant in understanding who is involved in criminality and how their treatment is mediated by "racial characteristics."

Finally, there has also been an energetic debate within this literature on whether or not statistics on race and ethnicity should be collected and published. Julian Roberts's contribution in this volume is testimony to the ongoing discussions that were first sparked in the print media and gained ever greater momentum through the publication of articles in a 1994 issue of the *Canadian Journal of Criminology*. The various positions taken in this issue concern how such statistics would be used and for what purposes. The desire not to exacerbate discrimination against racialized minorities is of key concern to many who opposed the collection of race statistics, as are the methodological problems of how people have been racially categorized (Hatt, 1994; Johnston, 1994). Proponents of gathering race statistics claim that suppressing this type of information violates the public's right of access to such information (Gabor, 1994). Judging that the harms do not outweigh the gains to be made from having access, such information should be made publicly available. Roberts (1994) argues for a compromise approach through periodic gathering of race statistics under special circumstances. Such an approach would ensure that safeguards are in place to prevent the abuse of this information while also making it possible to have access to race statistics.

From this brief overview, it is clear that the topic of "race" and crime in Canadian criminological writings has given priority to an empirical focus. More theoretical accounts have tended to be taken up by critical race scholars working outside of criminology. Although the contributions thus far have sustained interest in this area of study, much of the work has remained within a "race relations" framework and there is a paucity of work that challenges our understanding of how "race" is problematized in relation to crime. This collection represents an attempt to move beyond the uncritical acceptance of the concepts of "race" and "race relations" within the Canadian criminological literature to "render primary, contentious and problematic notions which are often treated as secondary, noncontentious and unproblematic" (Small, 1994:34).

From Race to Racialization and Crime to Criminalization

THE PROCESSES OF RACIALIZATION

"Race," within much of Canadian criminology to date, is rarely defined; when it is, it is conceptualized as a "trait" possessed by individuals and groups. In order to move towards an understanding of "race" as a process rather than a trait, we argue for the need for a shift in the debate from "race" to "racialization."

Robert Miles defines "racialization" as a "process of categorization through which social relations between people [are] structured by the signification of human biological characteristics in such a way as to define and construct differentiated social collectivities" (1989:75). The focus on process draws attention to the occurrence of continuous and ongoing acts that relate systematically to one another to produce difference and hierarchy. It also highlights the historical influences of colonization and conquest in shaping the ideological frameworks developed around categories of "race" (Small, 1999). Processes of characterization take place through representations (symbols, images), micro-interactions (norms, stereotypes), and social structures through which resources are allocated (Glenn, 1999:9). Within such an approach, discussions of crime are situated within understandings of how racialized identities are constructed and reconstructed through media images rather than merely represent individuals' actions (Van Dijk, 1988); how discourses of crime form and enact racial hierarchies; and how the criminalization of certain racialized groups is intrinsically situated within and connected to class and gender positions normalized through a variety of social structures and institutions.

The focus on processes of racialization also draws attention to the ways in which connections between race and crime are neither universal nor fixed. Small argues that the notion of racialization provides greater analytical strength for two reasons. First, it "emphasizes the continuing need to see the intricate relationship between 'racial' meanings and other (economic, political, religious) meanings" (1994:36). Second, unlike the focus on race relations, which "assumes that 'races' exist and seeks to understand relations between them," it focuses on "how groups not previously defined as 'races' have come to be defined in this way and assesses the various factors involved in such processes" (1994:30).

Such an analysis allows for the exploration of the ways in which connections between "race" and crime are as much about the characterization of an "other" as they are about the characterization of "self." Anthias (1998a:558) notes that the use of terms such as "ethnic minority" masks the fact that dominant groups, too, possess ethnicities. Miles (1989:75) makes a similar point, arguing that European explorers who used skin colour to define Africans as "Black" in fact differentiated themselves in terms of skin colour as well. "Black" and "White" "were bound together, each giving meaning to the other." As Small (1994:30) summarizes, "the problem is not 'race' but 'racisms', not relations between 'races' but relations which have been racialized, not the physical attributes of Blacks or their presumed inferiority, but the motivations of non-Blacks, and the obstacles they impose." The focus on racialization allows for a consideration of the ways in which individuals and groups can be understood as racialized only vis-à-vis one another and in particular historical and geographical contexts. Again, according to Miles, "Racialization refers to the historical emergence of the idea of 'race' and to its subsequent reproduction and application" (1989:76). This suggests that the criminalization of certain racialized groups within the Canadian context can be understood, first, in light of the ways in which White, majority groups have been constructed as race-less, and second, within the context of historical relations between First Nations people, early settlers, and recent immigrants and migrants.

Conceptualizing racialization as a process also allows for an analysis of how "privilege and oppression are often not absolute categories but, rather, shift in relation to different axes of power and powerlessness" (Friedman, 1995:114). Racialization is part of a broader process whereby "categories of the population are constructed, differentiated, inferiorized and excluded" (Anthias, 1998b:7). Processes of racialization, economic inequality, gendering, and criminalization are fundamentally interlocked and inseparable; at the same time the exact meaning and configuration of these processes depend on the local, historically specific contexts within which they exist (Razack, 1998). Bhavani and Coulson (1986:84-89) demonstrate this point through their analysis of demands made at Take Back the Night marches for safer streets through better policing. They explain:

> many black mothers are in a different set of relationships to the police from white mothers.... The worries black mothers may have about their children being late home from school can be as much to do with fears of police harassment as with fears of sexual assault.

This is likely to be more so for mothers of children who are young, Black, and male.

Examining the interlocking of processes of stratification raises issues about the politics through which individuals may be slotted into categories such as "Black," "visible minority," "Asian," "Aboriginal." As Smith and Feagin (1995:6) note:

> racial and ethnic identities are locally constructed at particu-
> lar historical times and places through a politics of represen-
> tation in which the role of the state looms large.... State
> policies [have often been] the means used to enforce rela-
> tions of racial and ethnic domination-subordination.

Understanding state responses to activities defined as criminal requires constant attention to how such definitions are shaped by questions of con-trol and consent, of legitimation and conformity, of legality and illegality. The over-criminalization of racialized "minorities" is already a heavily politicized issue in Canada and many other Western industrialized coun-tries. The public furore, for example, about illegal migration, youth gangs, and homeless people is deeply racialized and demonstrates that issues of race and crime have not disappeared from the political agenda. The exam-ination of how these issues and groups merge in such ways as to produce legal and public policy responses that continue to reinforce social, eco-nomic, and political inequalities is a central concern in this collection.

CRIME AND THE CRIMINALIZATION OF RACIALIZED GROUPS

The aim of challenging the social dynamics of hierarchical power is a cen-tral concern of many Marxist, feminist, and critical race scholars in the realization of social justice. How crime is conceptualized and defined has serious implications for how we understand the relationship between the powerful and the powerless in a given social context. Critical theorists point out that those activities defined as "criminal" are intricately tied to "the material and symbolic relationship between power, social control and actions which resist control" (Pfohl, 1994:404). The relationship between crime and the historical and social structures that shape our understand-ing has resulted in socially constructed definitions of crime that maintain gender, race, and class divisions. That is to say, these definitions of crime and categories of criminality are neither fixed nor natural. Labelling an activity, person, or group of persons as "criminal" "is often part of a broader strategy of repression and control, only some aspects of which belong to the exercise of crime-prevention and control in any normal sense" (Hall et al., 1978:187). The role of criminalization in this process of labelling is to target those activities of groups that authorities deem it necessary to control, thus making the process inherently political.

There are many historical and contemporary examples of activities and groups that have come under the scrutiny and control of authorities. The recent emphasis on "illegal" migrants in British Columbia is but one example of how the state can construct an activity as criminal. Cloaked in the rhetoric of public interest and concerns about maintaining social stability and order, the Chinese migrants seeking a better life in North America were labelled as "undesirable, cheaters, and illegitimate claimants" by both media and state institutions.[1] Through predominantly negative media attention, the Canadian government was able to obtain public support for its position. By attaching the label of criminal to the migrants the government claimed legitimacy for imprisoning and eventually deporting the migrants. Not only was its approach characterized by racist overtones, but framing the problem as a threat to public order and safety effectively stifled any opposition to the management of the issue.

The idea that state control agencies are less than neutral is widely accepted by many critical race scholars, who have been scathing in regard to how discriminatory and biased treatment has led to the over-policing of street crimes, but has left corporate and white-collar crime virtually untouched (Box, 1989; Lea and Young, 1993; Nelken, 1997). Feminists have pointed to the double standard in criminal law where male defendants are judged for their behaviour but female defendants are judged for whether or not they meet the standards of a "good" woman (Chesney-Lind, 1997; Gelsthorpe and Morris, 1990; Heidensohn, 1985). Similarly, critical race scholars point to the violation of procedural rules and wrongful convictions when minority defendants are on trial as evidence that the judiciary is not able to impart justice fairly (Gilroy, 1991). Racism, it is argued, is rife in the justice system and this has led to whole communities expressing distrust and suspicion when they confront state control agencies.

The racialized nature of social problems in Canada is a trend that is neither new nor original. Racialized groups have been historically the targets of moral panics and continue to be stereotyped as the criminal "other." It has been well documented that of the diverse ethnic groups in Canada, Aboriginal people and communities comprise one of the most heavily targeted groups by state control agencies (Moyer, 1992; O'Reilly-Fleming, 1994). Similarly, scholars in the United States and Britain also have remarked on the way in which Black people have been constructed as criminals in the eyes of the general public to such an extent that entire communities of Black people have been subject to repressive state laws without much protest or resistance from outside social groups (Chambliss, 1995; Davis, 1998; Mann, 1993; Pitts, 1993; Solomos, 1993; Walker, Spohn, and DeLone, 2000). Both Chambliss (1995) and Davis (1998) note with concern the implications for minority groups of increasing the allocation of resources in the criminal justice system. Governments are able to legitimize the criminalization of entire populations by arguing that crime is on the increase and warrants more attention and public resources. The expansion of crime control through such measures as increased levels of policing, greater police powers, and more prisons is likely to lead to both furthering the overrepresentation of racialized groups and sanctioning even harsher treatment in the criminal justice system. Accusations and charges of racism in the criminal justice system are not without merit. Aboriginal people continue to suffer the effects of law-and-order agendas of successive governments.

The measures taken to control and contain the threat posed by crime and criminals have led to the construction and institutionalization of minority peoples as a problem group responsible for social disorder and unrest. For example, the image of the young, racialized male committing a range of crimes and threatening the safety and security of citizens is imprinted on the minds of many as the cause of a law-and-order breakdown. As Angela Davis (1998:270), remarks, "the figure of the 'criminal' — the racialized figure of the criminal — has come to represent the most menacing enemy of 'American society.'" Critiquing how the process of criminalization is racialized in ways that maintain the oppression and subordination of minority people is the purpose of these essays. We seek to discover, through the examination of different sites of investigation, how the process of criminalization occurs, how resistance is achieved, and how we can understand the implications of these connections in striving for social justice.

The Overlapping Narratives of Racialization and Criminalization

This collection begins with several historical essays contextualizing the treatment of racialized people in Canada. Andrea McCalla and Vic Satzewich trace the history of processes through which First Nations people, immigrants, and people of colour have been defined in racialized terms. Through early twentieth-century state policy (such as the Indian Act and immigration policy), certain groups were negatively evaluated and some of their behaviour was criminalized through a "widening" of the "net of illegal behaviour." Joan Sangster explores another way in which state policy historically racialized individuals and groups through a discussion of the Ontario Female Refuges Act (1947) that served to regulate women's sexuality. Implicit in the criminalization of "sexual promiscuity" was a moral revulsion towards sexual relations between Whites and non-Whites. The historical backdrop provided by these chapters situates discussions of the positions that First Nations people and people of colour currently occupy vis-à-vis the criminal justice system. Sangster's analysis also provides an example of the ways in which understandings of both gender and class are intrinsic to the processes of racialization.

Understanding how individuals are racialized in the legal system forms the main theme of the chapters by Yasmin Jiwani, Audrey Macklin, and Julian Roberts. Yasmin Jiwani identifies four processes through which racialized groups and individuals are criminalized—erasure, trivialization, categorization, and culturalization. Through these processes, groups and individuals are reproduced as "other" in legal discourse and, consequently, racial stereotypes are either reinforced or the problems of racism are ignored. The result is a continued denial that racism in the Canadian justice system is pervasive or systemic. Audrey Macklin discusses one of these processes, culturalization, in detail and traces the ways in which provocation is a "culture defence" that contains features of Anglo-Saxon culture, although it is constructed and interpreted as "objective" and non-racialized. Macklin challenges the racial neutrality within legal discourse by suggesting that provocation is indeed a cultural defence for those whose behaviour fits within the current criteria. Julian Roberts's contribution is a timely reminder of how the relevance of racial characteristics is socially constructed in criminal justice policies. He argues against the routine collection of race-crime statistics on the grounds that information about the offender's "race" does not aid in the development of crime-control policies. Rather, periodic "special studies" can adequately fill the gap left behind. Such an approach, argues Roberts, is capable of avoiding the negative assumptions made about ethnic and racial groups when race-crime statistics are routinely published without compromising the access and availability of this type of information.

The processes of racialization and criminalization come together in many contexts. Whether it is through various criminal justice institutions like the police or social institutions such as the media, how racial groups have been constructed form the main focus of the remaining chapters in the collection. Gladys Symons's contribution is on the intersections between racialization and gendering in police constructions of street gangs in Montreal. She demonstrates how certain youth gangs are categorized by police in terms of their ethnicity while other gangs are characterized in terms of the activities they engage in. Girls are seen as occupying peripheral and sexualized locations within gangs.

Both Colleen Dell's and John Hylton's chapters give particular attention to the relationship between Aboriginal people and the justice system. Dell provides a vivid illustration of the workings of the processes of racialization by drawing on her work with the Elizabeth Fry Society of Manitoba. She notes that there is little understanding of the multiple and sometimes contradictory subject positions occupied by Aboriginal women. Through specific examples of women who have been in conflict with the law, Dell demonstrates how racialized understandings of criminal behaviour are embedded in responses to violence faced by Aboriginal women, how proper legal counsel is denied to these women, and how court norms during trial criminalize certain behaviours, which often has a direct effect on sentencing. Hylton describes the systemic discrimination against Aboriginal people in the justice system, reinforcing many of the arguments made that the process of racialization results overwhelmingly in the negative treatment of racialized groups when they come into conflict with the law. Hylton draws on a variety of statistical and governmental reports as evidence of the discriminatory and prejudicial treatment Aboriginal people continue to encounter at all levels of the legal system. His call for a more thorough understanding of the circumstances and contexts of Aboriginal communities and peoples involves moving beyond a preoccupation with their conflicts with the law towards longer-term solutions that are both enabling and inclusive.

Attention to the treatment and portrayal of Canada's Black[2] community has escalated in the last decade. Changes to Canada's immigration laws in the last decade, coupled with a number of police shootings in Ontario and elsewhere, have reinforced prevailing beliefs that citizens receive differential treatment from the justice system on the basis of physical racial traits. Three chapters in this book attest to the complex issues and controversies surrounding the problems of racism and discrimination. Chris Doran discusses moral panics and the construction of the contemporary "folk devil." Using the work of Stuart Hall and his colleagues with regard to the workings of ideology, culture, and representation, Doran argues that explanations of moral panics require an understanding of the deeper social structures at play if we are to make adequate sense of the relationship between late-capitalism and moral panics.

Annmarie Barnes explores the links between state deportation practices and the criminalization of Jamaican Canadians. She highlights how they have been the primary targets of recent amendments to Canada's immigration laws–changes that have resulted in increased rates of deportation of Jamaicans. The moral and legal implications of Canada's deportation practices can be felt globally, with many developing countries having to absorb the costs of accepting deportees who have committed serious crimes in Canada. For the deportee caught in the middle of debates about which country he/she is genuinely a member of, the notion of "home" no longer exists. As Barnes notes, current deportation practices are reminiscent of earlier government policies of transportation and banishment.

The theme of banishment is picked up also by Akua Benjamin, who examines how the news media's reinforcement of racist ideologies has contributed to the continued marginalization of Blacks. Through a process of discrediting and criminalizing Black organizations and Black leaders, the government's dismissal of their concerns and ideas is identified with the notion of banishment. Banishment occurs at two levels–social banishment, which is linked to the negation of issues important to the Black community, and legal banishment, which includes both the deportation of citizens and the lack of access to democratic rights. Benjamin argues that so long as problems of racism are dismissed, Black communities will face difficulties in gaining an equal footing in all aspects of Canadian society. Finally, the brief Appendix provides short summaries of reports and legal cases referred to by a number of the authors.

Notes

1. During the summer of 1999, news stories abounded over the migration of Chinese refugees to Canada's west coast. For the most part the stories cast the migrants and their attempts to seek refugee status negatively. See, for example, "Canada considers sending police to China in effort to stop migrants" (Canadian Press, 11 September 1999); "New detention facility awaits potential migrants" (Canadian Press, 16 September 1999); "Get tough with illegal migrants, says Manning" (Canadian Press, 16 September 1999). The introduction of Bill C-31 is a direct effort by the federal government to make significant changes to the 1978 Immigration Act in order to control the entry of "cheats and frauds" into Canada.

2. "Black" is used in reference to persons from both Africa and the Caribbean. It is acknowledged, as Annemarie Barnes notes, that such terms are deeply coded racially and cannot be used neutrally, nor are they apolitical in connotation.

References

Anderson, C. 1996. "Understanding the Inequality Problematic: From Scholarly Rhetoric to Theoretical Reconstruction," *Gender and Society* 10, 6:729-46.

Anthias, F. 1998a. "Rethinking social divisions: Some notes towards a theoretical framework," *Sociological Review* 63:505-33.

—. 1998b. "The limits of 'ethnic diversity,'" *Patterns of Prejudice* 32, 4:6-19.

Bhavani, K.K. and M. Coulson. 1986. "Transforming socialist feminism: The challenge of racism," *Feminist Studies*, 23:81-92.

Box, S. 1989. *Power, Crime and Mystification*. London: Routledge.

"Canada considers sending police to China in effort to stop migrants." 1999. Canadian Press, 11 September.

Chambliss, W.J. 1995. "Crime control and ethnic minorities: Legitimizing racial oppression by creating moral panics," in D.F. Hawkins, ed., *Ethnicity, Race and Crime: Perspectives Across Time and Place* Albany: State University of New York Press.

Chesney-Lind, M. 1997. *The Female Offender: Girls, Women, and Crime*. Thousand Oaks, CA: Sage.

Cheung, Y.W. 1980. "Explaining ethnic and racial variation in criminality rates: A review and critique," *Canadian Criminology Forum* 3:1-14.

Davis, A. 1998. "Race and criminalization: Black Americans and the punishment industry," in W. Lubiano, ed., *The House That Race Built*. New York: Vintage Books.

Doob, A. 1994. "Race, Bail and Imprisonment: Draft Working Paper." Toronto: Commission on Systemic Racism in the Ontario Criminal Justice System.

Friedman, S.S. 1995. "Beyond white and other: Relationality and narratives of race in feminist discourse," *Signs* 21, 1:109-57.

Gabor, T. 1994. "The suppression of crime statistics on race and ethnicity: The price of political correctness," *Canadian Journal of Criminology* (April):153-63.

Gelsthorpe, L. and A. Morris, eds. 1990. *Feminist Perspectives in Criminology*. Buckingham: Open University Press.

"Get tough with illegal migrants, says Manning." 1999. Canadian Press, 16 September.

Gilroy, P. 1991 [1987]. *There Ain't No Black in the Union Jack: The Cultural Politics of Race and Nation*. Chicago: University of Chicago Press.

Glenn, E.N. 1999. "The social construction and institutionalization of gender and race: An integrative framework," in M.M. Ferree, J. Lorber, and B.B. Hess, eds., *Revisioning Gender*. Thousand Oaks, CA: Sage.

Gordon, R., and J. Nelson. 1996. "Crime, ethnicity and immigration," in R. Silverman et al., eds., *Crime in Canadian Society*, 5th ed. Toronto: Harcourt Brace.

Hall, S., C. Critcher, et al. 1978. *Policing the Crisis: Mugging, the State and Law and Order*. London: Macmillan.

Hagen, J. 1985. "Toward a structural theory of crime, race and gender: The Canadian case," *Crime and Delinquency* 31, 1:129-46.

Hatt, K. 1994. "Reservations about race and crime statistics," *Canadian Journal of Criminology* (April):164-65.

Heidensohn, F. 1985. *Women and Crime*. Basingstoke: Macmillan.

Henry, F., P. Hastings, and B. Freer. 1996. "Perceptions of race and crime in Ontario: Empirical evidence from Toronto and the Durham region," *Canadian Journal of Criminology* (October):469-76.

Hill, M. 1999. Letter to the editor. Toronto Star, October 9.

Jackson, P. 1994. "Constructions of criminality: Police-community relations in Toronto," *Antipode* 26:216.

Johnston, J.P. 1994. "Academic approaches to race-crime statistics do not justify their collection," *Canadian Journal of Criminology* (April):166-74.

Lea, J. and Y. Jock. 1993. *What's To Be Done about Law and Order?* London: Pluto Press.

Mann, C. 1993. *Unequal Justice: A Question of Colour*. Bloomington: Indiana University Press.

Miles, R. 1989. *Racism*. London: Routledge.

Mosher, C. 1996. "Minorities and misdemeanours: The treatment of black public order offenders in Ontario's criminal justice system, 1892-1930," *Canadian Journal of Criminology* (October):413-38.

Moyer, S. 1992. "Race, gender and homicide: Comparisons between aboriginals and other Canadians," *Canadian Journal of Criminology*: 387-402.

Nelken, D. 1997. "White-Collar Crime," in M. Maguire, R. Morgan, and R. Reiner, eds, *The Oxford Handbook of Criminology*, 2nd ed. Oxford: Oxford University Press.

"New detention facility awaits potential migrants." 1999. Canadian Press, 16 September.

O'Reilly-Fleming, T. 1994. "The Mohawk-Canada crisis: Native peoples, criminalization and the justice system," in D. Baker, ed., *Reading Racism in the Criminal Justice System*. Toronto: Canadian Scholar's Press.

Ontario. 1989. *Report of Race Relations and Policing Task Force*. Toronto: Solicitor General's Office.

Pfohl, S. 1994. *Images of Deviance and Social Control*, 2nd ed. New York: McGraw-Hill.

Pitts, J. 1993. "Stereotyping: Anti-racism, criminology and black young people," in D. Cook and B. Hudson, eds., *Racism and Criminology*. London: Sage.

Razack, S. 1998. *Looking White People in the Eye: Gender, Race and Culture in Courtrooms and Classrooms*. Toronto: University of Toronto Press.

Roberts, J. 1994. "Crime and race statistics: Toward a Canadian solution," *Canadian Journal of Criminology*: 175-85.

Small, S. 1994. *The Black Experience in the United States and England in the 1980s*. London: Routledge.

—. 1999. "The contours of racialization: Private structures, representations and resistance in the United States," in R. Torres, J. Inda, and L. Miron, eds., *Race, Identity, and Citizenship: A Reader*. Malden, MA: Blackwells.

Smith, M.P., and J.R. Feagin. 1995. "Putting race in its place," in M.P. Smith and J.R. Feagin, eds., *The Bubbling Cauldron: Race, Ethnicity and the Urban Crisis.* Minneapolis: University of Minnesota Press.

Solomos, J. 1993. "Constructions of black criminality: Racialisation and criminalisation in perspective," in D. Cook and B. Hudson, eds., *Racism and Criminology.* London: Sage.

Ungerleider, C. 1994. "Police, race and community conflict in Vancouver," *Canadian Ethnic Studies* 26, 3:91-104.

Van Dijk, T.A. 1988. *News Analysis.* Hillsdale, NJ: Lawrence Erlbaum.

Walker, S., C. Spohn, and M. DeLone. 2000. *The Colour of Justice*, 2nd ed. Scarborough, ON: Wadsworth.

Part I
History

2

Settler Capitalism and the Construction of Immigrants and "Indians" as Racialized Others

ANDREA McCALLA AND VIC SATZEWICH

Settler capitalist societies like Canada were formed through the interrelated processes of colonization and repopulation through large-scale immigration (Denoon, 1983; Stasiulis and Yuval-Davis, 1995). In Canada, colonization and population-through-immigration historically involved at least three distinct contact situations. First, European colonizers confronted existing indigenous societies. The relationships that were established between Europeans and Aboriginal peoples were multifaceted and depended in part on the material interests of the respective parties. During the eighteenth and first half of the nineteenth centuries, indigenous peoples were sought as military allies and were incorporated into various aspects of the commercial fur trade. By the mid-nineteenth century, indigenous peoples came to be defined as obstacles to the development of capitalist industry and agriculture, and so their presence came to be increasingly defined as a problem by state authorities. Second, European interest in Canada was differentiated between English and French colonizers. The French wanted to establish a permanent physical presence in the colony of New France, whereas the British were initially more interested in the seasonal extraction of raw materials from the environment. The French lost their North American colony in 1760, but many of the French settlers and their descendants stayed. After the conquest of 1760 the British and French élites arrived at an unequal accommodation in which the former controlled politics and economic development, while the latter controlled civil society. Third, when the fur trade was on its last legs, in the mid-nineteenth century British authorities began to define British North America as a suitable location for large-scale settlement. Since then, successive governments have struggled with the issue of the kinds of immigrants that should be let into Canada.

Until the middle of the twentieth century, notions of "race" framed many of the ways in which groups and their interrelations in these contact situations were understood. This chapter will examine only two of these sets of racialized relations: Aboriginal/non-Aboriginal and immigrant/state relations, first with a historical analysis of how Aboriginal people were constructed in racial terms within early twentieth-century Indian policy. It also maps how the racialization of Aboriginal peoples resulted in multiple and diverse relationships to the criminal process. In particular, we show that the racialization of Aboriginal people led to the creation of certain kinds of status offences; that in some cases Aboriginal people engaged in criminal behaviour as a way of resisting state policy; and that the process of racialization had diverse consequences for policing and sentencing. The second part of this chapter considers how human difference was constituted as "race" difference within immigration policy. It delimits some of the social consequences of the racialization of immigrants by examining the ways "race" was used as a basis for immigrant inclusion and exclusion, immigrant allocation, and immigrant social control between the late nineteenth century and late 1960s.

The Racialization of "Indian"

The entrenchment of Aboriginal rights in the constitution of Canada in 1982 has generated considerable debate about the special rights of Indian, Inuit, and Métis people.[1] For much of this century, though, being defined as an Indian did not entail special rights. Rather, it meant a variety of special controls, regulations, restrictions, laws, and administrative practices. Many of these restrictions came from the Indian Act, which encapsulated much of the federal government's Indian policy. Until the early 1950s that policy was specifically framed by the assumption that Indian people and their culture were inferior, that social problems were the result of their stubbornly hanging onto their outmoded cultures, and that no effort should be spared to promote their assimilation into wider social relations (Gibbins and Ponting, 1986; Ponting and Gibbins, 1980).

The 1876 Indian Act defined who was an Indian and specified how someone could lose status as an Indian. In the Act, an Indian "was defined as any male person of Indian blood reputed to belong to a particular band, any child of such a person and any woman who is lawfully married to such a person" (Gibbins and Ponting, 1986:21). The definition of an Indian, therefore, was based on a combination of patriarchally defined lineage, "blood," and social acceptance. Even though "blood" seemed to be a euphemism for "race," the social and cultural characteristics of Indian people were not necessarily regarded as biologically grounded and fixed. Thus, even though Indians were the objects of a process of racialization, government officials nevertheless believed that is was possible for Indian people to change. This is evident in the enfranchisement provisions of the Indian Act. Enfranchisement referred to how Indian people, by becoming eligible to vote as Canadian citizens, could lose their status as Indians and stop coming under the domain of the Indian Act. It was premised on the assumption that with careful guidance from the state, Indian people could become like Euro-Canadians in their attitudes, values, and behaviours (Satzewich and Zong, 1996:277). The provisions for enfranchisement were pursued with varying intensity over the years. For a time in the 1920s the government had the power to enfranchise, without their consent, more "advanced" Indians (Titley, 1986:49). Until 1985, Indian women who married non-Indian men automatically lost their status as Indians, as did their children. The practice of enfranchisement led to the creation of the social category of "non-status Indians" — people who still considered themselves to be Indians but who were not recognized as Indians by the federal government.

The creation of a legal and racialized category of Indian within the Indian Act also meant that for much of the previous century Indian people faced a unique set of constraints and controls on their social, political, and economic rights that many other Canadians took for granted. For example, status Indians could not vote in provincial elections in British Columbia and Newfoundland until 1949, in Quebec until 1969, and in federal elections until 1960. Indian people could not take up homesteads in the late nineteenth and early twentieth centuries and remain Indian in the eyes of the government. Indians also faced special restrictions on their mobility: during the first half of the twentieth century they were prohibited from leaving their reserves without securing permission from the Indian agent (Barron, 1988). They also faced restrictions on their ability to market commodities off their reserves (Carter, 1990).

The legal categorization of Indian also entailed the criminalization of certain aspects of Indian peoples' behaviour. The federal government passed a series of laws and regulations meant to eradicate cultural and religious practices seen as contributing to the reproduction of distinctive, and inferior, ways of life. These status offences were created by the Canadian government to facilitate the assimilation of Indian people into Canadian society.

One of the first instances where state power was used to legislate against Indian cultural practices was an 1884 amendment to the Indian Act that provided that Aboriginal Potlatch and Tamanawas ceremonies were unlawful and subject to between two and six months' imprisonment. Both the Tamanawas and Potlatch were complex religio-cultural ceremonies practised by Indians on the Northwest Coast of British Columbia. The Tamanawas was a medicine, or healing, ceremony and the Potlatch involved ceremonial gift-giving and the transfer of material goods as a way of solidifying mutual bonds among households and publicly validating social status (Pettipas, 1995:91-93; Cole and Chaikin, 1990).

In 1895, a legislative amendment further widened the net of illegal behaviour to religio-cultural practices of prairie Indians. One of the ceremonies practised by Indian people on the prairies that drew the particular attention and ire of European authorities was the Sun Dance. The Sun Dance or Thirst Dance was a large summer ceremonial gathering that involved giving away goods and piercing the flesh. Europeans believed that the pace of assimilation would be slowed if Indian people continued these practices. Thus, the amendment, which became section 114 of the 1895 Indian Act, as quoted by Pettipas (1995:95-96), provided that:

> Every Indian or other person who engages in celebrating or encourages either directly or indirectly another to celebrate, any Indian festival, dance or other ceremony of which the giving away or paying or giving back of money, goods, or articles of any sort forms a part, or is a feature whether such gift of money, goods or articles takes place before, at, or after the celebration of the same, and every Indian or other person who engages or assists in any celebration or dance of which the wounding or mutilation of the dead or living body of any human being or animal forms a part or is a feature, is guilty of an indictable offense.

As with the earlier legislation, the term of imprisonment was set at between two and six months for those convicted of violating the law.

Later, the net was widened yet again to prohibit "Indian dancing" at prairie agricultural exhibitions such as the Calgary Stampede. In 1914 Parliament amended the Indian Act by providing for penalties of $25 or one month's imprisonment for Indians who "danced" outside of their own reserves or who appeared in shows or exhibitions in "aboriginal costume" (Titley, 1986:175).

The existence of these kinds of status offences that targeted the religious and cultural practices of Indian people raises at least three implications for the analysis of their relationship with the justice system. First, the social origins of these laws can, in part, be traced to the lobbying activities of groups within Euro-Canadian society. Moral entrepreneurs influenced the problematization and criminalization of certain aspects of indigenous culture and behaviour. In particular, missionaries saw the persistence of rituals associated with the Potlatch, Tamanawas, and Sun Dance to be inimical to what they saw as civilized Christian behaviour. An Anglican missionary who wrote to the Department of Indian Affairs about his first encounter with the people he was supposed to convert explained that when

> I first made the acquaintance of the Blackfoot ... I arrived in July when that great heathen festival, the Sun Dance, was in full swing.... The fantastic costumes, of the people, the paint and feathers, the then to me foreign tongue, made my heart sink within me, and if I ever felt the hopelessness of a task set me to do it was then. (Pettipas, 1995:97)

Such concerns were raised repeatedly by missionaries in the late nineteenth and early twentieth centuries and both Protestants and Catholics lobbied the government to take action to help eradicate these forms of "devil worship" (Pettipas, 1995:216).

Many senior officials within the Department of Indian Affairs were sympathetic to the concerns of these moral entrepreneurs, but they also had their own problems with the ceremonies. They were particularly vexed that the "giveaways" worked against their efforts to instil capitalist ethics and values such as respect for private property, the pursuit of individual accumulation, and working for the sake of individual and household gain. They were also concerned that since the preparation for and participation in the ceremonies could take several weeks, valuable time was lost for what Indian people should "really" have been doing: fishing, and working for wages (Pettipas, 1995:99; Titley, 1986).

Second, criminologists know it is one thing to pass a law prohibiting behaviour but quite another thing to enforce that law. Criminologists have also noted that control agents within the criminal justice system, such as police, judges, and parole boards, often have discretion as to how they enforce legal codes. The sheer existence of status offences that prohibited the Potlatch, Sun Dance, and Tamanawas were in themselves discriminatory, but were violations of these kinds of laws necessarily subject to strict enforcement on the part of social control agents at the time?

While contemporary debates about Aboriginal overrepresentation in provincial and federal prisons tend to focus on the issues of over-policing and more harsh sentencing at the hands of control agents (Royal Commission on Aboriginal Peoples, 1996), the historical record reveals a more mixed picture. Enforcement of the laws prohibiting the Potlatch, Tamanawas, and Sun Dance was left largely to Indian agents. Enforcement depended, in part, on the Indian agent's own personal beliefs and values. It also depended on their relationship with missionaries in the surrounding area, their own commitment to Christianity, their commitment to the overall goals and objectives of Department of Indian Affairs, and their desire for promotion. Many Indian agents tried vigorously to uphold the law, but others were more flexible. Some agents turned a blind eye on the assumption that efforts to maintain the strict letter of the law would be too disruptive of social order in the community; some felt that unsuccessful attempts to curtail such ceremonies would lead only to the further undermining of any legitimate authority they had in Indian peoples' eyes; and some felt that such ceremonies would eventually disappear on their own and so there was little to be gained by provoking the communities through strict enforcement (Pettipas, 1995).

Enforcement also depended on the bureaucratic structure of the Department of Indian Affairs. In the late nineteenth and early twentieth centuries, the main administrative unit within Indian Affairs was the Indian agency. Indian agencies were made up of both bands and reserves. On the prairies agents could be responsible for as many as 10 different reserves while in British Columbia some agents were responsible for dozens of small communities (Satzewich and Mahood, 1994). Some Indian agents, therefore, had only minimal contact with their isolated and inaccessible communities. In these cases, Indian agents were fortunate if they could visit some communities once or twice a calendar year. It was at

times extraordinarily difficult for Indian agents to stay on top of the daily
or even weekly happenings on many reserves, let alone police the sections
of the Indian Act that prohibited participation in certain ceremonial
events (Pettipas, 1995).

Also, the sometimes conflictual relationships between Department of
Indian Affairs personnel and the North West Mounted Police produced
variations in enforcement. James Macleod, the Commissioner of the
NWMP, for example, criticized members of the force for arresting Sun
Dance participants. He insisted that despite the "barbaric" nature of the
ceremony "what [the police] ... had done was akin to making arrests in a
church" (Pettipas, 1994:111). At times, NWMP constables seemed to counsel participants about loopholes in the law that would allow them to avoid
arrest. In at least one instance a local police detachment gave permission
to hold a Sun Dance against the wishes of the Indian agent (Pettipas,
1995:111).

The third implication of the creation of status offences that targeted
Indian peoples' cultural and religious ceremonies was that these offences
inevitably provoked resistance (Brownlie and Kelm, 1994). Resistance took
a number of different forms. People in some communities refused to give
up their religious and cultural ceremonies despite knowing that they were
likely to be caught and face legal sanctions. It is difficult to determine the
extent to which Indian people were incarcerated for the violation of these
status offences, in part because offenders often were charged and convicted on a number of interrelated grounds. However, even though they
are imperfect, the available records show that there were arrests, convictions, fines, and terms of imprisonment for those who violated the law. For
example, in 1902 there were nine arrests and convictions for "holding
dances"; another 27 individuals were arrested but given suspended sentences for their participation in "heathen dances." In 1903, there were 10
arrests and nine convictions for "holding dances" (Pettipas, 1995:122; see
also Titley, 1986:175).

Another form of resistance consisted of organized protests and petitions
directed to lawmakers, Indian agents, and senior officials of the
Department of Indian Affairs. This kind of resistance was more widespread
in the late nineteenth and early twentieth centuries than is sometimes recognized. Pettipas (1995:127–43) documents numerous cases in which
Indian people protested that the regulations prohibiting their cultural and
religious practices were contrary to their understanding of the terms of the
treaties. In other cases, Indian people submitted requests to the

Department of Indian Affairs for permission to hold ceremonies and petitions that pointed out the discriminatory nature of the prohibitions. In some cases, they petitioned for the removal of Indian agents who were particularly hard-nosed in their enforcement of the law. There was at least one case in which the legal status of the regulations was tested in court (Pettipas, 1995:133).

More often than not, this kind of political resistance had little effect and was off-handedly dismissed by Indian Affairs officials. In some other cases resistance was met with more harsh repression. In 1927, for example, after efforts were made to form an organized Indian lobby, the Indian Act prohibited the national political organizing of Indian people (Ponting and Gibbins, 1980:196). Also in 1927, the government made it illegal for Indian people to raise money or use band funds to help bring land claims disputes before the courts (Patterson, 1978:50). However, even though the political victories associated with these official forms of resistance were few and far between, it is clear that Indian people were not passive bystanders when it came to Euro-Canadian efforts to alter and criminalize their behaviour.

A final form of resistance involved changing certain aspects of the ceremonies to make them more acceptable to European eyes. For example, communities modified the self-mortification aspects of the some rituals, shortened the time required to complete the rituals, held ceremonies less often and in more remote locations, made the ceremonies more local in their scope, and changed the composition of commodities that were "given away." In other cases, communities grafted certain rituals onto Christian holidays, such as Christmas, or incorporated elements of traditional rituals into secular events such as Treaty Days, sports days, and agricultural fairs in the communities surrounding reserves (Pettipas, 1995:223).

In sum, Indian people were constituted as racialized subjects within federal Indian policy. While they were racialized, many of the policies and practices underlying the federal government's attempt to eradicate the so-called "Indian problem" were in fact based on the assumption that they could be culturally transformed into ideal-typical "Europeans." Efforts to criminalize certain religious and cultural ceremonies of Indian people in western Canada in the late nineteenth and early twentieth centuries resulted in a number of different kinds of relationships between Aboriginal people and the criminal justice system. In the next section, we want to consider the racialization of immigration control in Canada during the late nineteenth century and the first two-thirds of the twentieth century, and begin to indicate how that racialization structured immigrants' relationship with the criminal justice system.

Immigration and State Formation

In settler capitalist societies, immigration is a tool of both labour force expansion and of state formation. Canadian government decisions about who should be let into the country have been guided by two fundamental, if not always explicitly stated, questions: "Are certain immigrants better suited than others for certain kinds of jobs?" and "Are certain immigrants better candidates than others for participation in Canadian social and political life?" This dual significance to immigration means that immigration policies have been shaped by economic, demographic, social, political, and ideological factors (Fleras and Elliott, 1990:53). Since Confederation, the answers to these questions have constituted the basis for the processes of immigrant inclusion and exclusion, immigrant allocation in the labour force, and immigrants' treatment in Canadian society.

Until the mid-1960s, "race" was one of the main criteria used to understand the social, political, and economic capacities of immigrants (Ongley and Pearson, 1995:770). Many different segments of Canadian society, including government officials, politicians, business leaders, and representatives of labour organizations maintained a belief in "race" (Fleras and Elliott, 1996:44-45) as a legitimate category of immigrant selection. It was a category that accorded better opportunities to most classes of British and Northern European settlers (Hughes and Kallen, 1974:7); fewer opportunities for groups whose status as Whites was uncertain or questionable; and even fewer opportunities for those who were deemed to be non-White[2] (Satzewich, 1991:124). In this section we want to consider how notions of "race" informed decisions about who should be let into Canada, and how they in turn shaped decisions about how different groups should be treated once here.

The Immigration Act of 1869 was the first Canadian-born legislation to regulate immigration. At that time, the main concern for government officials was not the immigration of non-Whites, but rather the immigration of British paupers. While concerns over the class background of immigrants have remained evident in subsequent legislation, by the 1880s groups who were defined as non-White increasingly became the targets of government legislation. In 1885, a federal head tax was charged to incoming Chinese immigrants as a condition of entry. The rate started at $50 and increased to $500 by 1904 (Davis and Krauter, 1978:63). In addition, in 1903 Parliament required every Asian to possess $200 upon landing in Canada. Following that, the power to exclude immigrants in certain categories and of certain origins became law in the Immigration Act of 1910. Clause (c) stated that the governor-in-council could prohibit the landing in Canada of immigrants belonging to any race deemed unsuited to the climate or requirements of Canada, or of immigrants of any specified class, occupation, or character (Hawkins, 1991:17). These restrictions slowed, but did not stop, Chinese entry into Canada. The Chinese Immigration Act of 1923 came into effect on Dominion Day, July 1, which was known within the Chinese community at the time as "Humiliation Day." This legislation stopped the entry of Chinese almost entirely until 1947, when the Act was repealed (Davis and Krauter, 1978:63).

The Japanese did not face such overtly racist barriers, though they, too, were the objects of concern of Canadian officials and confronted more informal exclusionary measures. At the initiative of Canadian officials, the Japanese government entered into a gentleman's agreement with Canada, which had the effect of limiting Japanese entry without making Canada seem discriminatory in policy. A quota was set to allow 400 Japanese families per year, and was later reduced to 150. This substantially restricted the flow of Japanese immigrants to Canada (Davis and Krauter, 1971:62).

In 1906, a "continuous journey" provision was added to the Immigration Act, and effectively excluded potential immigrants from the Indian subcontinent (Knowles, 1996:904). The provision required that anyone wishing to immigrate to Canada had to do so via one continuous ocean journey. Since there were no direct steamship connections between Canada and India at the time, Indian immigrants had to make at least two separate journeys: first to Japan on one ship and then to Canada on a different ship. This continuous journey rule remained in effect for 40 years (Hawkins, 1991:17-21). Canadian government officials were reluctant to speak ill of East Indians publicly, for fear of putting the British colonial government in India in an awkward position. However, like the Chinese and Japanese, East Indians were conceptualized "as the bearers of lower standards of civilization, as a heathen debased class of people oblivious to the higher cultural forms of White settlers with which they could never assimilate" (Knowles, 1996:905). In 1947, Canada's Prime Minister, W.L. Mackenzie King, tried to defend the policy of Indian exclusion by claiming that Canada really had the best interests of Indians at heart. He claimed that the native of India is not suited to this country because of the difference in climate and customs and an assumed inability of Indians to adapt readily to new surroundings. Thus, he stated, a discontinuance of emigration from the Indian subcontinent to Canada would be most desirable in the interests of the Indians themselves (Hawkins, 1991:18).

Immigration policy also restricted the admission of other visible minority people to Canada, both formally and informally (Satzewich, 1991:126). In the early 1900s the Canadian government tried to deny American Blacks access to Canada without directly upsetting American officials. In fact, immigration officials admitted privately that they did everything in their power to bar Blacks from western Canada. For example, when farm applicants were sought to settle the Canadian West, Black American farmers were rejected by the Immigration Branch on medical and other non-racial grounds. In 1909 Blacks from Oklahoma began settling in Saskatchewan and Manitoba. Soon after, the Canadian government attempted to prevent additional Black settlement. It subjected them to unwarranted medical examinations and claimed that the climate was too severe. Eventually it was discovered that at least one medical examiner was paid a bonus for every Black applicant he rejected (Davis and Krauter, 1978:45). At the same time, extensive advertising campaigns targeted White Americans for migration (Henry et al., 1995:66).

In 1912, the Great Northern Railway sent notices to its employees that Blacks would not be admitted to Canada under any circumstances and that ticket sales to them for journeys between St. Paul, Minnesota, and the Canadian border should be discouraged. Restrictions on Black immigration were later extended to include visits by Blacks to Canada, since "visitors" might attempt to remain permanently in the country (Davis and Krauter, 1978:46). The fear of uncontrolled Black population growth made it difficult for Blacks to become citizens. Black men had to show proof of marriage within 30 days or risk deportation because Black immigration was defined as the cause of "race relations" problems in the country (Satzewich, 1991:141-45). In 1914, Immigration Superintendent W.D. Scott stated:

> the government does not encourage the immigration of coloured people. There are certain countries from which immigration is encouraged and certain races of people considered as suited to this [country] and its conditions, but Africans, no matter where they come from are not among the

> races sought, and hence, Africans no matter from what coun-
> try they come are in common with the uninvited races, not
> admitted to Canada. (Calliste, 1996:74)

Immigration agents were privately advised to refuse Caribbean Blacks entry even when they complied with the Immigration Act, mainly because "Blacks were identified as potential public charges because of economic reasons and racism in immigration policy and employment." In his advice to his colleagues, the Inspector of Immigration Agencies in the Maritimes suggested that "every obstacle is to be put in their way, and if everything else fails ... reject them as 'likely to become a public charge'" (Calliste, 1996:75).

The 1952 Immigration Act reaffirmed the cabinet's power over immigrant admission and selection. In the legislation cabinet retained its considerable leeway in how it could construct and define problematic immigrants. It could "refuse admission on grounds of nationality, geographical area of origin, peculiar customs, habits and modes of life, unsuitability with regard to the climate, probable inability to become readily assimilated, and other similar reasons" (Hawkins, 1991:38). While "race" was notably absent from this list, groups who were defined as non-White were nevertheless the main targets of exclusion. In the 1950s, immigration officials regularly used "climatic" and "social unsuitability" to stop Caribbean immigration, claiming that Blacks cannot handle the competitiveness of the country and that their entry would lead to racial problems (Satzewich, 1991:127). Eventually, in an attempt to improve Canada's international standing, when some countries were beginning to see Canadian immigration policy as racist, changes to the Immigration Act removed many of the blatant vestiges of racial discrimination. Canada was essentially forced to remove most country-of-origin and racial restrictions on paper, but for a time the government continued to explicitly recruit immigrants from predominantly White countries (Ramcharan, 1982:15). In 1967, further changes to the Immigration Act spelled out a set of more precise and transparent selection criterion. The 1967 "points system" changed the policy from an ethnically based set of criteria to a more universalistic skill-based policy (Avery, 1995:176-85), although it took several more years for the government to open immigration offices in the Caribbean. When it did, it was to control Black immigration to Canada, not to promote it (Satzewich, 1991:134-40).

Social Inequality and Social Control

In the mid-1960s, sociologist John Porter described Canada as a vertical mosaic. He used the concept as a metaphor to describe the structure of social inequality in Canada. He stressed that there was a reciprocal relationship between ethnicity and social class: British immigrants and their descendants and members of the French-Canadian political élite were at the top of the socio-economic hierarchy. As "charter groups," they could define the terms and conditions of entry for other immigrants to Canada. Other immigrants were accorded an "entrance status": ethnic groups from Northern Europe who were seen to be close to the British in terms of "race" and culture were in the middle of the socio-economic hierarchy; Southern and Eastern Europeans were ranked near the bottom; Aboriginal people and the few non-Whites who did manage to get into Canada were at the bottom. While there are debates about how well the concept of a vertical mosaic applies to Canada today, there are strong grounds to suggest that until the 1960s the "entrance status" accorded to Southern and Eastern Europeans, visible minorities, and Aboriginal people meant their allocation to the lowest occupational roles and their social and political marginalization.

Numerous cases in Canadian history show that class, race, and ethnicity have been important factors in determining both Canada's policy towards different groups of immigrant workers and where foreign-born men and women subsequently found employment (Avery, 1995:17). At various times the government encouraged the flow of immigrants from particular countries in order to help fill specific jobs.

In the 1870s the Immigration Branch began importing European immigrants as household servants. At this time selection was limited mainly to British women since they were considered to be of the right "racial"/ethnic stock. Due to intolerable working conditions many of them left those positions. After World War I the demand for domestic workers remained strong, and recruitment was broadened to Northern and Western European women. As with their earlier British counterparts, they found the low pay and poor working conditions unacceptable.

In this context, recruitment had to be broadened yet again. During the 1950s a Caribbean Domestic Scheme was established to circumvent the racially restrictive immigration policy. In 1955, well-educated women from Jamaica and Barbados were considered a success "since a high proportion of the immigrants remained in domestic service, not necessarily because they liked the work but because racism excluded them from other jobs" (Avery, 1995:209). This period marked a shift from domestic work being seen as largely White women's work to its current association with women of colour from developing countries (England and Stiell, 1997:199). Working as a domestic meant that one was vulnerable to employer control. For example, regulations introduced in 1973 restricted domestics from changing employers or occupations; if they did change employers, they were subject to deportation. The goal was to isolate these women so that they could not fight for better wages and working conditions (Avery, 1995:210). The government also tried to ensure that domestic positions would be filled by migrant women and these women would no longer be guaranteed landed immigrant status (England and Stiell, 1997:199-200).

Visible minorities were not the only ones allocated to specific realms of production. In the 1920s the Empire Settlement Act encouraged immigration from Britain, Norway, Sweden, Germany, and France. Immigrants from non-preferred countries, listed as Austria, Hungary, Poland, Romania, Lithuania, Estonia, Latvia, Bulgaria, Yugoslavia, and Czechoslovakia, were allowed in only as agricultural workers, domestics, or family-sponsored applicants. Those who arrived who fell outside of these categories were shown to the door and told to return to their countries of origin (Hawkins, 1991:27). Furthermore, although "race" prevented Jews from being banned by law, they did face discrimination affecting their business, employment, and education. Universities maintained restrictive quotas, and anti-Semitism restricted where they could live and acquire property (Henry et al., 1995:74).

As noted in the previous section, Black immigration was generally not desired. However, there were times when the demands for labour were so urgent that some flexibility in immigrant admissions was needed. In 1916, for example, the Dominion Iron and Steel Company in Nova Scotia was given permission to import 1,000 Caribbean labourers since other labour sources were said to be unavailable (Calliste, 1996:73). Even though they were needed desperately for operations to continue, the Black men working in the Sydney steel plant were "restricted to working around the coke ovens or blast furnaces, relegated to the hottest, most physically demanding, and lowest paid jobs in the plant" (Calliste, 1996:71).

These kinds of restrictions were not isolated anomalies in an otherwise free labour market. Racial discrimination in the area of work limited the job opportunities of many different immigrant groups. Chinese and Japanese entered Canada when their labour was needed to work in railroad construction and the lumber and mining industries. When the work ended they did not return to their homelands, and where their numbers made them visible, Canadians began to see them as a threat. As a result, the Chinese and Japanese became subject to severe job and social discrimination. They faced measures that prevented them from taking up jobs in certain industries. In 1878, for example, the British Columbia legislature passed a law prohibiting them from working on provincial projects and required every Chinese person aged 12 and older to obtain a $10 licence every three months. The penalty was set at a fine of 10 times the cost of a licence, or imprisonment. In 1884, "the Chinese Regulation Act prohibited any employer from hiring an unlicensed Chinese person. In 1890, under the guise of a safety measure, it sought to block Chinese employment in the mining industry through the Coal Mines Regulation Amendment Act" (Davis and Krauter, 1971:63). In addition to the 26 statutes aimed at restricting Chinese settlement passed by the British Columbia legislature between 1878 and 1899, in 1900 immigrants to the province were required to write an application to the provincial secretary in a European language if so ordered. Inability to do so could result in a $500 fine, a year's imprisonment, or deportation. Only after protest did the federal government disallow this legislation. When Chinese people tried to escape the discrimination in the labour market by becoming self-employed or small shop owners, they continued to face discriminatory barriers (Davis and Krauter, 1978:75). Saskatchewan, for instance, passed a law in 1912 that prohibited White women from working in Chinese- or Japanese-owned restaurants, laundries, or other businesses (Davis and Krauter, 1971:63).

In both British Columbia and Saskatchewan voting exclusion was based on race, not nationality. In the late nineteenth century, "Asian migrants were deemed, at best, to be a source of sojourner labour and their presence inspired widespread xenophobia, racism, and strict regulation" (Ongley and Pearson, 1995:787). Chinese residents of British Columbia and Saskatchewan were not allowed to vote in 1875. By 1896 this prohibition was extended to other Asians. These provincial barriers were extended to the federal level in the Dominion Franchise Bill of 1920, which read: "Persons who by the laws of any province of Canada, are disqualified from voting (for) a member of the Legislative Assembly of such province in respect of race, shall not be qualified to vote in such province under the provisions of this act" (Davis and Krauter, 1971:64).

The presence in Canada of people from India was often termed the "Hindu problem." As a result, laws were amended to include "other Asians" or "other Orientals," which also made voting, obtaining licences, and employment difficult if not impossible for many East Indians (Davis and Krauter, 1978:86-88).

It was only in 1947 that voting restrictions, at both the federal and provincial levels, were removed for the Chinese; restrictions on Japanese enfranchisement were lifted in 1949. After the Japanese bombing of Pearl Harbor in 1941, many Japanese Canadians were detained without trial, expelled from British Columbia, and interned in camps until 1947. Property was confiscated and sold at public auctions without the owners' consent; people were arrested and their property searched without warrant (Davis and Krauter, 1978:68). Only in 1988 were 12,000 Japanese paid $21,000 in compensation and given a formal apology from Parliament (Henry et al., 1995:70).

One of the more blatant examples of the link between "race" and labour market placement is the split labour market that existed for sleeping-car porters in Canada. By the 1920s the Canadian National Railway (CNR) and the Canadian Brotherhood of Railway Transport Workers agreed to a group classification system that restricted Blacks solely to porter positions. These men were forced into lower-paying positions and denied equal participation in the union. Higher-paying "Group I" positions consisted of dining-car employees and sleeping-car conductors. Lower-paying "Group II" positions were sleeping- and parlour-car porters. In this system, Blacks were hired to fill only Group II positions. When the CNR took over the Grand Trunk Railway in 1923, the Black employees in the Grand Trunk's dining-car service were replaced by White employees (Calliste, 1987:3).

Why were Blacks restricted to positions as porters? According to Agnes Calliste, "first they were cheaper, both in terms of wage rates and degree of unionization ... second, the assumed social distance that existed between whites and blacks meant that the presence of black porters on sleeping cars was considered as impersonal and did not serve as a complicating factor in the intimacies which travel by sleeping cars necessitated ... [and] third, Pullman officials were aware that blacks had been traditionally assigned service roles, and that it was a sign of status among whites to be waited on by them" (Calliste, 1987:2-3).

Only with the passage of the Canada Fair Employment Practices Act in 1953 were porters able successfully to combat discrimination in their employment (Calliste, 1987:1). Surprisingly, since the abolition of slavery[3] in the Emancipation Act of 1833, Blacks who were Canadian citizens enjoyed many legal rights and privileges on par with other Canadians. For example, Blacks have always been able to vote in both federal and provincial elections. On the other hand, they have faced racially based discrimination in housing, education, employment, and public accommodations not only in practice, but also under the safeguard of the law (Davis and Krauter, 1978:48). Separate schools for Blacks had been legalized in 1849. By 1850, segregated schools were operating in Nova Scotia and Ontario. In Chatham, Ontario, a court upheld the total exclusion of Blacks from ordinary public schools in 1861, and it took 100 years before legally segregated education ended in Ontario and Nova Scotia (Davis and Krauter, 1978:48-51).

Conclusion

Racism played an important role in forming Canadian society. The social definition of groups as racially different and the corresponding hierarchical evaluation of those differences had a variety of consequences for groups who were located at the frontiers of colonization and immigration. The definition of "Indians" in racial terms marked them as fundamentally different from Euro-Canadians. Yet, they were also seen to be capable of becoming "European" in both character and attitudes. In the Canadian government's effort to transform them into Europeans, Indians came to be the objects of a number of pieces of legislation in which their cultural and religious practices were defined as problematic. The criminalization of Aboriginal culture and religion resulted in a complicated relationship between Indian people and the justice system in this country. The particular trajectories of those relationships require more research.

Canada's immigration policy was historically framed by racial considerations. Head taxes, continuous passage stipulations, and theories about the relationship between "race" and climate were used to try to sustain Canada as a White person's country. The manner in which immigration policy and practice has changed over the years reveals the multiple ways in which human difference was interpreted as "race" difference. Policies were formulated to include and exclude certain immigrants, allocate and control them, and help further the development of what was envisioned to be a White-dominated society.

Through the liberalization of Canadian immigration policy it appears that exclusion and marginalization based on "race" no longer occur. Certainly, the passage of the Canadian Charter of Rights and Freedoms, the Multiculturalism Act, and employment equity legislation has helped alleviate some of the more blatant and obvious forms of racial discrimination. But Canada arguably remains a "stratified society where differences in skin colour or ethnic background continue to make a difference" (Fleras and Elliott, 1996:100). Many people argue that the reality in Canada is that "racial, Aboriginal, and ethnocultural groups continue to be sorted out unequally against a 'mosaic' of raised (dominant) and lowered (subordinate) tiles. Pyramids of privilege exist that elevate white, male, [heterosexual], middle-class, middle-aged, and the able-bodied to the top of the scale, and others, to the bottom" (Fleras and Elliott, 1996:100). The complex reality of racial discrimination, coupled with equally complex and contradictory perceptions of the extent to which racial discrimination is a continuing problem, illustrates how and why Canadian "race relations" remain tense.

Notes

1. The term "Aboriginal peoples" came into widespread use in the 1980s. It is an inclusive term that tends to be used to refer to people who historically were defined as status Indians, non-status Indians, Inuit, and Métis. In historical perspective, the terms "Indian" and "Aboriginal" are not interchangeable. Government legislation and the Indian Act between the late nineteenth and mid twentieth centuries specifically targeted "status Indians" and not Métis people, non-status Indians, the Inuit, or "Aboriginal people." Since our paper is historical, we use the term Indian to reflect the way the term was applied at the time.

2. Today "non-White" groups are most often referred to as "visible minorities" in Canada. Similarly, the terminology referring to certain racial groups has become outdated. As with our choice to use the term "Indian" in the first section of this chapter, we use terms such as "Black," "Chinese," and "coloured" as reflections of the historical context in which they are presented.

3. Slavery is a system of domination or enforced servitude of one person to another or one group to another. Black slavery was introduced into Canada as early as 1608 and continued into the nineteenth century. Research indicates that the enslavement of Blacks was practised in Quebec, New Brunswick, Nova Scotia, and Ontario. Although the institution of slavery ended after the US Fugitive Slave Act in 1850 and the Emancipation Proclamation of 1863, the treatment of Blacks continued to be marked by overt prejudice and discrimination. This dislike of Blacks created an inhospitable environment leading to residential segregation and legally enforced racially restrictive policies (Henry et al., 1995; see also Hill, 1981; Walker, 1980; Winks 1971).

References

Avery, D.H. 1995. *Reluctant Host: Canada's Response to Immigrant Workers, 1896-1994.* Toronto: McClelland & Stewart.

Barron, L. 1988. "The Indian pass system in the Canadian West, 1882-1935," *Prairie Forum* 13:25-42.

Brownlie, R., and M.E. Kelm. 1994. "Desperately seeking absolution: Native agency as colonial alibi," *Canadian Historical Review* 75:543-56.

Calliste, A. 1987. "Sleeping car porters in Canada: An ethnically submerged split labour market," *Canadian Ethnic Studies* 19, 1:1-20.

—. 1996. "Race, gender and Canadian immigration policy: Blacks from the Caribbean, 1900-1932," *Journal of Canadian Studies* 16, 1:70-87.

Carter, S. 1990. *Lost Harvests: Prairie Indian Reserve Farmers and Government Policy.* Montreal and Kingston: McGill-Queen's University Press.

Cole, D., and I. Chaikin. 1990. *An Iron Hand upon the People: The Law against the Potlatch on the Northwest Coast.* Vancouver: Douglas & McIntyre.

Davis, M., and J.F. Krauter. 1971. *The Other Canadians: Profiles of Six Minorities.* Toronto: Methuen.

—. 1978. *Minority Canadians: Ethnic Groups.* Toronto: Methuen.

Denoon, D. 1983. *Settler Capitalism: the Dynamics of Dependent Development in the Southern Hemisphere.* Oxford: Clarendon Press.

England, K., and B. Stiell. 1997. "They think you are as stupid as your English is: Constructing foreign domestic workers in Toronto," *Environment and Planning* A 29:195-215.

Fleras, A. and J.L. Elliott. 1990. "Immigration and the Canadian ethnic mosaic," in P.S. Li, ed., *Race and Ethnic Relations in Canada.* Toronto: Oxford University Press, 51-76.

—. 1996. *Unequal Relations: An introduction to Race, Ethnic, and Aboriginal Dynamics in Canada,* 2nd ed. Scarborough, ON: Prentice Hall.

Gibbins, R. and R. Ponting. 1986. "Historical background and overview," in Ponting, ed., *Arduous Journey.* Toronto: McClelland & Stewart.

Hawkins, F. 1991. *Critical Years in Immigration: Canada and Australia Compared* 2nd ed. Montreal and Kingston: McGill-Queen's University Press.

Henry, F., C. Tator, W. Mattis, and T. Rees. 1995. *The Colour of Democracy: Racism in Canadian Society.* Toronto: Harcourt Brace & Company.

Hill, D. 1981. *The Freedom Seekers: Blacks in Early Canada.* Agincourt, ON: Book Society of Canada.

Hughes, D.R., and E. Kallen. 1974. *The Anatomy of Racism: Canadian Dimensions.* Montreal: Harvest House.

Knowles, C. 1996. "The symbolic empire and the history of racial inequality," *Ethnic and Racial Studies* 19, 4:896-911.

Ongley, P., and D. Pearson. 1995. "Post-1945 International migration: New Zealand, Australia and Canada compared," *International Migration Review* 29 (Fall):765-93.

Patterson, E.P. 1978. "Andrew Paull and the early history of B.C. Indian organizations," in I. Getty and D. Smith, eds., *One Century Later: Western Canadian Reserve Indians since Treaty 7.* Vancouver: University of British Columbia Press.

Pettipas, K. 1995. *Severing the Ties That Bind: Government Repression of Indigenous Religious Ceremonies on the Prairies.* Winnipeg: University of Manitoba Press.

Ponting, J.R., and R. Gibbins. 1980. *Out of Irrelevance: A Sociopolitical Introduction to Indian Affairs.* Toronto: Butterworths.

Ramcharan, S. 1982. *Racism: Nonwhites in Canada.* Scarborough, ON: Butterworths.

Royal Commission on Aboriginal Peoples. 1996. *Bridging the Cultural Divide: A Report on Aboriginal People and the Criminal Justice System in Canada*. Ottawa. Supply and Services Canada.

Satzewich, V. 1991. *Racism and the Incorporation of Foreign Labour: Farm Labour Migration to Canada since 1945*. New York: Routledge.

Satzewich, V., and L. Mahood. 1994. "Indian affairs and band governance: Deposing Indian chiefs in western Canada, 1896-1911," *Canadian Ethnic Studies* 26:40-58.

Satzewich, V., and L. Zong. 1996. "Social control and the historical construction of 'race,'" In B. Schissel and L. Mahood, eds., *Social Control in Canada: A Reader on the Social Construction of Deviance*. Toronto: Oxford University Press.

Stasiulis, D., and N. Yuval-Davis, eds. 1995. *Unsettling Settler Societies: Articulations of Gender, Race, Ethnicity and Class*. London: Sage.

Titley, E.B. 1986. *A Narrow Vision: Duncan Campbell Scott and the Administration of Indian Affairs in Canada*. Vancouver: University of British Columbia Press.

Walker, J. 1980. *The History of Blacks in Canada: A Study Guide for Teachers and Students*. Ottawa: Minister of State for Multiculturalism.

Winks, R. 1971. *Blacks in Canada*. New Haven: Yale University Press.

3

Defining Sexual Promiscuity: "Race," Gender, and Class in the Operation of Ontario's Female Refuges Act, 1930-1960

JOAN SANGSTER

In 1942 an 18-year-old dishwasher, Anna, from Kenora, was put on a train to Toronto by the police to be transported to the Andrew Mercer Reformatory for Females for a period of one to two years. Removal from this northern community came after charges had been laid against her under the Female Refuges Act (FRA) because of her "idle and dissolute" life. Drunkenness and sexual promiscuity were supposedly the crimes that led to her incarceration. After receiving complaints that she was wandering the streets intoxicated, the local police had followed her from café to hotel to boarding house, at first removing her to the police station when she became ill after drinking, later collecting information on her liaisons with various men (Archives of Ontario [AO], 9332).

Like other young women, Anna was the focus of legal regulation under the FRA because her public alcohol consumption and sexual behaviour offended "community standards" and, in the view of police and court authorities, required drastic alteration. Yet, Anna's trial before a magistrate also took on a distinct character because she was of Native origin. The police chief claimed that she "had been seen in cafés with white boys ... coming in and out ... going into men's rooms.... [and that] she was a regular at the train station with white boys" (AO, 9332). His racial designation of her partners was significant: miscegenation implied her sexual debasement and was intended to spur the court into offering her "protection" (in the form of incarceration) from White men likely to take advantage of her. Also, one of those testifying against Anna was the local Indian agent, whose immense power of surveillance provided the court with ample information to be used against her. The agent testified that he had already charged her three times with liquor offences under the Indian Act, and he complained that she had been "fined and warned," to no avail (AO, 9332). He also claimed that a doctor had informed him of Anna's pregnancy, and on the stand he offered information on her family and background, which helped to persuade the magistrate to convict her. Hearing that Anna had been in an Anglican residential school confirmed the magistrate's view that she was incorrigible and in need of incarceration. "You went to Indian school for ten years, he said to her, "so you should know right from wrong" (AO, 9332). Anna's one-word answer in the affirmative probably had little effect on the magistrate, who sentenced her to an indefinite term in the Reformatory.

Anna's case also bears some strong similarities to those of other young women, from all racial and ethnic backgrounds, who were convicted under the FRA. Most of these women came from impoverished or work-ing-class backgrounds and were perceived to be part of an "underclass" with weak or non-existent sexual morality and in dire need of character transformation and social (and reproductive) control. At first glance, mas-culinist definitions appear to be the defining character of all the FRA con-victions. This law proscribed women's sexuality within a gender order based on hegemonic masculinity, the rejection of women's sexual activity outside of marriage, and the sanctification of the nuclear, father-headed family. However, the law was also applied in a class-specific manner. Women's material impoverishment always encouraged the likelihood of their arrest and was intertwined with expert discourses on what constituted "dissolute" sexual behaviour. Psychiatric and social work definitions of "sex delinquency," throughout this period, for example, were usually fused with images of working-class and poor women, and the criteria used by penal workers to assess women's rehabilitation were permeated with class biases. As Michel Foucault (1980:121) argued, sexual control is often most "intense and meticulous when it is directed at the lower classes."

While class and gender were crucial elements shaping the use of the FRA, race, too, was important. Indeed, the "simultaneity" of these factors in shaping women's experience of sexual regulation through the law should be the focus of our inquiry (Brewer, 1993; Roediger, 1993). As many Black feminists have argued, interrogating these categories alone may be unproductive, but in interplay, and in historical motion, the "paradigm becomes richer" (Brewer, 1993:27; see also Bannerji, 1993, 1995; Agnew, 1996). At the same time, capturing the complexity of "interlocking systems of domination" and the ways in which they "constitute each other," Sharene Razack (1998) has argued, remains an extremely difficult task.

Some systems of domination may remain less visible, and ironically, our very use of a "language of colour" contradicts our attempts to deconstruct race.[1]

While the vast majority of women convicted under this particular draconian statute were White, and often of Anglo-Celtic origin, the legal and social understandings of "promiscuity"—so central to the FRA—were racialized, reflecting a dominant ideological construction of women (and men) of colour as licentious and weak in moral conviction, and in contrast, White women as more moral and sexually pure.[2] It is the intention of this paper to outline, using two examples relating to the FRA, how the legal regulation of women's sexuality through this law was racialized and racist. On the one hand, convictions of White women who were sexually involved with Asian, Afro-Canadian, and Native men indicated fears that these women were especially debased and in need of carceral supervision because they had violated an important colour line. On the other hand, the increasing numbers of First Nations women convicted under the FRA, and the rationale for their incarceration, indicate that colonialism and racism made Native women more sexually suspect in the eyes of the law and more liable to legal prosecution.

As historians and legal scholars have repeatedly documented (for example, Backhouse, 1999; Tarnopolsky, 1982; Walker, 1997), Canadian law, through public policy, statute law, and judicial interpretation, played a significant role in constituting and reproducing racist ideologies, sanctioning discrimination, exclusion, and segregation based on race. Racial differentiation might be openly stated in legal statute, but also unfold as the effect of legal and judicial practices, in laws and policy relating to everything from the franchise to employment to recreation to morality to immigration. Because the law both constitutes society and reproduces prevailing cultural assumptions, "common sense" notions of race were firmly embedded in the operation of Canadian law from colonial times through the twentieth century.[3] Although ideological constructions of race did alter over time, a persisting theme in legal discourse and practice was the assumption of White superiority and imperialist right.

Attempting to uncover the racial meanings created by law, and the power relations they reflect and reproduce, has been a central aim of critical race theory. A fundamental premise of this theory is that "race is socially constructed, and the law is central to that construction" (Haney Lopez, 1996:9). Racial meaning systems are grounded in both "the world of ideas and in the material geography of social life" (17) and they are sustained by both subtle ideological consent—clothed in rationales ranging from "necessity" to "protection," to "fairness"—as well as by repressive coercion.[4] The construction of race is also interconnected with class, gender, and sexuality (Anthias, 1990; Anthias and Yuval-Davis, 1992; Raczack, 1998). In the latter case, for instance, many Canadian laws ostensibly about employment (such as those barring White women from working for Chinese men) emerged because of fears of the sexual corruption of White women by Asian men.[5] Similarly, though the letter of the FRA statute never mentioned race, it was one factor shaping how the law was implemented, and in the process it, too, "created" race and racism.

What Was the Female Refuges Act?

The Female Refuges Act was enacted in 1897 to regulate the Industrial Houses of Refuge, which held women sentenced or "*liable* to be sentenced" by magistrates under local bylaw or Criminal Code infractions.[6] Specifically aimed at women between the ages of 16 and 35, presumably because these were women's more active sexual and reproductive years, the FRA designated refuges or correctional institutions as places where women were offered shelter, work, and reform as a means of counteracting their "unmanageability and incorrigibility." The initial FRA allowed a sentence of up to five years; this was amended to two years less a day in 1919, following a coroner's inquest into an inmate's death, after she tried to escape by jumping from a window of Toronto's Belmont Refuge (*Globe and Mail*, 12 April 1919).

In 1919, the Act was also broadened with a clause giving magistrates and judges new wide-ranging powers. Any person could bring before a magistrate "any female under the age of 35 ... who is a habitual drunkard or by reasons of other vices is leading an idle and dissolute life." All that was needed was a sworn statement about the woman's behaviour, or in the case of parents and guardians, a claim that their daughter was "unmanageable and incorrigible."[7] No formal charge and trial were needed, and hearings were in private, although written evidence was supposedly required. Faced with criticisms about the Act, a 1942 amendment allowed sentences to be appealed before the Court of Appeal—though this appears to have been seldom used. In 1958, these sections were finally deleted after persistent lobbying of the government by the Elizabeth Fry Society, though in public, the government simply claimed that the issues involved were adequately covered by other Criminal Code and provincial statutes (Ontario Legislative Assembly Debates, March 1958).

The FRA allowed parents, police, welfare authorities, and the Children's Aid Society (CAS) to incarcerate women perceived to be out of sexual control. Although some women were also targeted when they were destitute, alcoholic, or had resorted to petty theft, the Act was used primarily to police women's sexual behaviour. For teenage girls already serving time in industrial or, later, training schools, the Act could increase their punishment by sending them to the Mercer Reformatory for up to two more years. Indeed, rather than sending convicted women to "low security" refuges where the indigent also lived, such as Belmont House or the Catholic Good Shepherd, some magistrates sent women straight to the Mercer Reformatory.

Although the total number of women convicted under the Act was small in comparison to other charges, such as public order and petty theft, the operation of the FRA provides important insight into the dominant definitions of sexual "promiscuity," or non-conformity, employed by the courts, social workers, and the medical profession at this time. These definitions not only punished "bad" girls, but were part of a broader web of moral regulation, setting out the ideal of "good" feminine sexuality against which all women, even those untouched by the criminal justice system, were judged.

The peak of FRA prosecutions came during the 1930s and World War II, though Native women increased as a percentage of the overall convictions in the post-World War II period.[8] Youth was the most distinguishing feature of all the women involved; indeed, the vast majority of those convicted were under 21. Most were Canadian-born and of Anglo-Celtic background, including first-generation British immigrants, though the presence of the latter group was not surprising given the influx of such immigrants to Ontario just before World War I and the tendency of immigrants to face economic and social dislocation.[9] Almost all the women came from either working-class or poverty-stricken backgrounds, with parents crossing the spectrum from the criminal classes to the skilled artisan. These young women usually had little education, having left school by 15, and their occupations, if they had one (and they often did not), were listed as domestic or, less often, waitress or factory worker.

The vast majority of FRA incarcerations resulted from three, often intertwined, factors: sexual promiscuity (termed here, non-conformity), illegitimate pregnancies, and venereal disease. Some of the women incarcerated were simply destitute runaways or street women, but for the over-whelming majority, dissolute was equated with errant sexuality. For Native women, charges of alcohol abuse and sexual promiscuity were often linked together by the authorities. Many FRA women either had an illegitimate child or were pregnant when they entered the Reformatory, and a significant number were treated for venereal disease. Their sentences were also stiff, as both the Mercer authorities and judges and magistrates claimed women needed a long period of time to effect real change in their character. On average, they received from one to two years, and women did not secure release easily, often serving the majority of their sentences.

Defining Promiscuity: Interracial Liaisons

A number of recurring patterns were evident in FRA convictions. In general, they reflected deep-seated anxieties that poor and working-class women were unruly and oversexual, either led astray or leading men astray. To this end, women who engaged in sexual activity in "public" spaces, did not exhibit the appropriate remorse about their sexual liaisons, or even boasted about them were especially suspect. The sexual activity of young women was threatening to worried parents when daughters disobeyed their parents, stayed out all night, ran away, consorted with "criminal" men and women, or contacted venereal disease. Pregnancy might also be a problem, particularly if the woman did not know the father well, or even who he was. Women with "too many" illegitimate children were a special focus of concern, and even though the files rarely mention sterilization, eugenic concerns undoubtedly percolated beneath the surface of some convictions, especially in the 1930s and early 1940s. Women perceived to have too many partners, or the wrong kind of partner (such as older, married men) were also targeted, though even one man could be one too many if parents objected to someone they felt was a bad influence on their daughter.

The wrong kind of partner was also defined by race.[10] Indeed, the way in which the courts interpreted promiscuity and prostitution rested on racist assumptions about the "instinctual" sexual behaviour of different races and the dangers of miscegenation, even if these were not openly stated. By the 1930s, strictly biological explanations of race, so popular at the turn of the century, were being replaced by theories that claimed both culture and biology created racial difference. Because those differences were also equated with a hierarchy, and a somewhat inevitable one, discrimination against people of colour, as well as Jews, was often condoned in the courts and in society (Walker, 1997).[11] It was not until the aftermath of World War II that a discernible shift in attitude occurred, characterized by increasing antipathy to the concept of racial discrimination, though "cultural racism" remained well entrenched in Canadian society (Razack, 1998).

During the 1930s and the early 1940s, however, interracial sex was seen as unacceptable and dangerous. This was made evident in an appeal before the Ontario upper court in 1930, in which a young woman challenged her two-year sentence for vagrancy handed out by Toronto Magistrate Margaret Patterson. The woman's nighttime socializing with "coloured" and White men and the fact that she lived with a "coloured railway porter" were central in the court's reassessment of the verdict. Debate centred especially on whether she had any "means of subsistence" and whether she was a prostitute. As the judge noted, to confirm the latter, she "has to do with more than one man," yet he could only find evidence of the relationship with the porter. However, the definition of "subsistence" gave the Judge the loophole he was searching for: subsistence had to be not just legal, but "reputable," not contradicting "the moral standards of the community." Being supported by a coloured man, he concluded, is "not the kind of subsistence that the Criminal Code" had in mind! One can be excused for concluding that the judge was determined to follow any tortuous "logic" to find a way of upholding Patterson's conviction, based more fundamentally on his aversion to mixed-race couples than anything else (*Rex v. Davis*, 1930).

If the higher court was happy to set such standards, the lower courts were happy to follow, not only in official judgements but in the more general investigation, interviewing, and counselling of women by probation officers, doctors, and social workers. In another case presided over by Magistrate Margaret Patterson in the 1930s, a 17-year-old, who was described by her foster mother as "boy crazy" and untruthful, was found in a "bawdy house with a Chinaman" (AO, 6972). Patterson immediately remanded her into psychiatric care, a decision that underscored how women's sexual non-conformity was literally equated with their insanity. A young Toronto woman, who was arrested in 1940 on a charge of incorrigibility, was declared mentally slow by the court doctor. The court also heard that she was "not working" and refused to follow her stepfather's rules about a curfew, but her major crime seemed to be that she was living with "a coloured man." Sent first to the Salvation Army hostel, she ran away; when re-arrested, she was sent to the Mercer (AO, 8398).

White police, court workers, and some working-class families perceived men and women of colour, particularly Afro-Canadians, to be more sexually promiscuous, and feared Whites would become tainted or seduced by these lax morals; in cases involving Chinese men, fears also centred on their supposed roles as pimps and drug pushers (Murphy, 1923; Pon, 1996). It was often parents who called the police concerning their daughters' interracial liaisons, hoping to pressure their daughters into abandoning the relationship. Once the case was in motion, however, incarceration under the FRA became a distinct possibility. One father swore out a statement against his 19-year-old, who had left school at 14 and was employed as a mail clerk. Despite the apparent respectability of her wage labour, he noted she was "keeping bad company ... she is now with a coloured man and pregnant by him." The case was originally brought to the police by a Catholic welfare agency that the girl contacted, hoping for assistance so she could keep her baby. They alerted the police and parents, and urged the woman to give up her baby, facilitating her return home to her parents after her sentence was served (AO, 8700).

Women could also be the focus of legal concern if they were sexually involved with Native men, though this was a less common scenario in large urban centres. One young woman from northern Ontario was incarcerated in the 1940s after her sexual relationship with a Native man became an issue. The court deemed her mother a bad example as she was living common law, but the mother also participated in the complaint against her daughter, who she charged was "running around with an Indian boy and would not get a job." Mabel claimed that her boyfriend "wanted to marry her" but became abusive "and threatened to kill her if she saw anyone else." The magistrate, despite his disbelief in her charges of violence, agreed that Mabel's conduct was satisfactory until she "started seeing a young Indian boy.... We will put this girl in a home. We can't have her running around with Indian boys like that" (AO, 9404).

In responding to their sentences, White women involved with men of colour sometimes claimed they did not understand why they were being punished, but in other cases they clearly understood that they should either profess shame or coercion if they were to escape the Reformatory. One 22-year-old British immigrant nursemaid, Elise, for example, was convicted under the FRA based on police information that she was "going around with H and other Chinamen and is now pregnant." Although the

Attorney General later admitted that the evidence against her was "flimsy," Elise served three months before being released into the care of the Salvation Army. She had originally come to the attention of the police as a "public charge" sent to a hospital after taking quinine to try to induce an abortion. Trying to secure sympathy, she told the court that she came to Canada to join her sister, who was "living a bad life" and "forced" her to sleep with Chinese and Italian men (AO, 8634).[12] Whether this was true or not (and given her later, clever attempts to feign labour to escape from the police, it may not have been) mattered little: she clearly knew this was the expedient thing to declare.

Yet, another young woman, who later told her story to the Elizabeth Fry Society, claimed little understanding of the rationale for her arrest. Her recollections highlight how quickly decisions were made, with little regard for the due process of law. She was arrested when living with her Chinese boyfriend, after her father, who was actually from another province, came to town and sought out the help of the police. The police arrived one morning as she sat in her dressing gown, and she remembers being whisked away and kept very much in the dark during the whole process. Without counsel, she misjudged the best strategy for securing her release:

> I was taken into a room and asked by a woman if I had ever slept with anyone else. I felt I would have to damage my character to save my boyfriend from blame. I said, "Yes" ... [and] I told her I was pregnant hoping that would help. Almost immediately I was taken to a courtroom.... [In court] I didn't see anyone else until the policeman [who arrested me] spoke from behind me.

After a few curt questions from the judge about her pregnancy, she offered to "get married" to her Chinese boyfriend if they would just let her out. It was the wrong tactic. She was remanded for a week in jail, then returned to court to be quickly sentenced to one year in the Belmont Refuge; after it closed, she was transferred to the Mercer Reformatory (Elizabeth Fry Society of Toronto, Copeland).

Magistrates and court and penal workers all displayed paternalism, horror, or revulsion towards the sexual behaviour of White and non-White women; nonetheless, specifically racist suppositions about women and men of colour were apparent. For example, if the parents of a girl were non-White, or had sexual relations with a person of colour, this was seen by court professionals as a rationale for the "lax" morals of the daughter. A disposition to immorality, they believed, could be passed on through familial contact. This "culture of immorality theory" worked against a young woman accused under the FRA, since the risk involved in *not* incarcerating her was so often determined by how "immoral" her family was. One Toronto teen, who was not working or attending school, was suspected of immorality; she was sent first to Belmont and later transferred to the Mercer so that she could learn some "self discipline." The court clearly believed that, left at home, she would be unduly influenced by her Native mother. "The father seems decent," reported a CAS worker, "but the mother is Indian and easy going in the home … apparently the family can do anything it pleases. Mother is inefficient and unintelligent" (AO, 7223).

Although it was invariably the woman incarcerated, these cases also indicate how the sexuality of non-White men was supervised and censured more stringently than that of White men (Dubinsky, 1993:88-89; Odem, 1995:80-81; Strange, 1996:155-56). As other authors have documented, men of colour could become "villainized," the focus of intense suspicion concerning sexual crimes, as the image of their volatile, potentially lascivious sexuality was widely embraced across lines of class and gender (for example, Dubinsky, 1993; Dubinsky and Givertz, 1999; Murphy, 1923). The perceptions of men from "White ethnic" backgrounds who were not Anglo-Celtic sometimes played a role in the courts' perceptions of women's sexual morality, though in far more complex ways in these years. It was not simply ethnicity per se that determined the courts' views, but rather that of their overall assessment of the family's morality. White European immigrants who were employed, hard-working, and appeared to have embraced the "proper" moral values were not necessarily looked on with suspicion. However, if they *did* become involved in sexual "immorality," the fact of their ethnicity could be made an issue, their immorality blamed on their lack of "Canadian" values (Sangster, 1996).

First Nations Women and the FRA

Although relatively small numbers of women of colour were arrested for dissolute behaviour, their sexual behaviour was still perceived to be a threat, both to themselves and to the larger community (Sangster, 1999).[13] Native women and women of colour were almost always seen to be more prone to promiscuity, and Native women were believed to need paternalist protection. "She is a loose character, highly sexed, and particularly so when she is drunk" (AO, 11089), noted a fairly typical magistrate's report for an Aboriginal woman. By the 1950s, the FRA cases do not indicate White women singled out especially because of their liaisons with men of colour, reflecting marginally different attitudes towards interracial relationships in Canadian society. On the other hand, after the late 1940s, the number of Native women incarcerated under the FRA multiplied, contradicting the overall trend for FRA arrests and reflecting the increasing over-incarceration of Native women in general (LaPrairie, 1984; Canada, 1993; Sangster, 1999).

This escalating pattern of incarceration was related directly to the intensifying effects of colonialism on Native communities. It is true that colonialism was hardly new: the denigration of Native cultures and missionary and government attempts to supplant traditional social structures and practices had existed for over a century. However, the post-World War II period saw new threats to patterns of traditional subsistence practised by many communities, the opening up of northern, previously isolated communities to hostile White populations, and the increased presence of Aboriginal peoples in urban areas, where they faced unemployment and racism. Social tensions and economic impoverishment resulted in ill health, alcoholism, and conflicts with the law, and Aboriginal families found few sources of aid other than "outside" legal and welfare authorities, which they sometimes avoided, fearing loss of their children or imprisonment.

Most Native women arrested under the FRA were brought before the court by the RCMP, local police, or the Indian agent for alcohol-related infractions; these were linked to charges of sexual immorality and illegitimate births, perceived to be inevitable, corollary crimes. Many already had convictions or run-ins with policing authorities, and some were literally destitute. As a sentencing report noted, one woman literally had no place of residence and no employment, nor any immediate family to help her. Under the circumstances, she had few alternatives, save for occasional prostitution, to sustain herself and deal with her alcoholism. Another sentencing report that noted a theft charge for "stealing clothes off a clothesline" (AO, 14355) underlined how economically marginal these women were.

If women did not have immediate family members with the resources to take them in, as many did not, then they were more likely to face incarceration. Moreover, First Nations women could be caught in the no-win situation caused by their lack of "official" Indian status on some reserves. Women who married Whites, of course, could not return to their home reserve, but even those who married into another reserve could be left without aid—depending on the whim of the local Indian agent. One woman in these circumstances was initially deserted by her husband and had to send her two children to live with her parents. The agent had little interest in helping her, in part because she "did not have status" on her husband's reserve, in part because she had a number of intoxication charges against her. Her decision to live with a White man nearby who had a criminal record was the last straw: faced with her refusal to testify against this "bootlegger," she was arrested under the FRA and sentenced to the Reformatory (AO, 8982).

Indian agents, as the opening story indicated, could also be a factor in a woman's incarceration, testifying against her before a magistrate or judge. Women living on reserves were subject to the agent's ongoing surveillance of their own and their families' lives, and most agents were not hesitant to make judgements about Native morality. Agents could be called on to judge women's possibility of parole as well, and their long list of comments on the family's churchgoing, education, drinking, and sexual habits reflected their immense powers of surveillance. While the agents exercised power because of their moral and political stature, in contrast, Native women were disadvantaged by language barriers (some needed translators in court) and their cultural alienation from the adversarial court processes in which they were involved.

It was not simply that First Nations women were surveyed—for women on welfare were, too—but that they were also surveyed using racist assumptions. Native women were seen as weaker in moral outlook, prone to alcoholism, easily corrupted by White men offering them alcohol, and likely to barter with their sexuality (Carter, 1996; Kline, 1995; Monture-Angus, 1995; Tiffany and Adams, 1985). "It is just another case of a girl coming here and going wild after the soldiers" (AO, 9337) commented one police report of a young First Nations woman. Another young woman was told by the magistrate:

> It is too bad that such a good looking Indian like you should throw yourself away. Other men buy the liquor for you, then you suffer and they escape…. I hope if you are removed from unscrupulous white men and Indian soldiers you might start a new life. (AO, 9004)

Once incarcerated, Native women still encountered assumptions, shared by male and female medical and penal experts, that they lacked the moral introspection necessary to "reform" themselves.

Removing women who drank alcohol was often seen as a means of "saving" younger, impressionable women from the likelihood of corruption. In his testimony urging incarceration, one RCMP officer noted that a woman from the reserve "is a bad influence … she has led a fifteen year old astray" (AO, 9004; AO, 14212). In a similar manner, the authorities in a small city wanted a married woman, separated from her husband and two children, incarcerated, not simply because of her sexual activity but because she had let a minor share her apartment and engage in sexual activity with men (AO, 9900).

Many of the sentencing reports of Native women indicate experiences similar to those of non-Native women, shaped by impoverishment, addiction or ill health, violence, family dissolution, and experience with some form of state care, such as the Children's Aid Society, foster homes, or very occasionally, residential schools. Many Native women were "damned" by reports that their families had alcoholic or "immoral" members, who were offered up as explanations for the (inevitable) decline of these women, just as they were for other FRA women. "Her family history is a bad one," noted one sentencing report. "Her father is living with a woman not his wife … and her mother is possibly worse than her, and certainly partly at fault for her behaviour" (AO, 9434). Moreover, there was a strong concern that both Native and non-Native women convicted under the FRA would likely produce illegitimate children who would become a burden on the state. After repeated alcohol charges, a woman with five children was sent to Mercer from the north. Since illness at four years had left her deaf, the Reformatory psychologist was unable to test her IQ, but this did not stop him from concluding she was mentally "slow." "No doubt children will continue until the end of her productive age, or until a pathological process renders her sterile," he commented, adding that "improvement is remote … so to prevent future progeny institutionalization recommended" (AO, 16461).

Native families were less likely than White families to implicate their own daughters and wives to the authorities, but some certainly did. They were troubled, as White families were, with what they perceived to be women "out of control" and in desperate need of aid, so they turned to the Indian agent or local police for help. Communities and families did not always feel that they could help women who appeared to be suffering from addiction and were sexually "promiscuous," were destitute, and needed their children cared for as well. One single father from the north brought his daughter to Juvenile Court twice because he considered her a "bad influence on her sister and other girls." She had run away, had a baby, and according to the police "was picked up at drinking parties and was involved in a break and enter" (AO, 10637). Another mother swore out a warrant when her 21-year-old daughter was "found intoxicated in hotel with an Indian" (AO, 8432). Occasionally, family members wrote to the Mercer asking that the woman not receive parole (AO, 9161). Certainly, some families, no matter how meagre their resources, offered uncondi-tional aid to released women. In one case, a mother found that the penal authorities placed less faith in the healing powers of family if the family happened to be Native. She wrote to the Mercer Superintendent, asking to have her grandchild sent to her, but her wishes were disregarded and the child was put up for adoption (AO, 15166).

Families and communities were probably led to believe that the Reformatory was going to provide care and education. Judges and magistrates, when rendering their verdicts, constantly claimed that women would "learn a trade and ... be released ... to re-establish [themselves]" (AO, 14305) and that the Mercer was the place to send women who were "badly in need of care and treatment for alcoholism" (AO, 14176). Yet, these were precisely the things the Elizabeth Fry Society argued most women were *not* getting at the Mercer Reformatory. By the late 1950s, their political lobbying not only included attempts to abolish the FRA, but also requests for education, training, and addiction aid for women incarcerated in the Mercer. As well, they wanted both the federal and provincial governments to pay attention to the poverty in northern Native communities that was leading to over-incarceration (AO, RG 20, 13-185). The fact that Native women's over-incarceration increased in the years after this study indicates all too well that the Society's concerns were ignored, as well as the way in which incarceration only accentuated Native women's alienation (Sangster, 1999). Indeed, the final verdict on the FRA was summed up by the experiences of a Native woman, Alice, from a small Ontario town who was convicted under the FRA in the early 1940s. This was not her first sentence on a morality charge, and she had been destitute for some time, but the purpose of a lengthy FRA sentence was to "reform" her for good. Yet, after her release, Alice's name appeared repeatedly in the Mercer registers over the next decades, on vagrancy and alcohol charges

(AO, 12128). For her, the FRA had done little to help, and perhaps more to intensify her problems with poverty, ill health, addiction, and racism.

Conclusion

These FRA convictions offer examples of the way in which the definitions of promiscuity employed by the courts, circulating also within the wider social context, were shaped within the interconnected categories of race, class, and gender. Trying to disentangle these as separate strands to assign one absolute pre-eminence is difficult because they were usually interwoven, hinged together "symbiotically," though not without some hierarchy (Razack, 1998).

Convictions of both White and Native women revealed high levels of impoverishment and ill health in women's backgrounds, with the courts unable to recognize, on a structural level, the material and social dislocations shaping women's conflicts with the law: the damaging results of poverty, their problems with addiction, and their experience of violence and institutional care. While there was some attempt by court and penal workers to pinpoint the "environmental" causes of their immorality, these were more likely to focus on women's "feeble-mindedness" or "immorality"[14] not the material and social conditions of their lives.

At the same time, the FRA was a gender-specific piece of legislation, reflecting a double standard of sexuality that portrayed women's sexual activity as dangerous if it was expressed outside of heterosexual marriage; the protection of what were deemed "proper" familial roles was inextricably linked to the regulation of women's sexuality. The use of the FRA bolstered notions of inherent differences between male and female sexuality, linking natural female sexuality to passivity and premarital purity, and sanctifying an ideal family type in which the wife was constrained within monogamous domesticity and the daughter was a dutiful and chaste apprentice for this role.

Yet, the FRA convictions also reflected change over time; there was a declining concern with White women's interracial liaisons and intensified policing of Native women in the post- World War II period. The interaction of social knowledge about "race" with the law may have altered somewhat, but a general theme persisted: the very notion of which women were *likely* to be promiscuous, which women needed "protection," which women had a weaker moral constitution, was shaped by the equation of

Whiteness with the protection of purity, and Aboriginal and women of colour with potential moral laxity. Indeed, Aboriginal women were subject to extra surveillance and control in part for this reason, lending credence to Kimberlé Crenshaw's observation that, even if "consent and coercion" are both at work in the reproduction of racism through the law, coercion was often more salient for people of colour (Crenshaw, 1988). Although FRA convictions were clothed in protectionist language, in medical rationales, or even in reform rhetoric, they also worked, ideologically, to construct race and racism through the practice of the law.

Notes

1. In this paper, I have not explored sexual orientation and disability, which were less salient forces in the criminalization of women under the FRA.

2. Because this paper focuses on the Female Refuges Act, my discussion centres on the regulation of women's sexuality, though it is clear that male sexuality also was regulated according to race.

3. As James Walker and others emphasize, the legal construction of "race" in Canada was part of a broader historical and global process of European imperialism.

4. There is some debate about the relative importance of consent and coercion in this process. For one excellent exploration of this, see Crenshaw (1988).

5. There is also an argument that this had to do with Whites opposing the economic competition posed by Chinese businesses. For different statements on anti-Chinese laws and sentiment, see Backhouse (1994, 1996) and Walker (1998). Sexuality and race also converged in eugenic discourse and legislation. See McLaren (1990).

6. Royal Statutes of Ontario (RSO), 1897, c.311, An Act Respecting Houses of Refuge for Females; RSO 1919, c.84, An Act Respecting Industrial Refuges for Females (The Female Refuges Act), see especially section 15; RSO, 1927, c. 347, sections, 15-17. Emphasis added. Also see Dymond (1923: ch.9). Women could be put in a Refuge for "bad habits" like drunkenness, if they were unable "to protect themselves" (p. 84). In this paper, I draw on case files of women sent to the Mercer Reformatory under the FRA.

7. This applied to daughters who were under 21. Using other laws, parents had essentially been able to do this before 1919.

8. About 60 per cent of all incarcerations took place during these years. However, Native women were seldom arrested under the FRA in the 1930s, more often in the 1940s (10 per cent) and 1950s (13 per cent). The number of Native women sent to the Mercer under the FRA, therefore, was a small percentage of the overall numbers of Native women sent there: in the 1940s about 6 per cent, and in the 1950s, about 4 per cent. The overall number of intakes (repeaters or not) listed as Native in the Mercer went from 169 in the 1940s to 370 in the 1950s. Most Native women were convicted under alcohol and vagrancy laws. In a previous article (Sangster, 1999) detailing these numbers, a typographical error mistakenly rendered 169 into 109.

9. Many of the case files are incomplete in terms of such information. An immigrant was often noted as such if there was a possibility of deportation.

10. It is important to note, however, that these cases were a small minority of FRA cases.

11. Note that the Ontario government, even into the 1950s, kept statistics on training schools, which noted the "nationalities" of inmates, with Whites separated from three other "races: Hebrews, Negroes and Indians." See also AO, Dept. of Reform Institutions, RG 20-16-2, Container J9, letter to Supervisor of Training School for Boys, 24 Feb. 1953: "children born in Canada are Canadian unless they are Indian, Hebrew or Negro, when they are shown as the appropriate race."

12. In this explanation, she appears somewhat deferential, yet in other dealings with authorities, she was far less so, denouncing the CAS as "a bunch of bullies who just want me in jail."

13. It is important to note that the Ontario government did not keep statistics on the "race" of women sent to the Mercer Reformatory (though they did of girls sentenced to training schools). However, the prison registers usually noted, under complexion, "Indian," and it is clear from this designation that there were steady increases in First Nations women over time, increasingly so in the post-World War II period.

14. The fear of unregulated reproduction of "unsuitable" women (predominately framed by class, though also influenced by race) by middle-class professionals shaped some FRA prosecutions in the early years, though this probably persisted as an underlying concern in the 1940s and 1950s.

References

Agnew, V. 1996. *Resisting Discrimination: Women from Asia, Africa and the Caribbean and the Women's Movement in Canada.* Toronto: University of Toronto Press.

Anthias, F. 1990. "Race and class revisited," *Sociological Review* 28, 1:19-42.

Anthias, F., and N. Yuval-Davis, eds. 1992. *Racialized Boundaries: Race, Nation, Gender and Colour and Class and the Anti-Racist Struggle.* London: Routledge.

Backhouse, C. 1994. "White female help and Chinese Canadian employers: Race, class, gender and law in the case of Yee Clun, 1924," *Canadian Ethnic Studies* 26, 3:34-52.

—. 1996. "White women's labour laws: Anti-Chinese racism and early twentieth century Canada," *Law and History Review* 14:315-68.

—. 1999. *Colour Coded: A Legal history of Racism in Canada, 1900-1950.* Toronto: University of Toronto Press.

Bannerji, H., ed. 1993. *Returning the Gaze: Essays on Racism, Feminism and Politics.* Toronto: Sister Vision Press.

—. 1995. *Thinking It Through: Essays on Feminism, Marxism and Anti-Racism.* Toronto: Women's Press.

Brewer, R. 1993. "Theorizing race, class and gender: The new scholarship of black feminist intellectuals," in S. James and A. Busia, eds., *Theorizing Black Feminism: The Visionary Pragmatism of Black Women.* New York: Routledge.

Canada, Royal Commission on Aboriginal Peoples. 1993. *Aboriginal Peoples and the Justice System: Report of the National Round Table on Aboriginal Justice.* Ottawa.

Carter, S. 1996. "Categories and terrains of exclusion: Constructing the 'Indian Woman' in the early settlement era in western Canada," in J. Parr and M. Rosenfeld, eds., *Gender and Canadian History.* Toronto: Copp Clark, 40-61.

Copeland, J. "The Female Refuges Act," unpublished manuscript, Elizabeth Fry Society of Toronto Library.

Crenshaw, K.W. 1988. "Race, reform and retrenchment: Transformation and legitimation in antidiscrimination law," *Harvard Law Review* 101:1331-87.

Dubinsky, K. 1993. *Improper Advances: Rape and Heterosexual Conflict in Ontario, 1880-1929*. Chicago: University of Chicago Press.

Dubinsky, K., and A. Givertz. 1999. "'It Was Only a Matter of Passion': Masculinity and sexual danger," in K. McPherson, C. Morgan and N. Forestall, eds., *Gendered Pasts: Historical Essays in Femininity and Masculinity in Canada*. Toronto: Oxford University Press, 65-79.

Dymond, A. 1923. *The Laws of Ontario relating to Women and Children*. Toronto.

Foucault, M. 1980. *History of Sexuality*. New York: Vintage.

Haney Lopez, I. 1996. *White by Law: The Legal Construction of Race*. New York: New York University Press.

Kline, M. 1995. "Complicating the ideology of motherhood: Child welfare law and first nations women," in M. Fineman and I. Karpin, eds., *Mothers in Law: Feminist Theory and the Legal Regulation of Motherhood*. New York: Columbia University Press, 118-42.

LaPrairie, C. 1984. "Selected criminal justice and socio-economic data on native women," *Canadian Journal of Criminology* 26, 4:161-69.

McLaren, A. 1990. *Our Own Master Race: Eugenics in Canada, 1884-1945*. Toronto: McClelland & Stewart.

Monture-Angus, P. 1995. *Thunder in My Soul: A Mohawk Woman Speaks*. Halifax: Fernwood Press.

Murphy, E. 1923 [1973]. *The Black Candle*. Toronto: Coles Publishing.

Odem, M. 1995. *Delinquent Daughters: Protecting and Policing Adolescent Female Sexuality in the United States, 1885-1920*. Chapel Hill: University of North Carolina Press.

Ontario. 1897. Royal Statutes. c. 311.

—. 1919. An Act Respecting Houses of Refuge for Females. Royal Statutes, c. 84.

—. 1927. An Act Respecting Industrial Refuges for Females (The Female Refuges Act). Royal Statutes, c. 347, s. 15-17.

—. 1953. Department of Reform Institutions. *Report*.

—. 1958. *Legislative Assembly Debates*.

—. Ministry of Correctional Services 1930-1960. Andrew Mercer Reformatory for Females Case Files.

Pon, M. 1996. "Like a Chinese puzzle: The construction of Chinese masculinity in *Jack Canuck*," In J. Parr and M. Rosenfeld, eds., *Gender and History in Canada*. Toronto: Copp Clark, 88-100.

Rafter, N.H. 1985. "Chastising the unchaste: Social control functions of a women's reformatory, 1894-1931," in S. Cohen and A. Scull, eds., *Social Control and the State: Historical and Comparative Essays*. Oxford: Basil Blackwell, 288-311.

Razack, S. 1998. *Looking White People in the Eye: Gender, Race and Culture in Courtrooms and Classrooms*. Toronto: University of Toronto Press.

Rex v. Davis, 1930.

Roediger, D. 1993. "Race and the working-class past in the United States: Multiple identities and the future of labor history," *International Review of Social History* 38:127-43.

Sangster, J. 1996. "Incarcerating 'Bad Girls': The regulation of sexuality through the female refuges act in Ontario, 1920-1945," *Journal of the History of Sexuality* 7:2.

—. 1999. "Criminalizing the colonized: Ontario native women confront the criminal justice system, 1920-1960," *Canadian Historical Review* 80, 1:32-60.

Stephen, J. 1995. "The incorrigible, the bad and the immoral: Toronto's factory girls and the work of the Toronto Psychiatric Clinic," in L. Knafla and S. Binnie, eds., *Law, Society and the State: Essays in Modern Legal History*. Toronto: University of Toronto Press, 405-39.

Strange, C. 1996. *Toronto's Girl Problem: The Perils and Pleasures of the City, 1880-1930*. Toronto: University of Toronto Press.

Tarnopolsky, W. 1982. *Discrimination and the Law in Canada*. Toronto: Richard De Boo.

Tiffany, S. and K. Adams. 1985. *The Wild Woman: An Inquiry into the Anthropology of an Idea.* Cambridge: Shcenkman.

Walker, J.W. St. G. 1997. *'Race' Rights and the Law in the Supreme Court of Canada.* Toronto: University of Toronto Press.

Walker, J.W. St. G. 1998. "The Quong Wing Files," in F. Iacovetta and W. Mitchinson, eds., *On the Case: Explorations in Social History.* Toronto: University of Toronto Press, 204-23.

Part II
Racialization and the Legal System

4

The Criminalization of "Race," the Racialization of Crime

YASMIN JIWANI

"There are no 'race' shield laws." (Johnson, 1993:1740)

Introduction

The criminalization of race and of particular racial groups has drawn considerable attention in the United States and Britain (e.g., Cashmore and Mclaughlin, 1991; Gilroy, 1987; Hawkins, 1995; Johnson, 1993). However, in Canada, explicit attention to the issue has emerged relatively recently, and has been spurred in part by the public attention given to the findings of various commissions and provincial task forces. These include: the Royal Commission on the Donald Marshall Jr. Prosecution (Hickman, 1989), the Task Force on the Criminal Justice System and its Impact on the Indian and Métis People of Alberta (Alberta, 1991), the *Report on Aboriginal Peoples and Criminal Justice* by the Law Reform Commission of Canada (1991), the Report of the Aboriginal Justice Inquiry of Manitoba (1991), the Quebec task force on Investigation into Relations Between Police Forces, Visible and Other Ethnic Minorities (1988, as cited in Henry et al., 1995), and more recently, the *Report of the Commission on Systemic Racism in the Ontario Criminal Justice System* (Williams, 1996).

While these reports amply illustrate the racism inherent in the criminal justice system and its attendant outcome of criminalizing particular racialized groups, the bedrock upon which such criminalization rests has a long historical tradition grounded in colonialism (Gilroy, 1987; Hall et al., 1978; Huttenback, 1976). Beginning with the colonization of Canada and the processes of settlement, particular groups have been identified as "others," and the process of "othering" has involved their racialization and criminalization (Backhouse, 1999). As Hall (1990:14) has noted, the power co-ordinates of race and racism are predicated on three characteristic relationships—domination and subordination, superiority and inferiority, and the naturalization of differences: "Natural physical and racial characteristics become the unalterable signifiers of inferiority." Underpinning these co-ordinates is the Manichean opposition of "us versus them" prevalent in colonial literature (JanMohamed, 1985; van Dijk, 1993).

Colonial-based representations of Aboriginal people and people of colour in popular culture, government policies, and the legal system have been documented in recent Canadian scholarship (e.g., Anderson, 1991; Backhouse, 1999; Bolaria and Li, 1988; Buchignani et al., 1985; Indra, 1979, 1981; Kline, 1994; Mosher, 1996). These studies attest to the fact that the criminal justice system works in concert with other institutions in society to perpetuate the racialization and criminalization of specific groups. Studies also show that the criminal justice system is saturated with "common-sense" and taken-for-granted notions of race and racism. However, from the perspective of the "white eye" (Hall, 1990), which views and defines the world according to its own terms, concepts of race and racism are often denied legitimacy, trivialized, contained (through redefinition and categorization), or erased in the dominant discourses of the system. Thus, it is not surprising to hear one judge comment that:

> In Toronto, in these courtrooms, sometimes I send young men from Vietnam to jail rather severely on offences. They've been in Canada a short time, they've been here a year or two or three, and I have to work out a kind of sentence that appears to have no bias.
>
> We're supposed to treat everyone in front of us in the same way ... but often have to lay out sentences trying to make it clear that in the circumstances of the recent immigrants' arrival into Canada on a charge of threatening or extortion, that's sometimes connected with Vietnamese gangs, and sometimes with not too much evidence in front of me on a sentencing hearing, I lay out some severe sentences that perhaps wouldn't apply in the same set of facts with someone who has been in Canada 20 or 30 years. (Heller, 1995:316)

The everyday, "common-sense" racism that permeates comments such as these are based on the view that "they," meaning these "others," need to be taught a lesson, and that "they" need to conform to "Canadian" norms. "They" in this case refers to recent immigrants whose immigrant status is made obvious by a number of taken-for-granted identifiers—racial appearance being one, culture and language being the others. The overt nature of the racism in these comments also attests to notions that "Canadians" do not break the law, but racialized "immigrant" groups do. Racialized groups are "othered" in the process and cast as undeserving of cherished "Canadian" values such as magnanimity and tolerance.

This chapter offers an overview of some of the recent findings that explicitly make the links between the criminalization of racial groups and the "racialization" of specific crimes, that is, how particular crimes are attributed to specific groups and how these groups are perceived as being prone to committing crimes. It further explores the different types of legal discourses used to erase, trivialize, categorize, and culturalize race and racism.

Racialization of Crime

Henry et al. (1995) have argued that the decision to police certain kinds of crime over other types reflects the racism and classism inherent in élite institutions. Thus, rather than police white-collar crime, which exacts economic costs, the tendency has been to police crimes associated with poor and racial minority groups. Racial minority communities have charged that they are "overpoliced and under-protected" (Flynn and Crawford, 1998; Henry et al., 1995; Quigley as cited in the RCAP, 1996; Williams, 1996). The emphasis on policing certain groups of people and certain types of crimes is reflective of the social stratification system underpinning Canadian society. Those at the bottom are considered to be the most prone to crime, are seen as less credible and deserving, and are often perceived by the dominant society as dispossessed and disposable (Dulude, 2000; Jiwani, 1999a). Hence, more negative attention is paid towards them and to their demands.

The issue of the over-policing of stigmatized groups is reinforced by the results of Ungerleider's study (1992) of two metropolitan municipal forces in Canada. Based on a sample of 251 officers, Ungerleider found that 25 per cent expressed views that could be categorized as reflecting "confusion" and as being "irrationally negative" towards visible minorities. In a similar study focusing on the Metro Toronto police force, Andrews (as cited in Henry et al., 1995:110) found that police officers' views and attitudes changed after joining the force. Over time, they came to hold perceptions and views of particular groups that were consonant with the prevailing notions held by the majority in the force. These views tended to be more conservative and authoritarian. This finding was echoed in a study of police officers' attitudes towards female victims of domestic violence (Rigakos, 1995).

The differential treatment of racialized groups by various parts of the criminal justice system and their overrepresentation in carceral institutions (Faith, 1993; McGillivray and Comaskey, 1998) are evidence of over-policing. Drawing from figures from Statistics Canada, McGillivray and Comaskey (1998:132) found that:

> nineteen per cent of admissions to carceral institutions (up to 90 per cent in some areas) are Aboriginal men. Rates are even higher for Aboriginal women who account for 50 per cent of women incarcerated in provincial institutions, and 20 per cent of women housed in federal institutions.

The Royal Commission on Aboriginal Peoples noted in its report that the incarceration of Aboriginal peoples is based on their stigmatization and inferiorization in Canadian society. Aboriginal peoples are considered to be less respectable and more prone to crime than their white counterparts. These perceptions subsequently influence how the police, Crown, and judges treat them. The differential and negative treatment of Aboriginal peoples is apparent in this example from the Aboriginal Justice Inquiry in Manitoba regarding the fines and penalty for fines exacted from Aboriginal peoples:

> Our research indicates that Aboriginal men who defaulted were twice as likely to be incarcerated as non-Aboriginal men, and Aboriginal women were three times more likely to be incarcerated than non-Aboriginal women. According to our study, the typical fine defaulter is an Aboriginal male between the ages of 22 to 29, who is single, unemployed, has less than grade 12 education and resides in rural Manitoba. Aboriginal offenders were twice as likely to be incarcerated

for fine default for one outstanding fine than non-Aboriginal offenders. The average amount of unpaid fines that led to the incarceration of Aboriginal people was $201.20. Aboriginal inmates incarcerated for defaulting on their fines served an average of 23 days in custody. (as cited in the report of the Royal Commission on Aboriginal Peoples, 1996:44)

The Royal Commission also found that Aboriginal peoples were more often denied bail and subjected to pretrial detention. They were also more likely to plead guilty without knowing the consequences of doing so, and did not have the time and resources to plead their case effectively. The Aboriginal Justice Inquiry in Manitoba noted that education, fixed residence, and employment were significant variables in determining who was subjected to pretrial detention. Since most Aboriginal peoples are economically disadvantaged, these criteria often work against their interests and result in their incarceration.

The overrepresentation of Aboriginal peoples in penal institutions has led to the incorporation of section 718.2(e) in the Criminal Code. This section makes specific reference to Aboriginal offenders.[1] In a recent decision, the Supreme Court of Canada (in *R. v. Gladue*), noted that section 718.2(e) applies to all Aboriginal people living on and off reserves. The Court further recognized the systemic discrimination against Aboriginal peoples, stating:

the circumstances of aboriginal offenders differ from those of the majority because many aboriginal people are victims of systemic and direct discrimination, many suffer the legacy of dislocation, and many are substantially affected by poor social and economic conditions. Moreover, as has been emphasized repeatedly in studies and commission reports, aboriginal offenders are, as a result of these unique systemic and background factors, more adversely affected by incarceration and less likely to be "rehabilitated" thereby, because the internment milieu is often culturally inappropriate and regrettably discrimination towards them is so often rampant in penal institutions. (1999:42 at 68)

The criminalization of racialized groups is not confined to Aboriginal peoples. Black activists have consistently pointed to the differential treatment of blacks and other people of colour in metropolitan cities in Canada. In Toronto, over the last 19 years, 17 black males have been shot by the police and 11 have died as a result (Flynn and Crawford, 1998). The findings of the Commission on Systemic Racism in the Ontario Criminal Justice System also portray a similar picture with regard to the differential treatment of black people in Ontario (Williams, 1996). The results revealed a significant increase in the number of black males incarcerated over a six-year period. Similarly, the rate of admission of black women was found to be seven times that of white women, and for black men, five times that of white men. Black men were also heavily represented in the category of charges pertaining to the "trafficking/importing" of drugs. Police were more likely to stop and detain black males than white males, and black men were more likely to be imprisoned upon conviction. Williams (1996:14) has argued that the differential outcomes in sentencing are a result of a combination of direct and indirect forms of systemic racism. As she noted:

> the higher incarceration rate of black convicted men in this sample is partly due to discretion being exercised more harshly against black than white men who share the same personal and case characteristics (direct discrimination). Differences in rates of unemployment, detention before trial, not-guilty pleas and prosecution by indictment also contributed to disparity in sentencing outcomes. Thus the indirect (systemic) impact of these apparently neutral factors was more frequent resort to prison sentences for black than white men.

Surveys undertaken by the Commission found widespread perceptions of the discriminatory nature of the criminal justice system among black, Chinese, and white communities. Black respondents noted that they were targeted more frequently by the police. Respondents also mentioned the overwhelmingly white character of the justice system, as is observable from the racial character of the police, Crown attorneys, and judges in the courtrooms. This perception is borne out by statistics that show that across the country, 2 per cent or less of the police force (Henry et al., 1995:118) and judges (Omatsu, 1997)[2] are people of colour. This lack of representation contributes to the perception that justice is not equitable but rather premised on white, male, middle-class attitudes about deserving victims and undeserving perpetrators.

The pervasiveness of discriminatory attitudes is evident in the reasons given for not granting bail and in harsher sentencing for black people. Bail is often not granted on the basis that "racial minority offenders 'can't raise the money'" (Henry et al., 1995:139). When bail is granted, it is frequently of a higher amount than that granted to a white person (Westmoreland Traore, as cited in Henry et al., 1995). The cumulative impact of the differential treatment of black people often results in longer sentences. In a Nova Scotia study, researchers found disparities in the sentences accorded to black and white defendants, with black defendants receiving harsher sentences and no discharges, whereas white defendants received discharges in 23 per cent of the cases (Renner and Warner, 1981, as cited in Henry et al., 1995:144). This pattern was also observed in the Donald Marshall inquiry. As with the findings of the Royal Commission on Aboriginal Peoples, the Marshall inquiry revealed that employment, education, and access to counsel were significant variables in determining discharge. Black people in Nova Scotia are also among the economically disadvantaged with little access to resources, employment, and high levels of education (Henry et al., 1995).

Intersecting Oppressions: Race and Gender

While over-policing contributes to a greater scrutiny and criminalization of racialized peoples, under-protection renders the victims of crime within racialized groups more vulnerable. The situation of women of colour and Aboriginal women victims of violence exemplifies the complexities of these intersecting forms of oppression that combine to render particular groups more vulnerable to violence (Crenshaw, 1994; Razack, 1998).

Flynn and Crawford (1998) have argued that the particular positioning of racialized communities and the criminalization of men of colour increase the risk for women of colour in abusive relationships. For women of colour, their communities become sites of safety and belonging. Yet at the same time, patriarchal violence renders these communities unsafe. Systemic racism from external agencies and state authorities impedes women from seeking help (Canadian Panel on Violence, 1993; Musisi and Mukhtar, 1992, as cited in Agnew, 1998). To engage state authorities by calling on them to respond to violence in the home forces women of colour to betray their men, leave their communities, and engage in "race treason" (Flynn and Crawford, 1998:96). The fear and knowledge of the potential of the justice system to criminalize men of colour often forces these women to remain silent.

Added to this, many women of colour are immigrant women who have arrived as dependants or temporary workers. Thus, their official status in terms of citizenship rights and privileges is tenuous, rendering them vulnerable to deportation (Dosanjh et al., 1994). Racism from the dominant society, combined with patriarchal violence from both within and outside their communities, creates a situation of extreme vulnerability. Many women are unable to call for police intervention for fear of losing their status and their children, and because they are dependent on their spouses, who consequently may be incarcerated and hence unable to sustain the family economically (Duclos, 1993; Martin and Mosher, 1995).

On the other hand, police response to calls for intervention in cases involving violence in racialized communities is also problematic. In many instances, police fail to respond or to follow protocol on the basis of an assumption that violence is a cultural problem (Agnew, 1998; Flynn and Crawford, 1998; Jiwani and Buhagiar, 1997). In their examination of the "Vernon massacre," which resulted in the deaths of nine people and injury to another two, Jiwani and Buhagiar (1997) found that the RCMP did not investigate prior complaints about violence and permitted the abusive partner to obtain gun permits. The media framing of the massacre used a cultural lens and sought to explain the violence as emanating from an arranged marriage (Jiwani, 1998). That "common-sense" understanding was also shared by the RCMP.

The racism that women of colour who are immigrants and refugees experience from external agencies and authorities is compounded by language barriers and prior histories with government agencies in their country of origin (MacLeod and Shin, 1993; Martin and Mosher, 1995). In many instances when they do turn to the justice system, women have to use interpreters. Interpretation becomes another site through which systemic racism (based on anti-immigrant sentiments) is introduced and which further criminalizes people of colour (Heller, 1995).

Moral Panic—Immigrants and Crime

The racialization of immigrants has been abundantly reported in the soci-ological literature (e.g., Jabukowski, 1999; Thobani, 1998). Similarly, the construction of immigrant communities as the site of social problems and criminality has been documented in Europe and Canada (e.g., Cottle, 1992; Hackett, 1989; Jiwani, 1993; Pearson, 1976; Tierney, 1982; van Dijk, 1993). Anti-immigrant sentiments are widely prevalent and most apparent in the treatment by the media of racialized immigrant minority groups (Jiwani, 1993). As an élite institution, the dominant media's messages and constructions not only inform the public imagination but also influence government policy. The media work in concert with other élite institutions to produce and reproduce a hegemonic view of reality. Racialized immi-grants are the media's latest moral panic, albeit a panic whose pitch varies according to international and national agendas dictated by globalization, migration, and the threat of invasion.[3] Immigrants are perceived to be an economic threat, by either taking away jobs or buying out Canadian firms and real estate; a social threat in terms of their presumed proclivity to crime; and a cultural threat in terms of dismantling Canadian traditions (Jiwani, 1993; see also van Dijk, 1993, for an elaboration of these themes in the European context).

The category "immigrant" has then come to signify a person of colour whose culture and language are perceived to be different. In this light, it is interesting to note that the Commission on Systemic Racism in the Ontario Criminal Justice System (Williams, 1996) found that questions about immigration status were often asked of racialized people, and refer-ences to foreignness were made in numerous court transcripts. Within the justice system, immigrants whose language is neither French nor English are treated differently.

In a study examining language bias, Heller (1995:356) analysed 118 files collected from January 1992 to January 1993 to determine whether the use of a court interpreter resulted in significant differences in sentencing. The files dealt with shoplifting cases handled by the legal aid clinic in a met-ropolitan Canadian city. Heller found that "blacks and whites receive lighter sentences than other non-whites," and further that the use of an interpreter resulted in sentences that were twice as harsh as those given to individuals not using an interpreter. Moreover, cases that involved inter-preters were often marked by a lack of preparation on the part of the Crown attorney. Heller further found that although interpreters started out with non-biased perspectives, over time they acquired and internalized the dominant perceptions pervasive in the justice system. They were more likely to view immigrants as engaging in illegal acts rather than as being innocent until proven guilty. Heller's study seems to suggest that immigrant groups who have not mastered the dominant language are seen as less deserving of justice, and further that the lighter sentences received by black individuals may have been the result of sensitivities raised by the Rodney King affair in the United States and the timing of the study that took place in the immediate aftermath.

Mapping the Legal Discourses on Race and Racism

Van Dijk (1993) has observed that there are continuities and changes marking the discourses[4] of race and racism. The continuities can be traced back to the colonial period (Said, 1978) and to the more explicit Manichean oppositions underpinning colonial literature. While the "us" versus "them" oppositional relation is explicit in the dominant media discourse on race and racism, Canadian legal discourses tend to be more subtle.[5] Contemporary legal discourses (as evidenced in reasons for judgement) also pivot on accepted notions of what constitutes Canadian law and the role of the judiciary, the courts, and legal personnel. Thus, impartiality, objectivity, neutrality, and the individualized focus on each case in isolation from its societal context define these accepted and taken-for-granted notions (Razack, 1998). The trend towards the inclusion of systemic, societal factors in making judicial decisions is observable in the recent rulings of the Supreme Court of Canada. However, in the lower courts, the inclusion of systemic, societal factors appears to vary according to individual judges.[6]

Contemporary legal discourses on race and racism can be defined in terms of: erasure, trivialization, categorization, culturalization, and inferiorization. These are ideal types (Weber, 1958), and hence, definitive cases illustrating these various types are not always available, though many cases will likely illustrate overlapping types of discourses.

ERASURE

In a recent case concerning the murder in Victoria, British Columbia, of a 14-year-old South Asian girl, Reena Virk, the judge's ruling in the trial involving the young man accused of the crime (*R. v. Warren Paul Glowatski*) made no mention of the racial character of the murder (Jiwani, 1999b). In fact, the accused had, on the night of the murder, boasted to his friends that he had killed a native man. Weeks later, he told his girlfriend that he had killed an "East Indian" girl whom he had never spoken to, in order to get back at other "East Indians" who had beaten him up. Despite the girlfriend's admission of this in the courtroom, her evidence regarding the racial motivation behind the killing was not considered by Macaulay J. in his reasons for judgement. In part, this erasure can be understood on the basis of the evidentiary requirements and the presumed lack of credibility of the witness. On the other hand, the sociological evidence on the prevalence of racism and the marginalization of those who are different suggests that such evidence should have been given more weight. Yet this same erasure continued to occur in the related case of Kelly Ellard, the co-accused in the murder of Reena Virk. Morrison J. clearly stated in her decisions regarding parole eligibility that racism was not a factor (Jiwani, 2000).

The erasure of race and racism can also be explained in terms of the law's preoccupation with the "reasonable person." Since justice has to be seen to be done in a manner that makes sense to the "reasonable person," the question becomes one of defining the characteristics of the "reasonable person." Much has been written about the "reasonable person" test, particularly from a feminist standpoint (Bhandar, 1997; Devlin, 1995). As Devlin (1995:419) has argued, "throughout the case law on judicial bias, the reasonable person is assumed to be without age, gender, or race. But this universal figure is like no one we know or can recognize." Nevertheless, it can be argued that the universal reasonable person is constructed from a white, male, middle-class perspective. In *R. v. Lavallée*, the Supreme Court of Canada acknowledged the androcentric nature of the reasonable person and argued for the inclusion of a gendered perspective (Bhandar, 1997). Devlin (1995) has affirmed this perspective but notes that race is also an important consideration (see also Backhouse, 1999).

TRIVIALIZATION

Unlike erasure, where the concepts of race and racism do not even enter in the discussion, in the case of trivialization, race and racism are mentioned but their import or systemic nature is not realized in its fullest sense. Thus, individual cases may be analysed and discussed but in reference to *other prevailing* considerations than racism, though this may be a common thread running through the case. For instance, in R. v. *Zundel*, the debate at the Supreme Court level included various contrary viewpoints on the distribution of hate literature, and more specifically, on whether section 181[7] of the Criminal Code violated section 2(b) on the freedom of expression in the Charter. Justices La Forest, L'Heureux-Dubé, Sopinka, and McLachlin argued that the case did not violate the constitutionality of the Charter and could be permitted under the banner of freedom of expression. McLachlin J. stated:

> the guarantee of freedom of expression serves to protect the right of the minority to express its view, however unpopular it may be; adapted to this context, it serves to preclude the majority's perception of "truth" or "public interest" from smothering the minority's perception. (29)

One could argue that decisions and judgements pertaining to the constitutionality of certain sections require an analysis that is not confined to the immediate situation but is cognizant of the future implications of any interpretation. However, from the minority point of view, and certainly from the perspective of the dissenting Justices Gonthier, Cory, and Iacobucci, the contextual issues and actual content of Zundel's publications far outweighed any concern with unfettered free speech. In fact, in the dissenting opinion, Cory J. and Iacobucci J. clearly identified the contextual impact of such unfettered free speech. Citing the expert opinion of Professor Mari Matsuda on the negative impact of racist speech on victims, the justices identified the potential of Zundel's publications to weaken the harmony between racial groups in Canadian society. They described, at length, the dubious nature of the content of Zundel's publications and the message of denial of a historical event and memory. Cory J. and Iacobucci J. also identified the prevalent racism in Canadian society and the increasing activity of hate groups, noting the negative impact on Canadian race relations. Thus, they employed a "realist" rather than a "formalist" concept of law (Devlin, 1995), taking into consideration the larger social context.

CATEGORIZATION

The discourse of categorization has been elucidated by Iyer (formerly Duclos; Duclos, 1993) in her examination of equality rights law, and by Razack (1998) in her analysis of the scripts used in the courts. Iyer (1993) pointed out that the categorical approach inherent in the legal approach to equality rights is a structural feature that inevitably works against claimants as it fails to take into consideration complex and often intersecting forms of oppression. Such intersections are not only negated, but also conflated so that difference is assumed to be lateral and mutually exclusive rather than hierarchical, intersecting, and relational. As a case in point, she refers to the categories of gender, race, and disability discrimination. Claimants are forced to choose between categories. Further, the categories are defined in reference to a dominant, yet invisible centre — the white, male, heterosexual, able-bodied norm. The criteria underpinning these categories are codified in the test of immutability. In other words, the difference has to be considered immutable — "natural" or "naturalized." As she stated:

> by focusing on immutability, the test reinforces an understanding of ascribed social characteristics as intrinsic to individuals, rather than comparative or relational; as inevitable rather than historically and geographically variable; and as neutral rather than reflecting a particular pattern of social relations (Iyer, 1993:183)

The categorical approach is underpinned by the notion that individuals fitting into a particular category are identical. Thus, all people of colour are alike, all women are alike, and so forth. The universalizing tendency of the categorical approach fails to take into consideration class differences or the hierarchical nature by which different groups are stratified in Canadian society. By negating differences, the categorical approach not only elides the impact of class but also forces claimants to caricature themselves in order to fit a particular mould that is considered acceptable. The result is that "[t]he claim will fail unless the claimant's experience of discrimination can be made to accord with how the dominant group imagines discrimination on the basis of a given characteristic" (Iyer, 1993:186).

On the basis of her examination of race and sex discrimination cases reported in the Canadian *Human Rights Reporter* (1980 to 1989), Iyer

(Duclos, 1993) demonstrated how women of colour disappear in the categorical approach that denies the complexity of compounding forms of discrimination faced by these women. The categorical approach then privileges one form of social identity over another. By denying differences within groups, the categorical approach invokes the classical racist notion of "they're all the same" (JanMohamed, 1985) and resonates with more classical forms of racism in which "they" are categorized according to perceived differences by an invisible yet dominant power.

CULTURALIZATION

Razack (1998:60) has defined culturalization as "a framework to pre-empt both racism and sexism." Discourses of race and racism, which pivot on the use of culture as a reference, highlight the following: (a) the conditions under which culture/cultural forms are considered legitimate and hence, acceptable, and (b) the reinforcement of an implicit distance between "us" and "them" where "they" have cultures that can be paraded and explained while the dominant culture remains invisible in the background.

In her insightful and complex analysis of cases involving violence against Aboriginal women and women of colour, Razack identified the differential conditions under which culture and cultural attributions are used in the courtroom to excuse and condone male violence and affirm white superiority. Thus, while culture is used to explain away male violence against Aboriginal women, it is significantly absented from any discussion of First Nations sovereignty or land claims issues. The representation of culture within the context of violence clearly inferiorizes the culture of "others," rendering them more primitive and backward.

In a critical and revealing analysis of cases involving gender persecution, Razack (1998:92-93) noted a similar pattern of the strategic use of culture that fits within the Western gaze. As she described it:

> women's claims are most likely to succeed when they present themselves as victims of dysfunctional, exceptionally patriarchal cultures and states. The successful asylum seeker must cast herself as a cultural Other, that is, as someone fleeing from a more primitive culture. That is to say, it is through various orientalist and imperialist lenses that women's gender-based persecution becomes visible in the West. Without the

imperial or colonial component, claims of gender persecution are less likely to succeed and asylum is denied.

With the entrenchment of a multicultural framework in the justice system, notions of equality and justice are now increasingly translated into the language of culture.[8] Systemic and everyday racism, as well as intersecting forms of oppression, are recuperated and presented in the form of cultural and gendered scripts that resonate with "common-sense" notions of discrimination and self-affirming stereotypes of other cultures.

The use of cultural scripts is also evident in the decision rendered in a recent case concerning the murder of Nirmal Singh Gill by members of a hate group (*R. v. Miloszewski, Synderek, Nikkel, LeBlanc, Kluch*). In his reasons for judgement, Stewart J. began with a description of the Sikh religion, identifying the particular characteristics of the victim's personality that made him an exemplary member of his faith. The subtext of the description suggests that the man did not deserve to die in such a violent way. The issue of racism is subsumed under the category of "hate crimes," where hate is defined according to the Supreme Court of Canada in *R. v. Keegstra*. Throughout, Stewart J. made no mention of the systemic nature of racism or of the continuum of racial violence to which people of colour are subjected. Rather, he concluded:

> I have heard evidence of truly hateful and sickening comments made by all of the accused as they disparaged ethnic minorities, homosexuals and members of the Jewish community. Clearly these views were fueled by hate, fear and ignorance. These are views which are antithetical to the principles upon which this country is based and which principles are adhered to by the overwhelming majority of our citizens. These are views which are alien to a tolerant, multicultural and civilized society. However, it must be remembered that another cherished principle of our democracy is freedom of speech. Individuals have a constitutional right to say things which are distasteful and unpopular subject only to the reasonable limits prescribed by law as can be demonstrably justified in a free and democratic society. (58)

Racism becomes an act of a few "loonies" out there, not a systemic phenomenon or one grounded in the very fabric of society.[9] The brutal murder is divorced from the actions that preceded it and from the language of hate that serves to dehumanize specific targeted groups rendering them more vulnerable to violence.

Conclusion: Justice or Just Us?

The criminalization of racialized groups rests ultimately on the continued production and reproduction of particular groups as "others." It also rests on a fundamental denial of racism and of the import of "race" as a sociological construct that is used for strategic ends.[10] These ends include the continued affirmation of the superiority of the dominant white, heterosexual, middle-class, and largely male perspective. The "us" versus "them" opposition underpins and supports the continued criminalization of racialized groups, where the latter represent a threat to be contained, trivialized, or erased.

Canadian society remains a stratified society, marked by those who are perceived as deserving, credible, and respectable at one end, and those who are disadvantaged and, therefore, seen as less credible and undeserving at the other end. This stratification system is evident in the economic and social distribution of wealth and resources. It is also a system that is classed, raced, and gendered. Within such a system, Aboriginal peoples and people of colour are ghettoized at the lower end and racism operates to keep them there. The criminal justice system works in concert with other institutions in society to maintain the status quo. As McCormick has observed: "rather than acting as a check on the rich and powerful, [the courts] in fact have privilege-reinforcing tendencies" (as cited in Omatsu, 1997:7).

Notes

This research was funded by Status of Women Canada and SSHRC (Grant number 829-1999-1002).

1. Section 718.2(e) of the Criminal Code states: "all available sanctions other than imprisonment that are reasonable in the circumstances should be considered for all offenders, with particular attention to the circumstances of aboriginal offenders."

2. Whether adequate representation would eliminate systemic racism in the system is a matter of debate (see Omatsu, 1997; Bhandar, 1997, for contrary views on this).

3. It can be argued that this panic is historically grounded in the very formation of the Canadian nation-state and its pitch varies according to the perceived threat that immigrants signify (see Jiwani, 1993; Thobani, 1998).

4. The term "discourse" is used to denote the evaluative categories of social thought and talk concerning and constructing a particular subject. It involves the use of language in specific ways, to communicate meanings organized around certain concepts and categories (Hartley, 1982).

5. In contrast to the American legal discourse, which tends to permit the evocation of more racial imagery in the courtroom (Johnson, 1993).

6. See Devlin's (1995) discussion of a case concerning Judge Spark's context-based ruling.

7. Section 181 of the Criminal Code states that "everyone who willfully publishes a statement, tale or news that he knows is false and causes or is likely to cause injury or mischief to a public interest is guilty of an indictable offence and liable to imprisonment."

8. The increasing use of a multicultural framework to comprehend issues of race and racism is evident in the title of a recent BC provincial judges conference. The conference was titled: The Court in a Multicultural Society.

9. It is interesting to note that one defence counsel for one of the accused made a similar argument: that since racism is a systemic phenomenon permeating society and saturating common attitudes, the accused was simply acting out what were common sentiments.

10. This denial is apparent in the discussion regarding the utility of crime-based statistics in a special issue of the *Canadian Journal of Criminology* 36 (1994).

References

Agnew, V. 1998. *In Search of a Safe Place: Abused Women and Culturally Sensitive Services*. Toronto: University of Toronto Press.

Alberta. *Report of the Task Force on the Criminal Justice System and its Impact on the Indian and Métis people of Alberta*. Main Report, vol. 1. Edmonton, 1991.

Anderson, K. 1991. *Race, Place and the Power of Definition in Vancouver's Chinatown: Racial Discourse in Canada, 1887-1980*. Montreal and Kingston: McGill-Queen's University Press.

Backhouse, C. 1999. *Colour-Coded: A Legal History of Racism in Canada, 1900-1950*. Toronto: University of Toronto Press.

Bhandar, B. 1997. "Race, identity and difference in the courts: Overcoming judicial 'bias,'" paper presented at The Court in a Multicultural Society, BC Provincial Court Judges Conference, Vancouver, 12 October.

Bolaria, B.S. and P.S. Li. 1988. *Racial Oppression in Canada*. Toronto: Garamond Press.

Buchignani, N., D. Indra, and R. Srivastava. 1985. *Continuous Journey: A Social History of South Asians in Canada*. Toronto: McClelland & Stewart.

Canadian Panel on Violence Against Women. 1993. *Changing the Landscape: Ending Violence—Achieving Equality. Final report*. Ottawa: Ministry of Supply and Services.

Cashmore, E., and E. McLaughlin, eds. 1991. *Out of Order: Policing Black People*. New York: Routledge.

Cornish, C., and A. Dutton. 1995. "Introduction: Racism, hate crime and the law," Proceedings of a Symposium held in Vancouver, 27-29 November 1992. Toronto and Vancouver: Praxis.

Cottle, S. 1992. "'Race,' racialization and the media: A review and update of research," *Sage Race Relations Abstracts* 17:2.

Crenshaw, K. 1994. "Mapping the Margins: Intersectionality, Identity Politics, and Violence Against Women of Color," in M. Fineman and R. Mykitiuk, eds., *The Public Nature of Private Violence: The Discovery of Domestic Abuse*. New York: Routledge, 93-118.

Devlin, R.F. 1995. "We can't go on together with suspicious minds: Judicial bias and racialized perspective in R. v. R.D.S.," *Dalhousie Law Journal* 18:408-35.

Dosanjh, R., S. Deo, and S. Sidhu. 1994. *Spousal Abuse: Experiences of 15 South Asian Canadian Women*. Vancouver: FREDA.

Duclos, N. 1993. "Disappearing women: Racial minority women in human rights cases," *Canadian Journal of Women and the Law* 6:25-51.

Dulude, L. 2000. *Justice and the Poor*. Ottawa: National Council of Welfare.

Entman, R.M. 1990. "Modern racism and the images of blacks in local television news," *Critical Studies in Mass Communication* 7:332-45.

Essed, P. 1990. *Everyday Racism. Reports from Women of Two Cultures*, trans. C. Jaffe. Claremont, CA: Hunter House.

Faith, K. 1993. *Unruly Women: The Politics of Confinement and Resistance*. Vancouver: Press Gang Publishers.

Flynn, K., and C. Crawford. 1998. "Committing 'Race Treason': Battered women and mandatory arrest in Toronto's Caribbean community," in K. Bonnycastle and G.S. Rigakos, eds., *Unsettling Truths: Battered Women, Policy, Politics, and Contemporary Research in Canada*. Vancouver: Collective Press, 93-102.

Gilmour, G.A. 1994. *Hate-Motivated Violence*. Working Document, Department of Justice Canada. Ottawa: Research and Statistics Directorate, May.

Gilroy, P. 1987. *"There Ain't No Black in the Union Jack": The Cultural Politics of Race and Nation*. London: Hutchinson Press.

Godin, J. 1994. *More Than a Crime: A Report on the Lack of Public Legal Information Materials for Immigrant Women Who Are Subject to Wife Assault*. Ottawa: Department of Justice Canada, Research and Statistics Directorate.

Hackett, R.A. 1989. "Coups, earthquakes and hostages? Foreign news on Canadian television," *Canadian Journal of Political Science* 22:809-25.

Hall, S. 1990. "The whites of their eyes," in M. Alvarado and J.O. Thompson, eds., *The Media Reader*. London: British Film Institute.

Hall, S., C. Critcher, T. Jefferson, J. Clarke, and B. Roberts. 1978. *Policing the Crisis: Mugging, the State, Law and Order*. London: Macmillan Press.

Hartley, J. 1982. *Understanding News*. London: Methuen.

Hawkins, D.F. 1995. "Ethnicity, race, and crime: A review of selected studies," in Hawkins, ed., *Ethnicity, Race, and Crime: Perspectives across Time and Place*. Albany: State University of New York Press, 11-45.

Heller, D.J. 1995. "Language bias in the criminal justice system," *Criminal Law Quarterly* 37:344-83.

Henry, F., C. Tator, W. Mattis, and T. Rees. 1995. *The Colour of Democracy: Racism in Canadian Society*. Toronto: Harcourt Brace.

Hickman, T.A. 1989. *Report of the Royal Commission on the Donald Marshall Jr. Prosecution: Commissioner's Report*. Halifax.

Huttenback, R.A. 1976. *Racism and Empire: White Settler and Colour Immigrants in the British Self-Governing Colonies, 1830-1910*. Ithaca, NY: Cornell University Press.

Indra, D. 1979. "South Asian stereotypes in the Vancouver press," *Ethnic and Racial Studies* 2:166-89.

—. 1981. "The invisible mosaic: Women, ethnicity and the Vancouver press, 1905-1976," *Canadian Ethnic Studies* 13:63-74.

Iyer, N. 1993. "Categorical denials: Equality rights and the shaping of social identity," *Queen's Law Journal* 19:179-207.

Jakubowski, L.M. 1999. "'Managing' Canadian immigration: Racism, ethnic selectivity, and the law," in E. Comack et al., eds., *Locating Law: Race/Class/Gender Connections*. Halifax: Fernwood, 98-124.

JanMohamed, A.R. 1985. "The economy of Manichean allegory: The function of racial difference in colonialist literature," *Critical Inquiry* 12:59-87.

Jiwani, Y. 1992. "To be or not to be: South Asians as victims and oppressors in the *Vancouver Sun*," *Sanvad* 5:13-15.

—. 1993. "By Omission and Commission: Race and Representation in Canadian Television News," Ph.D. thesis, Simon Fraser University.

—. 1998. "Culture, violence, and inequality," in L. Sherlock, ed., *Violence against Women: Meeting the Cross-Cultural Challenge*. Vancouver: BC Institute Against Family Violence.

—. 1999a. "Trafficking and the sexual exploitation of children and youth: An international/national perspective," Conference Proceedings of 'It's a Crime! An Act Local, Think Global' Conference on the Commercial Sexual Exploitation of Children and Youth, 30 April-1 May 1999. Vancouver: Vancouver Coalition of Children and Youth.

—. 1999b. "Erasing race: The story of Reena Virk," *Canadian Woman's Studies* 19, 3:178-84.

—. 2000. "Deconstructing the myth of girl violence: The denial of race in the murder of Reena Virk," *Kinesis* (May):7, 14.

Jiwani, Y., and L. Buhagiar. 1997. *Policing Violence against Women in Relationships: An Examination of Police Response to Violence against Women in British Columbia*. Vancouver: FREDA.

Johnson, S.L. 1993. "Racial imagery in criminal cases," *Tulane Law Review* 67:1739-1805.

Kline, M. 1994. "The colour of law: Ideological representations of First Nations in legal discourse," *Social and Legal Studies* 3:451-76.

Macaulay, J. 1999. Reasons for judgement in *R. v. Warren Paul Glowatski*. Supreme Court of British Columbia, Docket 95773, 2 June 1999.

MacLeod, L., and M. Shin. 1993. *Like a Wingless Bird: A Tribute to the Survival and Courage of Women Who Are Abused and Who Speak Neither English nor French*. Ottawa: National Clearing House on Family Violence.

Martin, D.L., and J.E. Mosher. 1995. "Unkept promises: Experiences of immigrant women with the neo-criminalization of wife abuse," *Canadian Journal of Women and the Law* 8:3-44.

McGillivray, A., and B. Comaskey. 1998. "'Everybody had black eyes ... nobody don't say nothing': Intimate Violence, Aboriginal Women, and Justice System Response," in K. Bonnycastle and G.S. Rigakos, eds., *Unsettling Truths: Battered Women, Policy, Politics, and Contemporary Research in Canada*. Vancouver: Collective Press, 131-42.

Mosher, C. 1996. "Minorities and misdemeanors: The treatment of black public order offenders in Ontario's criminal justice system, 1892-1930," *Canadian Journal of Criminology*: 413-38.

Omatsu, M. 1997. "The fiction of judicial impartiality," *Canadian Journal of Women and the Law* 9:1-16.

Pearson, G. 1976. "'Paki-Bashing' in a North East Lancashire cotton town: A case study and its history," in G. Mungham and G. Pearson, eds., *Working Class Youth Culture*. London: Routledge & Kegan Paul.

R. v. Gladue, [1999] 1 S.C.R. 688, file no. 26300.

R. v. Miloszewki, Synderek, Nikkel, LeBlanc and Kluch. Reasons for judgement before the Honourable William F. Stewart, file no. 96687-03-D2, Surrey Registry.

Razack, S.H. 1998. *Looking White People in the Eye: Gender, Race, and Culture in Courtrooms and Classrooms*. Toronto: University of Toronto Press.

Rigakos, G.S. 1995. "Constructing the symbolic complainant: Police sub-culture and the non-enforcement of protection orders for battered women," *Violence and Victims* 10:227-47.

Royal Commission on Aboriginal Peoples (RCAP). 1996. *Bridging the Cultural Divide: A Report on Aboriginal People and Criminal Justice in Canada*. Ottawa: RCAP, 26-53.

Said, E. 1978. *Orientalism*. New York: Pantheon Books.

Shaw, M., K. Rodgers, J. Blanchette, et al. 1991. *Survey of Federally Sentenced Women: Report to the Task Force on Federally Sentenced Women on the Prison Survey*. Ottawa: Solicitor General of Canada, Ministry Secretariat, User Report 1991-4.

Smitherman-Donaldson, G., and T. van Dijk. 1988. *Discourse and Discrimination*. Detroit: Wayne State University Press.

Thobani, S. 1998. "Nationalizing Citizens, Bordering Immigrant Women: Globalization and Racialization of Women's Citizenship in Late 20th Century Canada," Ph.D. thesis, Simon Fraser University.

Tierney, J. 1982. "Race, colonialism and migration," in J. Tierney, ed., *Race, Migration and Schooling*. London: Holt, Rinehart and Winston.

Ungerleider, C. 1992. *Issues in Police Intercultural and Race Relations Training in Canada*. Ottawa: Solicitor General of Canada.

van Dijk, T.A. 1987. *Communicating Racism: Ethnic Prejudice in Thought and Talk*. Newbury Park, CA: Sage.

—. 1993. *Elite Discourse and Racism*. Sage Series on Race and Ethnic Relations, vol. 6. Newbury Park, CA: Sage.

Weber, M. 1958. *The Protestant Ethic and the Spirit of Capitalism*, trans. T. Parsons. New York: Scribner.

Williams, T. 1996. Report of the Commission on Systemic Racism in the Ontario Criminal Justice System: Summary of Key Findings. Background notes for the Ontario Court of Justice (Provincial Division) annual convention, 21-23 May.

Yeager, M.G. 1997. "Immigrants and criminality: A cross-national review," *Criminal Justice Abstracts* 29:143-71.

5

Looking at Law through the Lens of Culture: A Provocative Case

AUDREY MACKLIN

Introduction

How is cultural difference constructed and performed in legal discourse? Today in Canada, "racial" and ethnocultural diversity is acknowledged as empirical fact, but multiculturalism as a political, institutional, and normative response to the phenomenon is highly contested. To what extent can and should Canadian society acknowledge, respect, and accommodate cultural difference? As philosopher Amy Gutmann (1994:3-4) asks:

> Is a democracy letting its citizens down, excluding or discriminating against us in some morally troubling way, when major institutions fail to take account of our particular identities? ... In what sense should our identities as men or women, African-American, Asian-Americans, or Native Americans, Christians, Jews or Muslims, English or French Canadians, *publicly* matter?

A few sentences later, Gutmann begins to answer her own questions. "Recognizing and treating members of some groups as equals now seems to require public institutions to acknowledge rather than ignore cultural particularities, at least for those people whose self-understanding depends on the vitality of their cultures" (5).

Yet the difficulty of applying theory to practice continues, especially in law. It is perhaps an indicator of confusion at the highest normative level that the Canadian Charter of Rights and Freedoms protects freedom of religion (s. 2), guarantees equality and freedom from discrimination based on, among other things, race, national or ethnic origin, or religion, promotes interpretation consistent with Canada's "multicultural heritage" (s. 27), and also states in its Preamble that "Canada is founded upon principles that recognize the supremacy of God."

Scholars such as Charles Taylor (1994) and Will Kymlicka (1995) engage in defining, theorizing, and justifying multiculturalism within liberal democracies, including Canada. One task identified by these (and other) authors is the demand to render justice to cultural minorities across a multi-ethnic society while respecting equality and autonomy as between individuals. Regardless of how one conceptualizes citizenship, one common premise apparently shared by theorists across disciplines is that a satisfactory account of citizenship includes/requires equality under and before the law. In Canadian legal discourse, scholars and the courts have agreed that the constitutional guarantee of equality requires more than formal sameness of treatment, and embraces treatment that recognizes and accommodates conditions of difference and disadvantage. This is sometimes referred to as substantive equality. For instance, Kymlicka's model of multicultural citizenship, which endorses certain group-differentiated rights, is not necessarily inconsistent with the idea of equality among citizens, if equality is understood in the richer, more substantive sense.

Of course, an abstract commitment to equality before the law must still grapple with the practical challenges arising from a multiplicity of identity claims and heterogeneity of the population. These features have challenged the legal system and its actors' claims to neutrality, objectivity, and fairness—the very qualities law invokes to legitimate its authority.

Inverting the Lens

I will begin by exploring one aspect of the criminal law in order to expose the limits of the conventional understanding of law as a "culture free" (read: objective) domain of analysis. This approach to law and culture treats culture as distinct from law and as a discrete object of legal scrutiny. This technique attempts to resolve various conflicts between law and culture by simply applying the former to the latter. I call this method "looking at culture through the lens of law."

People are lawfully abducted, confined, isolated, and sometimes even killed in many "liberal democracies." The criminal justice system calls these acts imprisonment, corporal punishment, solitary confinement, and capital punishment. It is critical to most legal systems that the state retains a monopoly on when and how these forms of violence are administered. The law punishes citizens who arrogate to themselves the power to inflict violence and constrains the defences available to those citizens. Where an accused commits an act of violence to preserve his/her own life or safety, the lives or safety of loved ones, or occasionally property, the law may excuse[1] the violence. The costs of avoidance may be so high that even if the law cannot formally approve of the act, it can understand and forgive it. Nevertheless, access to defences is strictly regulated,[2] and usually based on the idea that the accused subjectively believed she or he had no viable alternative but to commit an act of violence, and further that this belief was *objectively* valid when viewed from the perspective of the hypothetical "reasonable person."

One ongoing debate in North American criminal law concerns the so-called "cultural defence." Cases where it is raised involve situations of an accused, an immigrant from a non-European country, intentionally committing an act of violence and claiming as a defence that his/her actions were objectively reasonable when viewed from within the accused's particular cultural framework. Other cases raising this defence concern Aboriginal accused. I will not engage these situations for two reasons. First, the application of Canadian law to Aboriginal people is inextricably bound up with the question of Aboriginal self-government and related issues of sovereignty and jurisdiction over certain aspects of criminal law and punishment. These issues do not arise, or at least do not arise in the same terms, in the context of other ethnic and racialized minorities within Canada. Second, the most notable cases of Aboriginal culture being raised as a defence concerned property offences such as mischief or trespassing, not crimes of personal violence. Moreover, both instances have arisen in the context of organized political protest by Aboriginal people against non-recognition of Aboriginal title to land.[3]

In fact, there exists no separate and discrete cultural defence. Thus, the phrase is somewhat misleading. It is used to encompass the various legal analyses where the accused's culture is incorporated as a factor relevant to determining guilt. This is distinguishable from situations where the accused (and/or victim's) culture is introduced as a factor relevant to sentencing once the accused has been convicted of the offence. The deployment of culture to mitigate sentencing of persons convicted of a criminal offence has produced mixed results. Two notorious examples out of

Quebec featured sexual assault cases decided by White, Québécois women judges. In 1994, a man convicted of sodomizing his nine-year old stepdaughter (over a two-year period) was given a relatively light sentence because he had "spared" the girl's virginity, which the girl's mother had testified was an important attribute in Muslim culture. The sentence was overturned on appeal. In early 1998, another judge issued conditional (that is, non-custodial) sentences to two men convicted of raping a young woman. Both accused and complainant were of Haitian background. The judge commented that "the absence of regret of the two accused seems to be related more to the cultural context particularly with regard to relations with women, than a veritable problem of a sexual nature." Both decisions, and others like them, were widely criticized as denigrating the respective cultural communities generally and female members particularly.[4]

By and large, the explicit resort to culture as a means of negating culpability has failed in Canada. For reasons that I will elaborate below, I believe a cultural defence is conceptually doomed to failure. Apart from that, political objections to the use of culture as a legal defence to crimes of violence are compelling: the claims are usually asserted by male accused in defence of crimes of violence (sexual assault, domestic violence, homicide) committed against women and children. Perhaps the most highly publicized cases in North America involve so-called "honour killings," where male relatives kill a young female kin for actual or suspected behaviour that allegedly brought shame to the family. Another oft-cited case concerned a charge of abduction and rape brought against a Hmong[5] male, who claimed that the Hmong "marriage by capture" ritual required a woman to feign protest while the man abducts and forces intercourse on her.

Giving effect to a cultural defence in these cases diminishes the protection provided by law to the women and children of those communities who are often the victims of the violence, thereby denying *them* equal protection of the law. The alleged respect shown to the accused's culture by recognizing a so-called cultural defence undermines the equal status of his victims and the value law attaches to their right to life. In other words, assertion of a cultural defence in these circumstances places a higher value on the preservation of culture (as represented by the accused) than the preservation of women's lives and security. Of course, this feminist argument—powerful as it is—must contend with the occasional exceptional cases where women perpetrate the violence in the name of their culture. One notorious U.S. case concerned a woman charged with murdering her children. Upon learning of her husband's infidelity, she killed her children and unsuccessfully attempted to kill herself. Members of her community testified that parent-child suicide was an acceptable means of purging the shame of her husband's infidelity.[6]

Accused who assert a cultural defence typically rely on expert testimony to portray a static, monolithic, hermetically sealed culture that unambiguously authorizes violence against those who transgress cultural norms prevailing within the minority community. While such a patronizing depiction obviously serves the interests of the accused in the courtroom, the cultural portrait that the accused paints tends to be simplistic, inaccurate, reactively stereotypical, and ultimately promotes (rather than combats) contempt for minority cultures. Indeed, liberal critics such as Susan Moller Okin (1999) are quick to seize upon (and accept) these images as evidence that other cultures and religions are worse for women than secular Anglo-European culture and therefore undeserving of respect within a liberal framework.

Much has already been written—pro and con, with greater and lesser degrees of nuance and qualification—about whether the law ought to recognize a cultural defence. These analyses look at culture through the lens of law and ask if and where culture fits in the doctrinal picture. I do not propose to wade into the debate as it is currently framed. Instead, I pick up on the casual (and undeveloped) observation made by some scholars that reference to a cultural defence presumes that only certain immigrants, racialized minorities, have a "culture," whereas mainstream society—read White, Anglo-European society—in whose image law is created, does not. (In a sense, this complaint about the "othering" of culture mirrors one of the most common complaints levelled against the Canadian state policy of multiculturalism, namely, that it conveys a marginalizing rather than inclusive message about the place of cultural minorities in Canadian society.)

What I want to do here is unpack the observation about who has culture and demonstrate how law strategically ignores the cultural norms already embedded in criminal law defences. I contend that this oversight facilitates rejection of *other* cultural norms raised in the cultural defence while retaining access to the defence for those whose conduct comports with dominant norms of "mainstream" culture. I call this process looking at law through the lens of culture.

Commenting on the limits of liberal accommodation of cultural difference, Charles Taylor (1994:63) remarks in passing that "There would be no question of cultural differences determining the application of *habeas corpus*, for example." He makes a similar remark about homicide: "Even if, in the nature of things, compromise is close to impossible here—one either forbids murder or allows it." Of course, Taylor is well aware that the law of homicide contains defences that exempts certain intentional killings from the definition of murder. In this sense, the criminal law already compromises. The claim I wish to make here is that while cultural difference may not determine the application of certain doctrines, the very doctrines themselves instantiate certain culturally specific assumptions and norms. I pursue this argument by contending that the Anglo-European legal canon already recognizes a cultural defence.[7] We call it provocation. It only applies to murder (which carries a mandatory minimum life sentence) and it has the effect of reducing a charge of murder to manslaughter (which has no minimum sentence).

Of course, legal doctrine does not actually talk about provocation as a defence that reduces liability because an accused acted according to the dictates of the dominant culture when killing the victim, nor could it do so. Anglo-European law resists validating a higher source of authority than itself. It feels threatened by the claim that obedience to law may be subordinated to a conflicting cultural value embraced by the accused. People may be citizens (in the social sense) of many communities, but no communal or moral authority should claim superiority over the law of the sovereign.

The conventional law of provocation, then, is not conceptualized as a cultural defence. Moreover, jurisprudence emphatically denies that the defence implicitly sanctions killing motivated by rage[8] because the victim deserved it. What then does it say?

Section 232 of the Criminal Code sets out the requirements for the defence of provocation:

> (1) Culpable homicide that would otherwise be murder may be reduced to manslaughter if the person who committed it did so in the heat of passion caused by sudden provocation.

> (2) A wrongful act or insult that is of such a nature as to be sufficient to deprive an ordinary person of the power of self-control is provocation for the purposes of this section if the person acted on it on the sudden and before there was time for his [sic] passion to cool.

Reduced to its essential elements, the defence requires that the victim hurl an insult (by word, gesture, or action) that would deprive an "ordinary person" of self-control, and which in fact causes the accused to lose self-control. The accused must act on the sudden, lest provocation become a guise for premeditated revenge. Yet despite the reference to "loss of self-control," a provoked killing is not accidental: the accused intends his or her actions (though not always the consequence of death) and deliberately shoots the gun, plunges the knife, chokes the victim.

Provocation, then, is apparently not about culturally guided choices, it is about human nature and the loss of control. A insults B; B "naturally" loses self-control and kills A. The requirement that an "ordinary person" would lose self-control under the same circumstances is meant to ensure that the homicidal response really is somehow innate to the human condition. Notably, provocation invokes the "ordinary person" rather than the "reasonable person" (the usual objective standard against which accused are measured) because it is inherently unreasonable to fly into a rage and kill someone. Indeed, Cory J. of the Supreme Court of Canada explained recently:

> The objective aspect would at first reading appear to be contradictory for, as legal writers have noted, the "ordinary" person does not kill. Yet, I think the objective element should be taken as an attempt to weigh in the balance those very human frailties which sometimes lead people to act irrationally and impulsively against the need to protect society by discouraging acts of homicidal violence. (*R. v. Thibert*, 1996, para 4)

Without knowing anything about the criminal law or the provocation defence, most people can guess at least one or both of the scripts that recur most frequently in successful provocation cases: in the first, a man kills his intimate partner (and/or her paramour) because she has betrayed him sexually, usually by cheating on him but occasionally by mocking his sexual abilities.[9] Sometimes, the accused only suspects the infidelity. In the second, a young male subject to unwanted homosexual contact kills the man who made the advance. These are not the only scenarios, but they figure prominently in the jurisprudence and the public psyche.

I will now contrast two cases involving these narratives. In the Supreme Court of Canada case of *R. v. Hill* (1986), the victim was a 32-year-old man who had been a "Big Brother"[10] to the 16-year-old male accused. On the night of the killing, the accused was sleeping on the couch in the victim's apartment when, according to his testimony, he was awakened by an unexpected and unwelcome sexual advance—the victim was rubbing the accused's legs and chest. The accused grabbed a nearby hatchet and swung it at the victim, striking him in the head. The facts become somewhat more complicated thereafter,[11] but culminate in the accused grabbing two knives and stabbing the unarmed victim to death.

The second case, *R. v. Ly* (1987), was decided a year later by the British Columbia Court of Appeal. It concerned a man who had immigrated to Canada from Vietnam in 1980 and was living in a common-law relationship with a woman. Interestingly, her cultural origins are not revealed.[12] The accused suspected her of infidelity and confronted her with those suspicions on a couple of occasions. She denied the accusation and allegedly laughed when he described how he would "lose face" in his community if she was unfaithful. On the night of the killing, the victim returned home at 2:00 a.m. and told the accused her whereabouts that evening were none of his business. The accused testified that he then perceived the presence of a female apparition telling him to kill his partner, whereupon he strangled the victim. In both *Hill* and *Ly*, the accused raised the defence of provocation to the charge of murder.[13]

Because the test for provocation requires not only that the accused lose self-control, but also that the wrongful act or insult would cause an "ordinary person" to lose self-control, the critical issue in both cases is the construction of the ordinary person. In *Hill*, the question was whether the ordinary person was a young male (like the accused). In *Ly*, the issue was whether the ordinary person was a man of Vietnamese cultural background (like the accused).

The court in *Hill* determined that in assessing whether the ordinary person would have been provoked, it was necessary to hypothesize an ordinary 16-year-old male subject to a homosexual advance.[14]

Conversely, the court in *Ly* rejected the argument that the accused should be measured against the ordinary person of Vietnamese background, insisting instead that the appropriate standard was "the ordinary married man who, because of a history of the relationship between the spouses, had a belief that his wife was not being faithful to him" (39). The court ruled that the cultural background or racialized identity of the accused would only be apposite to constructing the ordinary person if the act or insult explicitly concerned that characteristic. That is to say, had the deceased insulted the accused by using a racial slur, then the ordinary person would be someone who bore the accused's racialized characteristic.

In effect, the court rejected a cultural defense in *Ly*. The court's rationale had nothing to do with concerns about the totalizing, essentialist, and caricatured presentation of Vietnamese culture or the one-dimensional description of the accused's relationship to his culture of origin. Neither did the court challenge the claim that the accused, in fact, lost self-control. Rather, the judgment derives its force from the principle that the level of self-control expected of people subject to the same law should not vary by culture. Quoting Lord Diplock from the British case of *DPP v. Camplin* (1978:37) the ordinary person is "possessed of such powers of self-control as everyone is entitled to expect that his fellow citizens will exercise in society as it is today."

Yet in *Hill* and *Ly*, the sex of the accused remains pertinent to construing how the ordinary person would react. Why? Surely not because males have less self-control than females. The proposition that men are inherently less rational, and thus more prone by nature to impulsive violence than women, is not one that judges tend to endorse. Indeed, Wilson J.[15] in *Hill* declares that any notion holding persons of different sex to different standards of self-control "would clearly be unacceptable" (para. 80), presumably because it would subvert crucial legal and social assumptions about male capacity for rationality and moral accountability. Why, then, is it crucial in a case like *Hill* to hypothesize that the ordinary person subject to an unwanted sexual advance is a young man? Why, for that matter, is it important to know that the victim was also male (or, to put it another way, that the insult was a *homosexual* advance)?

The Court avoids answering these questions. For our purposes, however, I think we can answer the question by imagining alternative scenarios. First, picture a 16-year-old female responding to an unwanted sexual advance from a 32-year-old male with homicidal rage.[16] Does this sound ordinary? How about a 16-year-old male responding to an unwanted sexual advance from a 32-year-old woman with homicidal rage? Try a 16-year-old female subject to an unwanted sexual advance from a 32-year-old woman. I know of no reported cases of provocation that feature these or like scenarios. If, as Wilson J. insists, men as a matter of principle do not naturally possess less self-control in general than women, then the only explanation left is that unwanted homosexual advances by men are "naturally" worse than any other kind of unwelcome sexual advance, and therefore elicit a stronger negative reaction from the targets. If one rejects a claim that homophobia is natural, one has difficulty resisting the conclusion that law projects as human nature the current of mainstream culture that defines masculinity in homophobic terms, and it is important to know that the accused in *Hill* is a young male subject to a homosexual advance because he is a product of that culture and his actions and reactions (including what causes him to "lose control") are shaped by it.

Now in *Ly*, the accused does not get the benefit of claiming that his cultural context explains why the conduct of his spouse was a worse insult to him than it might be to someone outside that cultural context. He still gets the benefit of his sex, so to speak, in the sense the standard is the ordinary *man* in the mainstream Canadian context who suspects his wife is unfaithful. In a recent analysis of this case, philosopher Arthur Ripstein (1997:220) endorses the court's result by asserting that the law "cannot make allowances for a man losing his temper because he regards a woman as his property, however deeply ingrained such a view may be in some cultures." One might reasonably query whether the current law of provocation does precisely that for men who are understood as members of mainstream culture.

As a purely empirical matter, most men in Canada (whatever their cultural context) who are confronted with an unwanted homosexual advance do not actually try to kill the other man. Similarly, only a small fraction of men (and an even smaller proportion of women) who discover their partners' infidelity *in flagrante* attempt to kill their partners or their partners' paramours. The "ordinary man" imagined in law does not purport to describe a statistical reality. It would thus appear to be a concession to human weakness that is not very ordinary at all. If the "ordinary person" is not a purely positive construct—a description of how ordinary people actually behave—it must contain a normative undercurrent. Despite its own stated objective of demonstrating compassion for past acts, the jurisprudence of provocation cannot avoid being read prospectively as an object lesson of what ordinary people might—and may—do to the partners who betray them and the gay men who proposition them.

Since fewer women than men actually kill, and women by definition will not be propositioned by gay men, the standard can pretend to be gender neutral while actually redounding to the benefit of male accused most of the time.[7] It bears reiterating that most ordinary men, according to this standard, are quite extraordinary.

I am not the first to criticize the existing application of the provocation defence as implicitly sanctioning violence against women and gay people.

And, as I noted at the outset, many have argued that recognizing a cultural defence would effectively heighten the vulnerability of women and children from within cultural minority communities. What I have tried to do is link the two streams, which have thus far been running parallel and *incommunicado*. This disjuncture is maintained discursively by characterizing the sexism and homophobia in the provocation defence as "political," (and therefore subject to challenge and transformation) while the sexism of culture defences is a matter of "culture" (and therefore immutable and monolithic).

Conclusion

I have attempted to problematize the tacit assumptions that law and culture occupy different conceptual spaces. I contend that the provocation defence purports to be a compassionate concession to the "reality" of human nature. In its application, however, it legitimates certain cultural norms about masculinity, notwithstanding that law purports not to accommodate cultural specificity in judging acts of lethal violence. The fact that this construction of human nature is challenged by critics as misogynistic and homophobic speaks to the reality that culture is an ever-shifting, contested, and unstable terrain, a feature that is regularly overlooked when discussing "other" cultures. It is beyond the scope of this chapter to address or resolve the important question of whether we ought to retain the partial defence of provocation at all and, if so, under what conditions. However, in respect of the cultural defence, I contend that the question "should the law recognize a cultural defence?" is the wrong question. What we should be asking is why law privileges one particular cultural defence above all others.

Notes

The author wishes to thank Richard Devlin, Leti Volpp, and Arthur Ripstein for their insightful comments and constructive suggestions.

1. Some scholars, such as George Fletcher, maintain a distinction between defences that excuse wrongful acts and those that justify what would otherwise be wrongful acts. Canadian legal doctrine does not implement the distinction, but in any event, the defence of provocation, which I discuss *infra*, is categorized as an excuse even by those who support the distinction.

2. For instance, self-defence may excuse X for killing the assailant Y, but the defence of duress will not excuse X for abducting Y under threat of death from Z.

3. See, for example, *R. v. Ashini* (1989), 2 C.N.L.R. 119; *R. v. Potts*, [1990] O.J. No. 2567 (Ontario Court of Justice, Provincial Division), 28 Nov. 1990. In the former case, Provincial Court Judge Igliolorte commented at p. 120 of his judgment that:

> Since the concept of land as property is a concept foreign to original people, the Court must not assume that a "reasonable" belief be founded on English and hence Canadian law standards. The Innu People must be allowed to express their understanding of a foreign concept on their terms, or simply express what they believe.

4. "Haitian Men Given Lenient Sentences on Cultural Grounds" (1998). Once again, it is important to note that s. 718.2(e) of the Criminal Code explicitly adopts sentencing principles that acknowledge Aboriginal cultural specificity by instructing judges that "all available sanctions other than imprisonment that are reasonable in the circumstances should be considered for all offenders, with particular attention to the circumstances of aboriginal offenders."

5. The Hmong are a Southeast Asian hill people concentrated mainly in Laos. During the Vietnam War, Hmong were recruited by the CIA as part of undercover operations in the region. Following the end of the war, Hmong fled to Thai refugee camps where they languished for many years. In the early 1980s, the United States finally consented to resettling several thousand Hmong in the U.S.

6. Some commentators have formulated an analysis that would salvage a culture defence in these cases. See Volpp (1994). I do not know of any North American cases in which women who commit or authorize female genital mutilation have been charged, although women have been charged and convicted in France.

7. Indeed, it is arguable that some or all other defences are culturally based. I focus on provocation here as a particularly clear example.

8. As opposed to self-defence or defence of others, or necessity, or under duress, which are other motives for killing that the law recognizes.

9. See, e.g., *R. v. Thibert*, [1996] 1 S.C.R. 37; *R. v. Stone*, [1999] 2 S.C.R. 290; *R. v. Tripodi*, [1955] S.C.R. 438; *R. v. Clark* (1974), 22 C.C.C. (2d) 1.

10. The Big Brother Organization matches boys (usually without adult male figures of authority/support in their lives) with volunteer men who befriend the boys and attempt to provide positive role models.

11. Among other things, the accused leaves the apartment and then returns, which certainly raises doubts about whether he could be said to have "acted on the sudden before there was time for his passion to cool."

12. One cannot help but wonder whether not naming her race invites the inference that the victim was a Canadian-born White woman. As such, she could be constructed as culturally and racially "neutral." While it may not ultimately alter the determination of legal culpability, I cannot avoid thinking that the racialized and cultural identity of the victim (whatever it was) was not a neutral factor in relationship and interaction between the two people, yet this dimension of the narrative is completely effaced.

13. Other possible defences, such as self-defence in the case of *Hill* or mental disorder in the case of *Ly*, either were not raised or were rejected at trial.

14. In fairness, *Hill* is not without ambiguity on this matter, but the more recent Supreme Court provocation case of *Thibert* note 10, advances this as the correct interpretation of the *Hill* judgment.

15. Who, incidentally, was the first woman appointed to the Supreme Court of Canada.

16. Suffice to say that if this was ordinary, the mortality rate for men would skyrocket.

17. But not all the time. There are various reported cases involving a woman killing her husband or her husband's paramour. Suffice to say, however, that these cases make up a small portion of the total. See, for example, *R. v. Daniels* (1983), 7 C.C.C. (3d) 542; *R. v. Gladue*, [1999] 1 S.C.R. 688.

References

Director of Public Prosecutions v. Camplin, [1978] A.C. 705.

Gutmann, A. 1992. "Introduction," in A. Gutmann et al., ed., *Multiculturalism and the Politics of Recognition*. Princeton, NJ: Princeton University Press.

"Haitian Men Given Lenient Sentences on Cultural Grounds." 1998. Canadian Press, 27 January.

Kymlicka, W. 1995. *Multicultural Citizenship: A Liberal Theory of Minority Rights*. Oxford: Oxford University Press.

Okin, S.M. 1999. "Is multiculturalism bad for women?" in S.M. Okin, ed., *Is Multiculturalism Bad for Women?* Princeton, NJ: Princeton University Press.

R. v. Thibert, [1996] 1 S.C.R. 37.

R. v. Hill (1985), 51 C.R. (3d) 97 (S.C.C.).

R. v. Ly (1987), 33 C.C.C. (3d) 31 (B.C.C.A.).

Ripstein, A. 1997. "Context, continuity and fairness," in R. McKim and J. McMahan, eds., *The Morality of Nationalism*. New York: Oxford University Press.

Taylor, C. 1994. "The politics of recognition," in A. Gutmann et al., eds., *Multiculturalism and the Politics of Recognition*. Princeton, NJ: Princeton University Press.

Volpp, L. 1994. "[Mis]Identifying culture: Asian women and the 'cultural defense'," *Harvard Women's Law Journal* 17:57.

6

Racism and the Collection of Statistics Relating to Race and Ethnicity

JULIAN V. ROBERTS

This chapter explores the issue of race-crime statistics, or, more accurately, race-criminal justice statistics, since the "crime" statistics come to us filtered through the decisions of criminal justice professionals such as the police. Before describing the nature of race-crime statistics in Canada, some brief background information about the issue of minorities and criminal justice may be of use to the reader.

Overrepresentation of Minorities in Criminal Justice Statistics

It is a fact of life that minorities, particularly visible minorities, are over-represented in the crime and criminal justice statistics in all Western nations. The specific minority varies from country to country, but everywhere some group accounts for a disproportionate number of convictions and admissions to prison (Tonry, 1997). There are two general explanations for this international phenomenon. First, minorities tend to have living conditions that put them at greater risk for offending. Second, it is clear that minorities attract a disproportionate degree of attention from police, and in some countries they are more likely to be sent to prison than would be expected in light of the crimes for which they have been convicted (e.g., Hood, 1992; Tonry, 1995).

Correctional statistics reveal the magnitude of the problem with respect to minorities and the criminal justice system. Although public knowledge of criminal justice trends is poor, a recent survey found that most Canadians are by now well aware that Aboriginal peoples represent a disproportionate percentage of admissions to custody (Nuffield et al.,

1999). At the federal level, the most recent statistics show that, although Aboriginal Canadians represent only 2 per cent of the general population, they account for 17 per cent of the penitentiary admissions (Reed and Roberts, 1999). In certain provinces, notably Ontario, Black Canadians are disproportionately represented in the admissions to custody. The Commission on Systemic Racism in the Ontario Criminal Justice System reported in 1994 that Blacks had a prison admission rate twice that of Whites (3,686 per 100,000 compared to 1,993). More recent statistics from the federal prison system reveal that the percentage of the prison population that is Black is three times higher than the percentage of Blacks in the general population (Wortley, 1998).

To what extent does this overrepresentation reflect discrimination against visible minorities? The invaluable work of the Commission on Systemic Racism in the Ontario Criminal Justice System demonstrated the existence of discrimination by the police: Blacks were significantly more likely to be detained in custody pretrial than were comparably situated White accused (Commission on Systemic Racism in the Ontario Criminal Justice System, 1995; Roberts and Doob, 1997). Although there was little evidence of discrimination by judges at the stage of sentencing, the Commission nevertheless uncovered evidence of racism against Black inmates in Ontario correctional institutions (Commission on Systemic Racism in the Ontario Criminal Justice System, 1994).

Public Perceptions of Racism in the Criminal Justice System

The discriminatory treatment of minorities by some (but by no means all) criminal justice professionals has not escaped the attention of the public. Surveys conducted by the Ontario Commission made it clear that the Ontario public were aware that justice in their province was not applied equally. This perception was not unique to Black residents of the province or to people with contact with the police. Over half the sample of Chinese respondents and White respondents agreed that Blacks are treated differently from Whites by the police in Ontario (Wortley, 1996). Not unexpectedly, a higher percentage (over three-quarters of the sample) of Black respondents held this view (Wortley, 1996: Table 2). It is also worth noting that Black respondents who reported having direct contact with the police were more likely to hold a perception of injustice.

Public Attributions of Criminality
to Visible Minorities and Immigrants

At the same time, there has been a tendency to "racialize" the crime issue in Canada and elsewhere. By this I mean a tendency to see links between crime and racial or ethnic origin. Although Canadians appear to be aware that the criminal justice system is not equitably administered, many people also believe that there is an inherent link between race and crime or culture and crime. This belief emerges clearly from a number of public opinion polls conducted over the past few years.

For example, surveys conducted in 1995 in Ontario revealed that nearly half (45 per cent) of the polled public believed there was a relationship between ethnicity and criminality. Of those who held this belief, the groups most often identified (by two-thirds of the sample) as being more responsible for crime were "West Indians" or "Blacks" (Henry, et al., 1996). The findings from the Ontario surveys make it clear that visible minorities, particularly Caribbean Blacks, are singled out by many members of the public as being responsible for a disproportionate amount of crime. However, there is a more general stereotyping at work. Other research has shown that many Canadians also see a link between immigrants and crime. For example, a national survey of Canadians conducted in 1989 found that 48 per cent of respondents agreed with the statement that "immigration increases the crime rate." If the individuals who responded "don't know" are not included, the percentage seeing a link between immigration and crime rises above 50 per cent (see Palmer, 1994, for a discussion of attitudes towards immigration).

These survey findings carry important practical consequences for visible minorities. One obvious danger concerns the decisions of members of the public in judicial proceedings. If members of the public believe that there is an inherent link between race and crime, what does this say about the chances of a Black accused receiving unbiased treatment from members of a jury? The decision in *R. v. Parks* recognized the right of counsel representing Black accuseds to pose questions to the jury regarding their ability to lay aside any prejudice they may hold with respect to Black accuseds. However, this step may prove insufficient to ensure equal treatment: a considerable volume of research has shown that judicial remedies to ensure that bias does not affect a trial have often proved ineffective (Roberts, 1997).

It is worth noting that this discussion concerning a link between race or ethnicity and crime is not new to Canada. In September 1929, the American Prison Association held its annual congress in Toronto. At that meeting, J.C. McRuer gave a talk in which he responded to assertions that there was a link between nationality and crime by stating, "I have heard it repeated times innumerable that the foreigner is responsible for our so-called lawlessness—but the figures do not bear this out." McRuer then presented ethnicity data for convicted persons and concluded:

> I am convinced that the Crime Problem we have in this country is our own problem. Foreigners may be contributing factors but the real problem is inherently Canadian in its origin as it is American in its origin in U.S.A., or French in its origin in France, or Italian in Italy. (American Prison Association, 1930:108)

Recently, the media have contributed to a worsening of this racialization of the crime issue. We know that most members of the public derive their information about crime and justice exclusively from the news media. News stories frequently link a specific crime report with the race or immigrant status of the suspect or accused. This is apparent from media coverage of high-profile cases such as the "Just Desserts" murder in Toronto in which the race of the offenders was prominent in most accounts of the crime and subsequent trial, but also from coverage of more mundane crimes.

Collection and Distribution of Race-Crime Statistics

This is the social context in which there have been calls for the annual collection and publication of statistics that would identify the race or ethnic origin of suspects, accused persons, and offenders (Roberts, 1994). At the present, race-crime statistics are not collected by the criminal justice system in Canada. What effect might the collection and publication of race-crime statistics have on public perceptions, both of injustice and of the relationship between race or ethnicity and crime? Before addressing this question, it is worth noting the practice with respect to collection of this kind of information in other countries. As will be seen, there is considerable variability.

The Practice in Other Countries
Regarding Race-Crime Statistics

The experience of criminal justice systems in other Western countries is variable: some jurisdictions, such as the U.S., routinely collect and publish arrest statistics broken down by the suspect's race or country of origin. Other countries, for example, France, carry an absolute prohibition against the collection of racial data but monitor nationality. But collecting crime statistics based on nationality or country of origin is no more useful than race. The same outcome will be seen. Over (and under) representations of various nationalities will always be found. In France for example, statistics show that 25 per cent of the inmate population in Paris were foreigners, while they account for only 7 per cent of the capital's population (Tournier and Robert, 1989). This obviously does not establish a causal link between nationality and criminality.

In other European countries, such as Belgium, this information is readily available to the police because it is contained on identification papers that all residents are obliged by law to carry. However, it is perhaps worth taking a closer look at the U.S. experience, for that is the model advocated by several politicians in Canada. In my view, the American example best illustrates the dangers of collecting and publishing crime statistics that are broken down by the race, ethnicity, or nationality of the suspect or accused.

The widely distributed annual publication provides information on several aspects of criminal justice in the U.S., including a breakdown of the percentage of arrests in which the suspect was Black, White or Amerindian. Thus, in a recent edition of this publication (U.S. Department of Justice, 1998: Table 4.10), we find that for a list of offences, Blacks accounted for 27 per cent of persons charged with an offence. On the same page, the U.S. Bureau of Justice Statistics presents census information showing that 13 per cent of the U.S. population are Black. Anyone who can subtract 13 from 27 can arrive at the "overrepresentation" of Black Americans in arrest statistics. This kind of statistical presentation may help to promote the idea that there is a causal link between race/ethnicity and crime.

It is not clear why this information needs to be published in this way. The race of the offender is not a useful research variable like criminal history. Knowing that a certain percentage of crimes are committed by people with a criminal record has obvious implications for crime-control policies. If recidivists commit a high percentage of recorded crime, judges may wish to impose much harsher penalties on such offenders. In contrast to this, knowing what percentage of crimes (or, more accurately, *alleged* crimes) involves visible minorities carries no implication for crime control policies. It does not help judges sentencing offenders to know whether crime rates are higher (or lower) for any particular ethnic group.

It may seem natural to an American audience to publish "crime" statistics presented in this way. Americans may have a different perspective, and may see the distinction between Black and White as being critical. Skin colour is perhaps the central defining personal characteristic of American society, therefore to present White/non-White arrest statistics, even if there is no basis in criminal justice policy development for such a practice is not remarkable. In Canada, we may be less inclined to define ourselves in this way because Canadians come from such a variety of cultures and such a high percentage of Canadians were born in another country.

Problems in Collecting Race-Crime Statistics

There are also insurmountable practical difficulties in terms of the collection of race-crime statistics. Classifying people according to their ethnic origins is far from easy in a multiracial society. It requires considerable juggling with the concepts of race, ethnicity, and country of origin, and some curious outcomes are the result. For example, I am a White, Anglophone resident of British ancestry, born and raised in a country in which 98 per cent of the population is Black. I travel on a European Community passport and hold Canadian citizenship. If I am charged with a crime, whose crime statistics go up? Whites? Kenyans? Immigrant Canadians? Anglophones? And this, of course, is central to the issue: a major reason *not* to routinely collect racial statistics is simply that they *cannot* be gathered with any reasonable degree of reliability or validity (Doob, 1991).

This difficulty is frequently overlooked by advocates of the collection of race-crime statistics, to whom the classification by their race of suspects, those accused, or offenders is as simple (and as uncontroversial) as classification by their gender.

The point can be illustrated by reference to the form employed by Statistics Canada when an attempt was made (in the early 1990s) to collect this information (Canadian Centre for Justice Statistics, 1991). The general definition of race used by Statistics Canada included a combination of two elements: common descent and common physical features. The coding options accompanying the form reflect the conceptual difficulties surrounding the definition of race. The general problem is that there are so many exceptions and so many problematic classifications. For example, consider those Jamaicans who have white skin. Are police officers going to classify them as Black or White? And what should be recorded when a police officer's classification does not coincide with the self-classification by the suspect or accused?

Classifying Native Canadians using the Statistics Canada system created even greater problems. A suspect with a North American Indian mother but a non-Indian father is to be classified as a "North American Indian." At the same time, there is a separate classification for the Métis, even though these latter are described on the form as "people of mixed Indian and European ancestry." Police officers—for it is they who are being asked to undertake this dubious anthropological exercise—are asked to distinguish also between South Asians and Southeast Asians. The internal logic becomes even more tortuous when the "other" category is examined, which lumps together Arabs, Turks, and Armenians (among others). Clearly there are severe limitations associated with the common features approach to classifying individuals.

Small wonder, then, that in those few Canadian jurisdictions that attempted to collect these data, race was seldom recorded and forwarded to the Canadian Centre for Justice Statistics. Police officers themselves—a group said to be in favour of collecting such data—have found the task impractical. And this was one reason why Statistics Canada abandoned the exercise of collecting crime statistics according to the race or ethnicity of the suspect. The only area in which racial origin data are routinely available now is with respect to the federal correctional population (Solicitor General Canada, 1998).

Dangers of Publishing Crime Statistics that Include Racial or Ethnic Origin

The reason for not collecting race-crime data goes beyond the level of technical difficulties. There are clear dangers for visible minority communities in Canada. Publication of crime statistics involving the race of the suspect or accused will inevitably lead to further stereotyping. If a particular minority happens to be overrepresented in these statistics, members of this minority group may well be seen by others as crime-prone.

Some proponents of race-based criminal justice statistics cannot see what all the fuss is about. But the dangers are real enough. In the not so distant past, early criminologist Cesare Lombroso collected so-called "crime statistics" by different ethnic groups. In his hands, these "data" provided the empirical justification for many racist statements about Gypsies and other minority groups.

Ultimately, the collection and dissemination of race-crime statistics add nothing to our knowledge about the nature of crime. Race is not a *cause* of crime, and publishing racial statistics does not help us develop better crime-control policies. Suppose, for example, that we knew that visible minority youth were overrepresented in the youth crime statistics. Knowing this would not help us address the problem of youth crime. On the other hand, knowing that a substantial number of young offenders have a troubled history of attending school, and drop out for protracted periods, has very clear implications in terms of our response to juvenile criminality. It points us towards developing better programs for helping students stay in school.

Police Reports and Crime Statistics Are Not the Same

The reference to Lombroso is not just a historical curiosity; it is important to understand the attraction of race-crime data and their power to misinform. Neither Lombroso more than 100 years ago nor the public today appreciate that *arrest* statistics are not *crime* statistics, and that while a relationship obviously exists between the two, one cannot use one as a substitute or proxy for the other. Almost every mass media article on this issue talks about *crime* and not about *criminal justice* statistics. Since the media constitute the primary source of information for most members of the public, the error is likely to be widely transmitted. Most people are likely to translate a statement like "Blacks account for 25 per cent of arrests" to mean that "Blacks commit 25 per cent of all crimes."

Criminal justice statistics reflect the influence of many factors, including differential policing and variable reporting rates across crimes. Consider the crime of robbery. One major victimization survey (Jefferson, 1988) found that only 8 per cent of robberies were recorded by the police.

This means that police-based statistics represent the proverbial tip of the iceberg. It would be very foolish to base estimates of offending by different groups on such statistics. Furthermore, the incidents that are recorded by the police may not be representative of all robberies. As Jefferson notes: "whatever the arrest figures ... the 'unknown' element is so great, especially for those crimes where black 'over-representation' is seen to be greatest, as to make all estimates of black offending strictly conjectural" (538; see Gabor and Roberts, 1990, for further discussion of the empirical research on race and crime).

If this were not compelling enough, we should recall what happens when we compare criminal justice statistics including race to the findings from victimization surveys. The overrepresentation of Blacks diminishes significantly, and in some cases disappears completely. Thus, the *Sourcebook* referred to earlier notes that 46 per cent of arrests for violent crimes involved Black Americans. Victimization surveys, however, reveal that the percentage of offenders who were identified (by the victim) as being Black was less than one in four (U.S. Department of Justice, 1986). Most people, however, including (and perhaps especially) the politicians who have called for the routine collection of racial statistics, believe arrest statistics to be a perfectly satisfactory index of criminality.

Argument in Favour of Collecting Race-Crime Statistics

There is one potent argument in favour of collecting and publishing criminal justice statistics involving race, and that is the protection of minorities through the documentation of bias within the criminal justice system. If the Toronto police had not recorded the race of the suspect/accused for a brief period in the early 1990s, the Ontario Commission on Racism would not have been able to conduct its research that ultimately demonstrated the existence of discrimination against Black accuseds at the level of bail. We need to track the treatment of minorities to ensure, for example, that judges or parole boards (or the police for that matter) do not discriminate against any particular group. The race or ethnic origin of the suspect or accused benefits from this context in the same way all do by ensuring that other extra-legal variables (e.g., socio-economic status, gender) do not affect criminal justice decision-making.

The solution lies not in the routine collection (and publication) of such information; this simply confers an undesirable status upon race.

Instead, the criminal justice system should conduct periodic "special studies" of limited scope and duration. (This is in fact the position currently endorsed by Statistics Canada.) A special study involves recording, over a limited period of time, the racial or ethnic origin of suspects, accuseds, and offenders. A sample of cases is followed as it makes its way through the criminal process, from the laying of a charge by the police to the release of the offender on parole, for the small subset of cases that proceed that far. A study of this nature permits researchers to determine whether the criminal justice system (at all stages) is treating people equally, but minimizes the degree of stigmatization that may occur. Of course, the practical problems of classifying people remain to be overcome, even in a "one-shot" study of this kind.

But if we can collect the data periodically, why not every time someone is charged with an offence? Put another way, what exactly is the difference between routine collection of race or ethnicity information and a so-called "special study"? There are important symbolic and practical differences between the two.

The symbolic message conveyed by the American practice of routinely publishing race-crime data is that a person's race (or ethnicity, or country of origin) is important to understanding why crime occurs, why some people offend, and how crime can be controlled. A special study, on the other hand, conveys a very different message. The focus of a special study is not on ascribed characteristics of the offender (such as race, ethnicity, or country of birth) but rather on the functioning of the criminal justice system itself. The goal of the special study is to document inequitable treatment, if it exists, not to document relative rates of participation in criminal justice statistics.

On a practical level, these special studies are far less likely to be used improperly. Routinely collecting race (or country of origin) at the arrest level leads easily to the association of crime and race. To avoid (or at least limit) such misuse, special studies would be released by Statistics Canada under separate cover and would include detailed explanation of exactly what the statistics do (and do not) mean. The potential for abuse is, of course, still there, but should be greatly reduced.

Conclusion

There is little justification for routinely collecting and disseminating race-crime statistics, and much to fear from such a practice. On the other hand, the use of special studies generates the necessary information to test for discrimination while providing safeguards to prevent the abuse of such data. This solution appears more appropriate for Canada than the American one or the blanket prohibition against such statistics that exists in certain European countries.

If race-crime statistics are collected and published annually as part of the crime statistics, a vicious circle will arise in which adverse social conditions, made worse by racism, will produce higher rates of crime in certain visible minority and immigrant populations. These elevated crime rates will draw the disproportionate attention of law enforcement agencies, which contributes to disproportionate rates of visible minorities in the official criminal justice statistics. Widespread publication of this disproportionate involvement in crime statistics without the interpretation that would accompany an academic discussion of the problem will inevitably lead to confirmation, in the public's mind, of a link between race and crime. It will further polarize Canadian society by stressing the gap between law-abiding Canadians raised in the host country and unlawful groups and cultures who come to Canada. The result will be an increase in calls for tighter immigration rules, as well as a number of other undesirable reactions. One inevitable result will be the stigmatization of whole communities. In light of this, it is particularly important to listen to the views of the communities most likely to be affected by the publication of these statistics. To date, most community representatives who have taken a position on the issue have opposed the publication of race-crime statistics. Finally, the general public also seems aware of the dangers posed by race-crime statistics: a survey conducted in 1994 found that half the respondents were of the opinion that the collection of race-crime statistics would be a bad idea because it could exacerbate racial tensions in Canadian society (Angus Reid Group, 1994).

References

American Prison Association. 1930. *Proceedings of the 59th Annual Congress.* Toronto, 20-26 Sept.

Angus Reid Group. 1994. *The National Angus Reid News Poll: Public Opinion on Reporting Crime Statistics by Race.* Ottawa: Angus Reid Group.

Canadian Centre for Justice Statistics. 1991. *Report from the Canadian Centre for Justice Statistics on the 'Racial Origin' Variable on the Revised UCR Survey.* Ottawa: Statistics Canada.

Commission on Systemic Racism in the Ontario Criminal Justice System. 1994. *Racism Behind Bars: The Treatment of Black and Other Racial Minority Prisoners in Ontario Prisons: Interim report.* Toronto: Queen's Printer for Ontario.

—. 1995. *Report of the Commission on Systemic Racism in the Ontario Criminal Justice System.* Toronto: Queen's Printer for Ontario.

Doob, A.N. 1991. *Workshop on Collecting Race and Ethnicity Statistics in the Criminal Justice System.* Toronto: Centre of Criminology, University of Toronto.

Gabor, T., and J. Roberts. 1990. "Rushton on race and crime: The evidence remains unconvincing," *Canadian Journal of Criminology* 32:335-43.

Henry, F., P. Hastings and B. Freer. 1996. "Perceptions of race and crime in Ontario: Empirical evidence from Toronto and the Durham region," *Canadian Journal of Criminology* 38:469-76.

Hood, R. 1992. *Race and Sentencing.* Oxford: Clarendon Press.

Jefferson, T. 1988. "Race, crime and policing: Empirical, theoretical and methodological issues," *International Journal of the Sociology of Law* 16:521-39.

Lombroso, C. 1911. *Crime: Its Causes and Remedies.* Montclair, NJ: Patterson Smith.

Nuffield, J., J. Roberts, R. Hann, M. Beare and P. Tremblay. 1999. *Report of a National Survey on Corrections in Canada.* Ottawa: Ministry of the Solicitor General Canada.

Palmer, D. 1994. *Anatomy of an Attitude: Origins of the Attitude toward the Level of Immigration in Canada.* Ottawa: Citizenship and Immigration Canada.

R. v. Parks 84 C.C.C. (3d) 354.

Reed, M., and J. Roberts. 1999. "Adult correctional services in Canada, 1997-98," *Juristat* 19.

Roberts, J. 1994. "Crime and race statistics: Toward a Canadian solution," *Canadian Journal of Criminology* 36:175-86.

—. 1997. *Challenge for Cause and the Question of Bias in Criminal Trials.* Ottawa: Department of Criminology, University of Ottawa.

Roberts, J., and A. Doob. 1997. "Race, ethnicity, and criminal justice in Canada," in, M. Tonry, ed., *Ethnicity, Crime and Immigration: Comparative and Cross-National Perspectives.* Chicago: University of Chicago Press, 469-522.

Solicitor General of Canada. 1998. *Corrections in Canada.* Ottawa: Solicitor General Canada.

Tonry, M. 1995. *Malign Neglect: Race, Crime and Punishment in America.* New York: Oxford University Press.

—, ed. 1997. *Ethnicity, Crime and Immigration: Comparative and Cross-National Perspectives.* Chicago: University of Chicago Press.

Tournier, P., and P. Robert. 1989. *Les étrangers dans les statistiques pénales. Constitution d'un corpus et analyse critique des donnees.* Paris: CESDIP.

U.S. Department of Justice 1986. *Criminal Victimization in the United States.* Washington: Bureau of Justice Statistics.

—. 1998. *Sourcebook of Criminal Justice Statistics—1997.* Washington: Bureau of Justice Statistics.

Wortley, S. 1996. "Justice for all? Race and perceptions of bias in the Ontario criminal justice system—A Toronto survey," *Canadian Journal of Criminology* 38:439-67.

—. 1998. Canadian federal incarceration rates by racial group. Table available from the author. Toronto: Centre of Criminology, University of Toronto.

Part III
Processes of Racialization and Criminalization

7

Police Constructions of Race
and Gender in Street Gangs

GLADYS L. SYMONS

This chapter examines police constructions of race and gender in street gangs in a major metropolitan centre; specifically, how the Montreal Police Department (SPCUM)[1] addresses the phenomenon of street gangs in that city. The analysis focuses on the processes of racialization and gendering of street gangs in Montreal. Since the police are often the first-line interventionists with youth on the street, their constructions of the street gang question are important to understand. Questions of racialization and gendering are significant in this context, for the police have an important role to play both in defining the street gang issue and in developing strategies to deal with it.

In 1996, the SPCUM declared the issue of "youth and street gangs" an organizational priority for the next five years. The Police Department reported that at the end of the previous year "59 street gangs were active in Montreal, with membership estimated at 1,300 teenagers ranging from 15 to 19 years of age" (SPCUM, 1995:2). It is therefore an opportune time to examine police attention to the phenomenon of youth and street gangs.

The present analysis is based on data from a qualitative, iterative study, using observation techniques,[2] documentary analysis, and verbatim transcriptions from 28 intensive interviews conducted with a theoretical sample[3] of the Montreal Police Department during 1997 and 1998. We have examined both official documentation and police discourse, analyzing the processes of the racialization and the gendering of street gangs. The repercussions of these perspectives concerning ethnic minority group members and women in gangs are discussed.

Police Definition of a Street Gang

The police in Montreal define a street gang as "a group of individuals, usually adolescents and/or young adults, who use the power of group intimidation in order to carry out, on a more or less regular basis, violent criminal acts" (Châles et al., 1996:2).[4] Six criteria identify a street gang, namely, an organized structure, an identifiable leadership, a defined territory, regular association of several juvenile delinquents, a specific goal, and involvement in illegal activities.

The "typical" young person attracted to or implicated in a street gang is described as a violent and unpredictable, poorly educated, unemployed male between 16 and 22 years of age who comes from an economically deprived background and belongs to a minority ethnic[5] group. Even at the age of 25 or 26, he can still be a member of a gang, becoming more violent as time goes on (Châles et al., 1996:6).

The structure of a street gang is depicted as a configuration of concentric circles consisting of a hard core, surrounded by a soft core, which is surrounded by a group of youth on the periphery. The hard core (10 to 15 per cent of the membership) is made up of criminally active youth who are virtually immune to rehabilitative influences. The soft core (30 to 40 per cent) is comprised of youth more loosely connected to the gang, for whom there is more hope for rehabilitation. The periphery (45 to 60 per cent) includes youth weakly affiliated with the gang. They may be simply attracted to it, victims of it, or witnesses to gang misdemeanours and hence intimidated by it (Châles et al., 1996:14-15). One policeman explained the situation:

> It is because the SPCUM and the *Conseil de sécurité publique* (Public Safety Committee) agree that street gangs constitute a threat to urban security that the phenomenon has been earmarked as an organizational priority for the next five years. The objective is to try to develop preventive strategies to target youth at risk, and to try, with the tools at our disposal to help them get out of the street gang. The goal is to give them other interests and other ways to feel good about themselves. Of course, here I am referring to the periphery gangs, because the hard core is often irrecoverable.... It [street gangs] is a priority and we are concerned about it. One not only sees an increase in the numbers of gangs in the jurisdic-

tion, but also an increase in the violence—an increase in violent crime.

Racialization and gendering of street gangs are two important components of the system of social stratification in complex societies, and it is important to specify the dynamics of these processes. Moreover, the articulation of race and gender in street gangs needs to be identified and addressed by the police, as well as by other interventionists in the field.

Racialization of the Street Gang Issue[6]

Holdaway (1997:70) defines racialization in the context of police work as "social processes that connote and denote relationships and other phenomena with the meaning of 'race.'" Racialization involves an ongoing process of negotiation. Says Holdaway:

> "Racialization" is a myriad of social processes related to but not wholly determined by the wider meanings of racialized groups within a particular society or by the related but particular ways in which the meaning of racialized categories are articulated within the police workforce.

He goes on to specify that "[t]here are wider, societally drawn meanings that encroach upon officers' use of racialized categories, and they are a powerful source of pressure playing upon the police workforce" (85). It is important to note the localization of the racialization process in the society within which police services (as well as other organizations) operate. We are not suggesting that the police invent racialized categories. Rather, they draw upon (and sometimes modify or reinforce) those racialized categories already constructed and firmly embedded in society at large.

Police documentation (SPCUM, n.d.) identifies five "ethnic groups" from which street gangs originate: Jamaican, Haitian, Asiatic, extreme right, and Latino. The inclusion of the "extreme right" as an ethnocultural group in this context denotes Caucasians (either Anglophone or Francophone) often involved in racist activity. The categorization of minority group gangs by "ethnicity," and the identification of majority group gangs by "activity" contribute to the racialization of the street gang issue. Also evident in the above citation is the homogenization of different

"Asiatic" groups and experiences as well as those of different "Latino" groups. On the other hand, Jamaican and Haitian experiences are differentiated (rather than subsumed under the term "Black") because of language. Jamaicans are Anglophone and Haitians are Francophone, and it would be somewhat of an understatement to point out that language is a critical marker in Quebec.

The street gang phenomenon is, in general, associated with ethnic minorities in the police discourse. Some police officers, however, do identify the presence of majority group gangs labelled "Québécois" gangs. Here, it is necessary to interject yet another note on language. Police in Montreal adopt the general linguistic usage of the majority group in Quebec society. Thus, "Québécois" refers to Francophone Québécois 'de souche,' that is, those French Canadians living in Quebec who can trace their origins to the early French settlers. "Ethnics," on the other hand, are the Others, that is, ethnocultural groups other than the Québécois 'de souche.'

Police define "Québécois" gangs as less structured, less durable, and involved in what is referred to as "the usual crime." One officer explained the police response to Québécois gangs before, as he put it, "the ethnic gangs arrived on the scene." He told us: "You didn't need any particular expertise, because they [crimes committed by these gangs] were the usual crimes." Apart from the Québécois gangs, some Francophone youth *de souche* are involved in "ethnic" gangs, but the police locate them more often on the periphery than in the hard core, the latter being made up of ethnic minority youth.

Racialization is present in police discourse when the link between gang behaviour and ethnicity is normalized. Some police, for example, contend that gang behaviour is "normal" for the youth of certain ethnic communities. It is considered to be a part of an "ethnic mentality" and part of the mores of particular ethnic groups. As one policeman explained, "It's directly related to the mentality of their origin." Police also speak about a "culture of violence" that the youth left behind in their "war-torn" country of origin (immigrant status being taken for granted). One policeman told us, "Here [in Quebec] our kids are born with a hockey puck in their hand, but there [a country of origin of immigrants] they come into the world with a grenade in their hands." These culturalist beliefs foster the racialization of the street gang question.

The notion that street gangs are imported from outside of Quebec is frequently articulated, hence subtly identifying "youth and street gangs" as an immigration issue. At least one officer openly blamed Canada's multi-cultural policies for the rise in street gangs. A frequently heard explanation for gang membership concerns the societal structure in the country of origin. Having been members of gangs in their home country, we are told, immigrant youth seek out gangs, or create new ones, when they arrive in Quebec. "They have gangs there [in the country of origin]," explains one policeman, "It's part of their mores."

While the racialization of the street gang issue is present in police discourse, there is also evidence of an awareness of this very practice. One policeman reflects on the racialization process in Quebec society at large:

> For sure the ethnics are more visible. When a street gang is made up of Jamaicans, Haitians, Asiatics or Latino-Americans, it's easy to say, for example, "Ah, there's a gang of Latinos. But perhaps the gang is mostly White, with twenty youths, fifteen Whites and five Latinos. People only notice the Latinos. It's the Latinos that the average Québécois sees, not the whole gang. So, if you have six Blacks and twenty Whites, people say, "Look at that Black gang." Because what strikes them, what draws the attention of the majority, is the minority.

Other studies suggest similar instances of the racialization of youth. For example, although not articulated as such, racializing youth is apparent in one American study (Wordes et al., 1994) of the impact of race on detention decisions. The authors found that even when the seriousness of the offence and other social factors were controlled for, at each decision point in the detention process African-American and Latino youth were more likely to be detained than were Caucasian youth. Moreover, it is worth noting that racialization is not restricted to youth. In our earlier study of policing in a multi-ethnic neighbourhood in Montreal (Symons, 1997) we found the racialization process at work. Police construct ethnocultural communities as the "Other," and the "we/they" dichotomy is clearly articulated in both language and practice.

Gendering the Street Gang Issue[7]

In this analysis, we use the term "gender" as an organizing principle (Ferree et al., 1999). Gender defines social relations between the sexes, where relationships of power and dependency are interwoven in a complex tapestry throughout the social structure. We see a hierarchy of male dominance and female subordination replicated in institutions, organizations, language, and practice (Symons, 1992). In the process of gendering, the abstract category of gender is translated into and embodied in experiences of everyday life. Gendering has important implications for men and women, boys and girls. As Kaschak (1992:5) points out:

> The most notable aspect of current gender arrangements is that the masculine always defines the feminine by naming, containing, engulfing, invading, and evaluating it. The feminine is never permitted to stand alone or to subsume the masculine…. Masculine meanings organize social and personal experience, so that women are consistently imbued with meanings not of their own making.

We are interested in how genderized categories are articulated by the police in the context of the youth and street gang phenomenon. Gendered categories are embedded in societal discourse and practice, and the police (as well as other members of the society) draw upon these categories to define and construct the experiences of boys and girls in gangs. We shall examine how societal definitions of gender and gendered behaviour impinge on categories used by the police.

Police discourse provides a particular perspective on the experiences and identities of girls in gangs. The following case, described to us by one policeman, is typical.

> This one young girl came to the city. She was a timid girl, and not particularly physically attractive. She has few friends. One day she finds herself being harassed by a Haitian boy. This goes on for a week or two, when suddenly another young man comes to her aid. He defends her against the abuse of the aggressor and sends him off. Essentially, he saves the young woman from her aggressor. The girl is very grateful to this young man, who treats her well and protects her from

harm. Now, she gets emotionally involved with him. As the months pass, she acquires the status of her boyfriend in the gang. They have little parties and many outings. And then one evening, she is invited to a party and her former aggressor appears.

She asks, "What are you doing here? I don't want to see you."

The boyfriend explains, "Ah, he's my friend now, everything is settled."

The aggressor had always been his friend. The whole thing was organized in advance. It's one of the tricks the gang uses.

Now, the girl's in love, but she is also afraid of those guys. She loves the guy but fears him and the gang. She hangs around with a bunch of other girls who are there, and then its "Ya, ya, come on this evening, we're going out." It looks very interesting. But the experience is very difficult for the girl, because she has become the property of the group. Everybody uses her. She is group property.

It was at this point that she dropped out of the gang, and then she asked for help. It took a long time before she would talk. In the space of six months, she had gone from a girl who had just arrived in Montreal, rather intellectual, then became a witness to criminal acts, attempted murder. All of this happened in the space of maybe six months. When she told her story to the social worker, the social worker couldn't believe it.

She said, "It's not possible for someone to live through as many incidents as you have in such a short period of time. You've made it up."

So the social worker called us [the police] and we started to look into it. We confirmed certain criminal acts and certain criminal complaints associated with what the girl said. She had not been lying!

In this discourse we can see the gendering process at work. Stereotypes of girls abound. To begin, attention to the physical attractiveness of the girl in question is the second descriptor (after her timidity) used to define her. "She was a timid girl, and not particularly physically attractive." In fact, girls are caught here in a double bind. Either they are not attractive enough to develop an authentic relationship with a boy, so are easily duped into false emotional attachments, or they are too pretty for their own good, and hence become victims of sexual aggressions.

A second theme running through the discourse is the girl's dependent status. Girls in gangs are identified solely in relation to the boys in these gangs. They are seen as the property of boys, their girlfriends, their sexual objects/partners, their tools, their accomplices, their hostages, and/or their victims. Girls in gangs are accorded no identity of their own, no purpose or meaning outside their relationships with boys.

Third, girls are seen as victims. Girls associated with gangs are depicted as vulnerable, powerless, timid, and passive. They are described as "prey," lured into the gang rather than joining it of their own accord. In the story told above, the girl is harassed by one young man, then "saved" by another. "Suddenly another young man comes to her aid. He defends her against the abuse of the aggressor and sends him off. Essentially, he saves the young woman from her aggressor," explains the policeman.

Fourth, girls are described as emotionally dependent on boys. The main reason given for girls' involvement in gangs is their (exaggerated) need for love and affection. Girls are depicted as emotionally starved, ready to jump at any sign of affection, real or imagined. Enticed by a display of false caring, the girl becomes emotionally attached to a boy in the gang. Once this happens, she will do his bidding.

A fifth theme running through this story, and our data in general, is the sexualization of girls' behaviour in gangs. "Everybody uses her. She is group property," the policeman tells us. Feminist researchers from the United States have noted the tendency of the American juvenile justice system to sexualize the behaviour of girls in gangs. Chesney-Lind (1989:5), for example, notes "the central role played by the juvenile justice system in the sexualization of female delinquency and the criminalization of girls' survival strategies." We see the process at work in our Canadian data as well. As a case in point, prostitution is construed only within a criminal context, rather than, for example, addressing the issue in terms of the contribution of girls' sex work to the economic livelihood of the gang.

When analysing discourse, what is left unsaid is often as revealing, if not more so, than what is said. This is certainly the case with respect to police constructions of girls in gangs. As we noted above, girls are considered peripheral to the boys' gangs. When asked about the question of girl gangs, the phenomenon was glossed over, either by negating the presence of girl gangs in Montreal or by identifying them simply as groups of girls affiliated with boys' gangs, once again defining the female in terms of the male.

The articulation of race and gender is important for a complex analysis of girls in gangs, as some American feminist researchers have suggested (Harris, 1994; Joe and Chesney-Lind, 1995). The most striking thing about the police discourse on race and girls in gangs (as well as race and girl gangs) is, in fact, the lack of it. The police seem unaware of the dynamics, or the consequences, of the articulation of race and gender for girls involved with gangs. Our queries about the ethnic origins of girls in gangs were answered with remarks such as "White, Black, it doesn't matter." Explained one policeman:

> The girls come from all milieux. For sure, they [the boys in the gang] will favour their own ethnicity for their girlfriends, but for prostitution they will take those who are the easiest.... But we find a lot of young White girls, because it's a status symbol to have a White girl.

Conclusion

Analysis of official organizational discourse of the SPCUM and conversations with police personnel reveal that the police construction of race and gender in street gangs involves the processes of both racialization and gendering. Images of violence-prone "ethnic youth" from war-torn countries (it is taken as given that the "ethnic youth" in question are male) and traditional representations of vulnerable, emotionally needy, dependent girls are examples of the racialization and gendering processes at work.

Repercussions of such constructions of youth in street gangs include the casting of ethnic minorities and women in stereotypical racial and gender roles. Consequences of such racialization and gendering must be examined, for definitions suggest outcomes. If ethnic youth are identified as "hard core" and violence-prone, hopes for and action aimed at their rehabilitation will be affected. With respect to girls in gangs, gendered categorizations are a double-edged sword. On the one hand, such constructions may safeguard the girls from police repression, given paternalistic depictions of girls as less dangerous than boys. On the other hand, these same constructions may mean that girls and young women are excluded from preventive community strategies that could improve their life chances and social condition. What is certain is that strategies for addressing the articulation of race and gender in street gangs will be lacking as long as the issue remains unspoken.

Notes

I would like to thank the administration and the police of the SPCUM for their co-operation and generous sharing of their time and perspectives. I also heartily thank my research assistants, Lise Beaudoin-Roy, Patricia Gazzoli, and Caroline Mohr, for their invaluable help and dedication to this project. Finally, I acknowledge, with gratitude, the financial assistance of Immigration et Metropole (SSHRCC), ENAP, and the GRES (Groupe de recherche ethnicité et société, Université de Montréal).

1. Service de police de la communauté urbaine de Montréal.
2. Including a day-long course on gangs for police officers and an evening seminar for interventionists. For further methodological details, see Symons (1999a).
3. A theoretical sample (or purposeful sample) is a non-probabilistic one, where rational criteria derived from theory are used to choose the sample studied (Strauss, 1994: 16). In this case we wanted to sample members of the police administration, the anti-gang squad, and constables on the street who were knowledgeable about the street gang issue in Montréal.
4. All citations from the police literature and interviews are the author's free translations from the French.
5. "Minority ethnic group" is often used by the police to designate racialized groups.
6. For an elaboration of the racialization issue, see Symons (1999a).
7. For a more detailed discussion of the gendering of street gangs, see Symons (1999b).

References

Châles, J., A. Duval, M. Fontaine, and Y. Jolicoeur. 1996. "Formation: Connais-tu ma gang?," Montreal: Unpublished manuscript. SPCUM.

Chesney-Lind, M. 1989. "Girls' crime and woman's place: Toward a feminist model of female delinquency," *Crime and Delinquency* 35, 1:5-29.

Ferree, M., J. Lorder, and B. Hess. 1999. *Revision Gender*. Thousand Oaks, CA: Sage.

Harris, M. 1994. "Cholas, Mexican-American girls, and gangs," *Sex Role* 30:289-301.

Holdaway, S. 1997. "Responding to racialized divisions within the workforce—the experience of black and Asian police officers in England," *Ethnic and Racial Studies* 20:69-90.

Joe, K., and M. Chesney-Lind. 1995. "Just every mother's angel: An analysis of gender and ethnic variations in youth gang membership," *Gender and Society* 9:408-31.

Kaschak, E. 1992. *Engendered Lives: A New Psychology of Women's Experience*. New York: Basic Books.

SPCUM. 1995. *Rapport d'activité*. Montréal: Service de police de la communauté urbaine de Montréal.

SPCUM. n.d. Cours: Formation anti-gang. Course outline. Montréal, unpublished manuscript.

Strauss, A.L. 1994. *Qualitative Analysis for Social Scientists*. Cambridge: Cambridge University Press.

Symons, G. 1992. "The glass ceiling is constructed over the gendered office," *Women in Management Review* 7, 1:18-22.

—. 1997 "Le contrôle social et la construction de l'Autre: la police dans un quartier multi-ethnique," in Deirdre Meintel, Victor Piché, Danielle et Sylvie Fortin, eds., *Le quartier Côte-des-Neiges à Montréal: les interfaces de la plurietnicité*. Paris: l'Harmattan, 173-89.

—. 1999a. "Racialization of the street gang issue in Montréal: A police perspective," *Canadian Ethnic Studies/Études ethniques au Canada* 31:124-38.

—. 1999b. "*Gendering the street gang issue: A police perspective.*" Paper presented at the 4th International Conference on the Child, Montreal, Oct.

Wordes, M., T. Bynum, and C. Corley, C. 1994. "Locking up youth: The impact of race on detention decisions," *Journal of Research in Crime and Delinquency* 31, 2:149-65.

8

The Criminalization of Aboriginal Women: Commentary by a Community Activist

COLLEEN ANNE DELL

The claim made in this chapter is disturbing: Aboriginal[1] women are criminalized within the Canadian criminal justice system. Two fundamental factors supporting this claim are identified: (1) the lack of acknowledgement of the influential relationship between race, gender, and class, and (2) the absence of research on, and understanding about, Aboriginal women in conflict with the law. Examples from my work as a community activist with the Elizabeth Fry Society of Manitoba illustrate my exposure to these factors. My experiences as an activist uniquely shaped and informed my understanding of the criminalization of Aboriginal women in the criminal justice system. The examples I have chosen display interrelated segments of the criminal justice process—police, courts,[2] and sentencing—and thus demonstrate the pervasiveness of the injustices that are my concern.

The Elizabeth Fry Society of Manitoba is one of 23 sister agencies across Canada whose mandate is to assist women and girls in conflict with the law. The agency network, allianced as the Canadian Association of Elizabeth Fry Societies (CAEFS), is founded on the pioneering work of Elizabeth Fry, an early nineteenth-century social activist who worked to educate prison officials and the public regarding the abhorrent conditions for women at the Newgate prison in London, England, and later, throughout Europe. In the early 1950s, the Manitoba branch of the Elizabeth Fry Societies was established, continuing Elizabeth Fry's legacy by promoting community education and awareness about women in conflict with the law as well as by offering supports, services, and programs to Manitoba women. Nearly a half a century later, this community-based agency continues to work to serve the needs of women and girls who are, have been, or may be at risk of becoming involved with the Canadian criminal justice system. A high percentage of the girls and women with whom the Manitoba agency works are Aboriginal.

My involvement with the Elizabeth Fry Society of Manitoba commenced in the early 1990s when I became an institutional volunteer. Since then I have been committed to the agency and the women for whom it works. Highlights of my work with the Society include creation and facilitation of the Families Moving Together program,[3] parole supervision in conjunction with the Correctional Service of Canada, initiation of the Precious Pals program,[4] Executive Director of the agency, and co-principal researcher on the study, entitled, "Prairie Women, Violence, and Self-Harm."[5]

Aboriginal Women in Conflict with the Law

A fundamental concern in working with women in conflict with the law is that understanding, in general, and research, in particular, are underdeveloped (Arbour, 1996; Faith, 1993; Gavigan, 1993; Pollock, 1999). A common "justification" is that federal female offenders,[6] in comparison to males, comprise only 2.5 per cent of the total offender population (Correctional Service of Canada, 1997; Johnson and Rodgers, 1993). On average, this figure is slightly higher at the provincial[7] level, approximately 13 per cent (Dell, 1995a). It is commonplace, therefore, for females to be excluded as subjects of research or simply to be added on as "correctional afterthoughts" (Comack, 1993).

Research on Aboriginal females in the Canadian criminal justice system is even more limited, it is primarily descriptive in nature, often concluding that Aboriginal women are overrepresented (Dubec, 1982). It is important to acknowledge that there has been growing attention paid to Aboriginal female offenders in recent years, including the resurrection of the 1991 *Report of the Aboriginal Justice Inquiry of Manitoba* by the current Manitoba provincial government and the research of scholars such as Patricia Monture-Angus (1999, 2000). The area in general, however, remains seriously under-researched. Aboriginal women comprise approximately 2 per cent of the Canadian population (Statistics Canada, 1997) and 35 per cent of the female prison and jail populations (Boritch, 1997). In Manitoba, Aboriginal women comprise approximately 14 per cent of the provincial population (Statistics Canada, 1991) and roughly 80 per cent of the female jail population[8] (Elizabeth Fry Society of Manitoba, 1999; *Report of the Aboriginal Justice Inquiry of Manitoba*, 1991). These statistics underlie the serious need for an understanding of *why* Aboriginal women are overrepresented. Canadian research, however, has neglected to problematize race as a research variable within the female offender category (Daly and Stephens, 1995; LaPrairie, 1992; Shaw, 1995; Sugar and Fox, 1990). Furthermore, there has not been acknowledgement of the relationship between class and the Aboriginal female offender. This, in turn, has facilitated the criminalization of Aboriginal women within the justice system. Aboriginal women are viewed, treated, and targeted as criminals for reasons that are yet to be thoroughly understood.

To help comprehend the complex process of criminalization of Aboriginal women in the Canadian criminal justice system, a range of approaches to understanding must be equally considered. These extend from the effects of the historic oppression of Aboriginal women within Canadian society, to accounting for current academic theoretical orientations, to acknowledging the experiences of front-line workers. The following examples reveal the pronounced need for increased understanding. Again, it is important to recognize that there is immense diversity among Aboriginal women as a group. Drawing on the words of Winona Stevenson (1999:75) "we [Aboriginal people] cannot be lumped into one all-encompassing category." The majority of Elizabeth Fry clients in Manitoba are urban Métis women.

Client Experiences

Having been employed in divergent realms of the criminal justice system in Canada, I can contest the varied interpretations and understandings each one offers regarding Aboriginal women's involvement with the law. In my opinion it is only through a melding of an array of perspectives and experiences that a grounded and encompassed understanding of Aboriginal women in the criminal justice system can be achieved. Presented in this section is *only one* facet of such an understanding—the criminalization of Aboriginal women from the perspective of a community activist.[9] The experiences of clientele at three stages of the criminal justice process are detailed: police, courts, and sentencing. Drawing upon these illustrations, a brief analysis is provided, highlighting the need for an understanding of the intersections between race, gender, and class and how a better outcome could have been effected for the women. The chapter concludes by identifying two key issues that would facilitate a move towards a more comprehensive and integrated understanding of the criminalization of Aboriginal women in Canada.

Typically, the first contact of a woman in conflict with the law is with the police. Although limited, Canadian research has pointed to racist, sexist, and classist conduct on the part of police agencies in response to Aboriginal women (Comack, 1999; Dell, 1996; Nahanee, 1993; *Report of the Aboriginal Justice Inquiry of Manitoba*, 1991). Within Manitoba, this likelihood is reflected in the reluctance of Aboriginal female clientele of the Elizabeth Fry Society to contact the police. Their reasons for this avoidance include fear that they will not be believed, especially if they are victims; that the police will be unresponsive; and that they will be embarrassed. The following experience exemplifies this.

On a Wednesday afternoon I entered the home of Lisa,[10] an Aboriginal female client of Elizabeth Fry and the mother of five children. Lisa's house is located in the North End of Winnipeg and within a few blocks of the Elizabeth Fry Society. The North End is disproportionately comprised of Aboriginal residents and is characterized by high social and economic disadvantage in comparison to the remainder of the city. Upon entering Lisa's home I found her huddled in a corner crying uncontrollably. She said she been sexually assaulted under threat with a weapon by her common-law husband. With the fear that her partner would soon return, Lisa and I hurriedly packed some clothes and gathered her children and a few of their toys. We arrived at the Elizabeth Fry office at approximately 5:00 p.m. Lisa soon after telephoned the police, answered some identifying questions (such as name, address, complaint), and was told to wait for the officers to arrive. At 7:00 p.m. Lisa made a follow-up call to the police and was told to continue waiting. At 9:00 p.m. no officer had yet arrived. Lisa was not surprised—this was not her first experience with the unresponsiveness of police. At 10:00 p.m. Lisa despaired and, to my consternation, returned home.

As I write an event has occurred in Winnipeg that reinforces my concern—the murder of two Aboriginal women. Early in the morning of 16 February 2000, two sisters, Doreen LeClair and Corrine McKeowen, were stabbed to death in their North End Winnipeg home by McKeowen's estranged boyfriend. Winnipeg police admitted to mishandling some of the *five* "911" calls made to the police in the eight hours preceding the murders, resulting in five staff being placed on administrative leave. In an interview with the *Winnipeg Free Press*, Arlene Meadows, a sister of the victims, suggested why the police did not attend to the *first* "911" call:

> "Because there is a law for the rich and a law for the poor," she said. "Manitoba Avenue. North End. They don't care ... So what? A couple of more Indians killing each other. Who cares? Two more less we have to worry about?" "Yes ... I'm Métis. My mother was a Cree Indian. We are Métis. I'm very proud of it." (Sinclair, 2000:A1, A4)

The second stage of the criminal justice process, after a woman is charged with an offence by the police, is to obtain legal counsel. A common obstacle in obtaining a defence lawyer for Aboriginal women is their lack of familiarity and distrust of a non-Aboriginal justice system. It has been suggested that this has resulted in few Aboriginal people availing themselves of legal counsel at the earliest opportunity (Barkwell et al., 1989). Elizabeth Fry workers witness this often with their clientele. Aboriginal women's obtaining of legal counsel is further complicated by constructions of their cultural distinctiveness.

Margaret, a middle-aged woman from a northern Manitoba reserve, was remanded on a charge at a custodial facility. I attended the custodial unit to facilitate the Families Moving Together program to the women incarcerated there and asked Margaret if she wished to participate. With the assistance of my volunteer, we determined that Margaret spoke and understood only Ojibwa. We further realized that Margaret was completely unfamiliar with what she referred to as a "White system." One week after Margaret's admittance to the facility she had yet to speak with a lawyer. Had the system been sensitive to Margaret's unique cultural needs, she would have had access to an interpreter and to legal counsel much sooner. The economically disadvantaged position of many Aboriginal peoples in Manitoba, must be considered equally because it, too, contributes to their alienation from the legal process.

The criminal justice system's lack of understanding of the unique needs of Aboriginal women is similarly present in the courtroom. There is a lack of knowledge of Aboriginal culture in general, and its pertinence to women in particular, despite the existence of some studies that have raised awareness of the necessity of such an understanding in the justice system (Dell, 1995b; Sugar and Fox, 1990; Monture-Angus, 1999).

Cathy, an Aboriginal woman, appeared in court on a violent offence charge. In response to questions posed to her, she often paused before answering and did not make eye contact with court personnel. The prosecution later suggested during his submission that the reason Cathy did not look at anyone while being questioned, and was hesitant in answering questions, was because she was attempting to hide something i.e., that she was lying. Neither the prosecutor nor Cathy's defence lawyer replied that Cathy's approach to justice, based in her Aboriginal traditions, was in direct conflict with the European tradition. Silence and uncommunicativeness in the Canadian system is seen as unco-operative, while in Cathy's cultural system it connotes the maintenance of personal dignity.

In addition to the lawyers' ineptness in understanding Cathy's cultural distinctiveness and how it affected her representation within the Eurocentric criminal justice system, her own attorney also reflected Cathy's disadvantaged class position; it was not economically feasible for Cathy to hire a senior lawyer. Consequently, the court appointed counsel for Cathy, from a junior class of lawyers who are commonly overworked and underpaid. It is a constitutional right of all persons charged with an offence in Canada to be treated equally before the law, but the system of legal representation works to the disadvantage of the poor, among them, poor Aboriginal women.

The final stage in the criminal justice process is judicial sentencing. In a 1988 CAEFS workshop on women and sentencing, community workers recounted examples of racist and sexist sentencing practices that reflected harsh sentencing of non-Caucasian, and often economically disadvantaged, women. This continues to be the case for some Aboriginal clientele of the Elizabeth Fry Society of Manitoba over a decade later. Consider the following, for example.

Rhonda, a young Aboriginal female client of the Elizabeth Fry Society and North End resident of Winnipeg, was given a life sentence for second-degree murder. In comparison to the average disposition for second-degree murder received by females and males in Canada, this is a harsh sentence (Dell and Boe, 1997; Sinclair, 1999; Sinclair and Boe, 1998). Rhonda also received a harsher sentence than her male co-accused who had committed the actual act that resulted in the victim's death, due to his plea bargain. In the judge's sentencing submission, he drew upon information from Rhonda's background, but dismissed her tormented upbringing and instead highlighted her past as a young offender. By dismissing Rhonda's upbringing, the judge discounted a life of extreme dysfunction, poverty, and neglect—physical, emotional, and financial. In doing so the judge dismissed the combined social effects of race, gender, and class for a young Aboriginal woman who came into conflict with the Canadian criminal justice system.

Intersecting Race, Gender, and Class

Historically, the Western feminist movement has assumed unity *across* groups, such as race and class. Following concerns of ethnocentrism, a re-examination of perspectives within feminism was initiated[11] (Bannerji, 1996). Feminism in general arrived at the understanding that the concepts of race and class needed to be unilaterally incorporated into its analyses of gender (Barrett and McIntosh, 1985; Segal, 1987). This understanding soon addressed similar interconnections of race and class for women in conflict with the law (Chesney-Lind, 1997; Daly, 1994; West, 1992). At the start of the new millennium such understandings remain to be fully translated into practice. The above glimpses into the lives of Aboriginal women who came into contact with the Canadian criminal justice system illustrate that assumptions about race, gender, and class and their interconnections remain embedded in the system and continue to perpetuate existing inequalities.

Reflecting on the above women's experiences, the outcomes may have been altered drastically had the interrelatedness of race, gender, and class been taken into account. This translates into practice through, for example, sensitivity to cultural distinctiveness, gender inclusivity—transcendence beyond the male, European, middle class perspective—and acknowledgement of the influence of economic class. Specifically, Lisa might have received the timely attention from the police that she required to leave an abusive relationship together with validation that as a female Aboriginal North End resident she had been wrongly violated. Margaret might have been spared a week of confusion and fear incarcerated within a "foreign justice system," with validation of her cultural needs as an Aboriginal woman from a northern Manitoba reserve. Cathy might have been spared not only confusion and fear but blatant misrepresentation and maligning of her behaviour. Rhonda might have received a sentence that accounted for the context of her life, validation of her tormented upbringing, rooted in race, gender, and class inequalities, and its impact on her coming into conflict with the law. And Doreen LeClair and Corrine

McKeowen, the two murdered sisters, might be alive today, validation of their lives as Aboriginal female North End residents. How much more *evidence*—which gives the Canadian criminal justice system its impetus—do we need to initiate change?

Conclusion

The absence of informed understanding about Aboriginal women and their culture, and the failure to acknowledge the influential relationship between race, gender, and class facilitate the criminalization of Aboriginal women within the Canadian criminal justice system. From the perspective of a community activist, two key measures are suggested for facilitating understanding of the effects of race, gender, and class and their intersections on the criminalization of Aboriginal women in Canada. First, any attempt to comprehend the complex process of criminalization of Aboriginal women in the Canadian justice system *must* account for a range of perspectives. The agents of the criminal justice system, ranging from system representatives to front-line workers, need to be communicating their perspectives with one another. For example, community activists need to share their views and experiences with academics, and vice versa. Second, the voices of Aboriginal women who come into contact with the criminal justice system must be heard. To this point, they have been overwhelmingly silenced, both figuratively and literally. If the women are not heard they cannot be assisted, as illustrated in Lisa's predicament. If the wealth of information and insight contained by each fragment of the criminal justice system was shared among the various agents, Aboriginal women who come into conflict with the law in Canada would stand in less danger of neglect, misunderstanding, and misrepresentation. In turn, this would assist not only Elizabeth Fry activists, but others as well, in questioning, challenging, and informing the "neutral" principles on which the Canadian criminal justice system is founded.

Notes

This chapter is dedicated to the memory of Norma Jean Sinclair, an Aboriginal woman who struggled within the Canadian criminal justice system. I am grateful for the support of the Social Sciences and Humanities Research Council of Canada, Carleton University Faculty of Arts and Social Sciences and Graduate Studies, and the Elizabeth Fry Society of Manitoba and Executive Director Debbie Blunderfield.

1. Approximately 3.6 per cent of Canada's population is Aboriginal. This is inclusive of First Nations people (59.9 per cent status and 15.3 per cent non-status), Métis (15.3 per cent), and Inuit (5.2 per cent). It is important to acknowledge that there is not one "type" of Aboriginal person. Categorical thinking such as this fosters discriminatory stereotypes and practices within Canadian society. Given the brevity necessary here, distinctions between the Aboriginal women are not recounted.

2. The court stage includes legal representation and prosecution.

3. The Families Moving Together program is an eight-session program designed to facilitate communication to help heal and strengthen the family unit and help women avoid re-involvement in the criminal justice system. The program focuses on the triad of self-love, communication, and the family unit.

4. The Precious Pals program matches up a child of an Elizabeth Fry agency client with a volunteer who is committed to spending quality time with the child, serving as a pro-social role model and providing positive social opportunities.

5. The Elizabeth Fry Society of Manitoba, in conjunction with Cathy Fillmore of the University of Winnipeg and Colleen Anne Dell of Carleton University, has done research on "Prairie Women, Violence, and Self–Harm." Understanding of the needs of women who self-harm within the institution and community settings should assist women in conflict with the law as well as the management of self-harm within these settings. The project is funded by the Prairie Women's Health Centre of Excellence.

6. Females serving a sentence of two years and greater.

7. Females serving a sentence of less than two years.

8. The Portage Correctional Institution, in Portage la Prairie, is the main correctional facility in Manitoba housing females sentenced to a term of incarceration. This rate of 80 per cent has remained relatively stable since the mid-1980s (*Report of the Aboriginal Justice Inquiry of Manitoba*, 1991: 498).

9. I cannot succinctly distinguish my role as a community activist from other roles I hold, such as researcher and academic; however, I can draw upon my experiences in the activist role and identify the unique perspective this contributed to my understanding of the criminalization of Aboriginal women in Canada. My perspective also is informed as a White (race), female (gender) resident of the working-class North End of Winnipeg (class). I describe my perspective as "lived," based on my class and gender experiences. I do not have a "lived" understanding of being Aboriginal. I do, however, have a grounded understanding based on 25 years of growing up in the North End of Winnipeg. This shaped who I am while teaching me the social roles of race, class, and gender and their intersections. My academic perspective is grounded foremost in my "lived" understanding.

10. Names and essential descriptive factors have been altered to protect the women's identities.

11. This initiation was primarily generated by Black feminism in the United States and subsequently filtered into the Canadian forum.

References

Arbour, L. 1996. *Commission of Inquiry into Certain Events at the Prison for Women in Kingston (Canada)*. Ottawa: Public Works and Government Services Canada.

Bannerji, H. 1996. *Thinking Through: Essays on Feminism, Marxism and Anti-Racism*. Toronto: Women's Press.

Barkwell, L., D. Gray, R. Richard, D. Chartrand and L. Longclaws. 1989 *Research and Analysis of the Impact of the Justice System on the Métis*. Winnipeg: Manitoba Métis Federation.

Barrett, M., and M. McIntosh. 1985. "Ethnocentrism and socialist-feminist theory," *Socialist Review* 20:22-47.

Boritch, H. 1997. *Fallen Women. Female Crime and Criminal Justice in Canada*. Toronto: ITP Nelson.

Canadian Association of Elizabeth Fry Societies. 1988. *Women and Sentencing: Workshop Proceedings*. Ottawa.

Chesney-Lind, M. 1997. *The Female Offender: Girls, Women and Crime*. London: Sage.

Comack, E. 1993. *Women Offenders' Experience with Physical and Sexual Abuse: A Preliminary Report*. Winnipeg: University of Manitoba.

—. 1999. *Locating Law: Race/Class/Gender Connections*. Halifax: Fernwood.

Correctional Service of Canada. 1997. *Basic Facts about Corrections in Canada*. Ottawa: Department of Solicitor General.

Daly, K. 1994. *Gender, Crime and Punishment*. New Haven: Yale University Press.

Daly, K., and D. Stephens. 1995. "The 'dark figure' of criminology: Towards a black and multi-ethnic feminist agenda for theory and research," in N. Rafter and H. Heidensohn, eds., *International Feminist Perspectives in Criminology: Engendering a Discipline*. Philadelphia: Open University Press, 189-215.

Dell, C. 1995a. *Searching for Success: Women, Children and the Criminal Justice System*. Winnipeg: Elizabeth Fry Society of Manitoba.

—. 1995b. *A Study of Participation, Employment and Training Potential Opportunities for Aboriginal Women within the Canadian Criminal Justice System*. Winnipeg: Elizabeth Fry Society of Manitoba/Winnipeg Aboriginal Management Board.

—. 1996. "Offending Women: Gender and Sentencing: An Analysis of the Criminal Justice Processing of Blue- and White-Collar Theft and Fraud Offenders," MA thesis, University of Manitoba.

Dell, C., and R. Boe. 1997. *Female Young Offenders in Canada: Recent Trends*. Ottawa: Correctional Service of Canada.

Dubec, B. 1982. *Native Women and the Criminal Justice System: An Increasing Minority*. Toronto: Ontario Native Women's Association.

Elizabeth Fry Society of Manitoba. 1999a. "Educational Conference. Creating a Path into the Millennium: Working with Women and Girls in the Justice System." Winnipeg.

—. 1999b. "Working with Women and the Criminal Justice System." Winnipeg information pamphlet.

Faith, K. 1993. *Unruly Women*. Vancouver: Press Gang.

Gavigan, S. 1993. "Women's crime: New perspectives and old theories," in E. Adelberg and C. Currie, eds., *Too Few to Count*. Vancouver: Press Gang, 215-34.

Hannah-Moffat, K., and M. Shaw. 2000. *An Ideal Prison? Critical Essays on Women's Imprisonment in Canada*. Halifax: Fernwood.

Indian and Northern Affairs. 1998. http://www.inac.gc.ca/stats/facts/1995/abocon.html.

Johnson, H., and K. Rodgers. 1993. "A statistical overview of women and crime in Canada," in E. Adelberg and C. Currie, eds., *Too Few to Count*. Vancouver: Press Gang, 95-116.

LaPrairie, C. 1992. "The role of sentencing in the over-representation of aboriginal people in correctional institutions," in R. Silverman and M. Nielsen, eds., *Aboriginal Peoples and Canadian Criminal Justice*. Toronto: Butterworths, 133-44.

Monture-Angus, P. 1999. "Standing against Canadian law: Naming omissions of race, culture, and gender," in E. Comack (1999:76-97).

—. 2000. "Aboriginal women and correctional practice: Reflections on the task force on federally sentenced women, In K. Hannah-Moffat and M. Shaw (2000:52-60).

Nahanee, T. 1993. *Aboriginal Women, Violence and Police Charging Policies in Canada*. Ottawa: Department of Solicitor General.

Pollock, J. 1999. *Criminal women*. Cincinnati: Anderson.

Report of the Aboriginal Justice Inquiry of Manitoba. 1991 Vol. 1: *The Justice System and Aboriginal People*. Winnipeg.

Segal, L. 1987. "Not advancing but retreating: What happened to socialist feminism?" in *Is the future female? Troubled thoughts on contemporary feminism*. London: Virago Press, 49-80.

Shaw, M. 1995. *Understanding Violent Women*. Ottawa: Correctional Service of Canada.

Sinclair, G., Jr. 2000. "Why, why, why? Victims' family asks whether 911 delay race-related," *Winnipeg Free Press*, A1, A4, 18 Feb. 2000.

Sinclair, R. 1999. "Male youth and women abuse: Learning from Canadian adult partner homicide and attempted murder offenders," paper presented at the American Society of Criminology annual general meeting, Toronto.

Sinclair, R., and R. Boe. 1998. *Male Young Offenders in Canada: Recent Trends*. Ottawa: Correctional Service of Canada.

Statistics Canada. 1991. *Census of Canada. Ethnic origin: The nation*. Ottawa.

—. 1997. *Census of Canada*. Ottawa.

Stevenson, W. 2000. "Colonialism and first nations in Canada," in E. Dua and A. Robertson, eds., *Scratching the Surface: Canadian Anti-Racist Feminist Thought*. Toronto: Women's Press.

Sugar, F., and L. Fox. 1990. *Survey of Federally Sentenced Aboriginal Women in the Community*. Ottawa: Native Women's Association of Canada.

West, L. 1992. "Feminist nationalist socialist movements: Beyond universalism and towards a gendered cultural relativism," *Women's Studies International Forum*, 50, 5-6:563-79. Vol. 128:70 18 Feb. 2000.

9

The Justice System and Canada's Aboriginal Peoples: The Persistence of Racial Discrimination

JOHN H. HYLTON

While there are important consequences of discriminatory treatment for all "racialized" groups, this chapter focuses on the experience of Canada's Aboriginal people.[1] It will be shown that discrimination against Aboriginal people pervades the operations of the justice system and that Aboriginal people are significantly disadvantaged as a result. Some of the reasons why this injustice persists, as well as some directions for the future, will also be discussed.

Justice System Discrimination against Aboriginal People

A very extensive research literature on Aboriginal people and the Canadian justice system has developed over the past three decades. In light of this literature, and the variety of ways in which an examination of discrimination against Aboriginal people can be approached, a comprehensive review is beyond the scope of this chapter. Rather, the focus here is on the most persuasive evidence from the research literature. In addition, some of the most comprehensive and authoritative reports produced as a result of public inquiries and commissions over the past decade will be referred to (see Appendix to this volume). Finally, some important recent court judgements, as well as several legislative reforms that acknowledge justice system discrimination against Aboriginal people, will also be discussed.

PERSUASIVE EVIDENCE CONCERNING SYSTEMIC
RACIAL DISCRIMINATION IN THE JUSTICE SYSTEM

Of the available evidence concerning systemic racial discrimination in the justice system, none is more persuasive than the body of research showing the large and growing disproportionate representation of Aboriginal people in Canada's correctional facilities. The Royal Commission on Aboriginal Peoples (1995) has referred to this as "injustice personified." Overrepresentation statistics are important not only because they point to disparities in the corrections field but also because what happens in corrections reflects decisions made at all the earlier stages of the criminal justice process.

1. *Studies consistently show that Aboriginal people are vastly overrepresented in correctional facilities throughout Canada.* Between 1989 and 1994, Aboriginal admissions to provincial correctional facilities in Saskatchewan were approximately 6.8 times higher than would be expected from the provincial Aboriginal population. Corresponding figures for other provinces include: 5.5 times higher in Alberta, 4.9 times higher in Manitoba, 1.5 times higher in the Northwest Territories, and 2 times higher in Ontario (La Prairie, 1996).

On 5 October 1996, Statistics Canada conducted a one-day "snapshot" of all offenders in Canadian correctional facilities (Canadian Centre for Justice Statistics, 1998). The findings show that while Aboriginal people account for approximately 2 per cent of the adult population in Canada, they account for 17 per cent of the inmates. In provincial/territorial facilities, Aboriginal persons accounted for 18 per cent of the inmates, while in federal facilities they made up 14 per cent. In Saskatchewan, the proportion of Aboriginal persons incarcerated was almost 10 times their proportion in the provincial population (76 per cent of the inmate population compared to 8 per cent of the provincial population). In Manitoba, 61 per cent of the inmates were Aboriginal persons (compared to 9 per cent in the provincial population) and in Alberta, over one-third (34 per cent) of the inmates were Aboriginal persons (compared to 4 per cent in the provincial population). In the other jurisdictions, the proportion ranged from twice to almost nine times the proportion in the provincial/territorial population.

In Saskatchewan, it has been shown that 70 per cent of 16-year old treaty Indian males would be incarcerated at least once by the time they reached the age of 25. The corresponding figure for non-status Indians and Métis was 34 per cent, while the figure for non-Aboriginals was 8 per cent (Hylton, 1981).

2. *Overrepresentation occurs in pretrial detention, as well as among sentenced inmates.* In a survey of Alberta, Saskatchewan, Manitoba, the Northwest Territories, and Ontario, Aboriginal persons admitted to pretrial detention were found to be from seven times higher in Saskatchewan to two times higher in Ontario (La Prairie, 1996); and between 1988 and 1995, Aboriginal remand admissions were much higher than the proportion of Aboriginal people in the general population—16 per cent of total admissions in B.C., 29 per cent in Alberta, 70 per cent in Saskatchewan, 55 per cent in Manitoba, and 6 per cent in Ontario (La Prairie, 1996).

3. *There is no indication that the extent of overrepresentation of Aboriginal people is diminishing over time.* In fact, all the available evidence points to an increasing disparity in admission rates. In Manitoba, between 1983 and 1999, Aboriginal admissions at the Headingly provincial correctional centre went from 37 per cent (Hamilton and Sinclair, 1991) to 66 per cent.[2] In Alberta, the Alberta Task Force (1991) projected that Aboriginal admissions would continue to increase, from 30 per cent of total admissions in 1989 to 39 per cent of admissions by 2011.In federal institutions across Canada, the percentage of Aboriginal offenders was 8 per cent in 1981, 9 per cent in 1983, 10 per cent in 1987, and 11 per cent in 1990 (McMahon, 1992). The Royal Commission (1995) reported the corresponding figure was 12 per cent in 1993-94 and 13 per cent in 1995. This represents an increase of 55 per cent in rates in less than 15 years.

In Saskatchewan, the number of Aboriginal people admitted to correctional centres increased from 3,082 to 4,757 between 1976-77 and 1992-93, an increase of 54 per cent (Hylton, 1994). Aboriginals comprised 65 per cent of the admissions in 1976-77 and 69 per cent in 1992-93. The Royal Commission (1995) reported that by 1993-94, the corresponding figure was 72 per cent. The most recent information for 1998-99 indicates that Aboriginal people now make up 76 per cent of sentence admissions and 78 per cent of remand admissions.[3]

4. *Overrepresentation of Aboriginal people is occurring not only among male adult offenders, but also among female offenders and among young offenders.* In provincial jails across Canada in 1989-90, 29 per cent of

women and 17 per cent of men were Aboriginal (McMahon, 1992). In 1991, nearly half the women admitted to provincial correctional institutions in Canada were Aboriginal (La Prairie, 1996). In Saskatchewan, figures for 1998-99 indicate that 89 per cent of female sentenced admissions and 89 per cent of female remand admissions were admissions of Aboriginal women.[4] In Alberta (Alberta Task Force, 1991), it has been reported that Aboriginal men made up 30 per cent of male provincial correctional centre admissions, but 45 per cent of female admissions were Aboriginal women. The situation with respect to young offenders was described as "even more dramatic," with projections indicating that 40 per cent of young offender admissions would be Aboriginal admissions by 2011.

Linn (1992) reported that 70 per cent of youth in custody in Saskatchewan were Aboriginal; and a review of Manitoba juvenile court records between 1930 and 1959 revealed that during this time less than 10 per cent of the caseload consisted of Aboriginal youth (Kaminski, 1991). In 1990, a review of custody facilities for young offenders indicated that 64 per cent of the Manitoba Youth Centre's population and 78 per cent of the Agassiz Youth Centre's population were Aboriginal (McMahon, 1992).

These data clearly show widespread systemic discrimination against Aboriginal people within the Canadian criminal justice system. As Manitoba's Aboriginal Justice Inquiry has pointed out (Hamilton and Sinclair, 1991:101), "the best evidence of systemic discrimination lies in the adverse impacts that the system has on Aboriginal people." Whether or not there is an intention to discriminate, the "standard practices" of the system have an adverse impact on Aboriginal people; this constitutes systemic discrimination.

OVERT DISCRIMINATION AGAINST ABORIGINAL
PEOPLE IN THE CRIMINAL JUSTICE SYSTEM

Some might be tempted to dismiss the importance of overrepresentation statistics by suggesting that they are the inevitable consequence of higher crime rates among Aboriginal people and other racialized groups. While this line of argument does not in any way diminish the importance of practices that systemically discriminate against Aboriginal people, it does raise an important additional question: Does overrepresentation result only from systemic discrimination, or is overt discrimination also important in explaining Aboriginal overrepresentation? Answering this question requires going beyond overrepresentation statistics. As Doob (1994:1) has pointed out, almost everyone who has ever tried to answer the apparently simple question—"Does the criminal justice system discriminate against certain groups?"—realizes quickly that this is not a simple question to answer. To determine if overt discrimination has occurred, it is necessary to show that, even when like cases are being dealt with by the system, members of racialized groups are adversely impacted by discretionary decisions.

Regrettably, systematic research that would allow for a definitive assessment of the extent of overt discrimination in the justice system has not been completed. Rather, a number of more limited studies and literature reviews have been completed that shed some light on the question. While each of these studies and reviews contains methodological and design weaknesses, they nonetheless represent the kinds of findings that are currently available. A sampling of some of these studies and reviews is provided below:

1. *Prejudice and discrimination involving the police.* Aboriginal people are more critical of the police in terms of their fairness and effectiveness (Forcese, 1999; Hamilton and Sinclair 1991; Griffiths and Verdun-Jones, 1994). Patrol officers have been found to act on the basis of stereotypes and discriminatory views of people and circumstances (for example, Commission on Systemic Racism, 1995; Hamilton and Sinclair, 1991; Lundman, 1980). Ericson (1982) found that in instances involving property loss or damage, formal action by the police was more likely to be taken when suspects were poor and non-white; Havemann et al. (1985) have reported that, in comparable cases, a lower proportion of Aboriginal children and youth are let off with police warnings compared to the national rate. Harding (1985) found different charge rates for drunkenness in Regina: 30 per cent for members of First Nations, 21 per cent for Métis, and 11 per cent for non-Aboriginal suspects.

In a study of police attitudes towards various criminal justice issues in a prairie city, Hylton (1979) found that police officers consistently reported negative attitudes towards Aboriginal people, more so even than members of the general public. Bala (2000:47) has noted, "There are many documented incidents of police and correctional workers using racial epithets and stereotyping": And Mosher (1998) has documented numerous instances of police bias in dealing with racialized groups in Ontario.

2. *Pretrial and crown decisions.* Hamilton and Sinclair (1991) found that Aboriginal people faced more charges on average than non-Aboriginal people. Linn (1992) reports that only 5 per cent of Crown referrals to mediation programs in Saskatchewan were Aboriginal offenders, even though 22 per cent of first-time offenders were Aboriginal.

In Alberta, the Alberta Task Force found Aboriginal adults and youth were less likely to be referred for diversionary programs. Studies in Alberta (Alberta Task Force, 1991) and Manitoba (Hamilton and Sinclair, 1991), as well as a review by the Law Reform Commission of Canada (1991), have reported that Aboriginal people are less likely than other accused to be given bail in similar offence circumstances, they are more likely to be detained prior to trial, and, on average, they spend a longer time in pretrial detention. Hamilton and Sinclair (1991) reported that Aboriginal accused more often plead guilty, are more often unrepresented or represented by legal aid (as opposed to private counsel), and spend less time with their lawyers than non-Aboriginal accused.

3. *Disparity in sentencing.* Studies in Manitoba (Hamilton and Sinclair, 1991) and Alberta (Alberta Task Force, 1991) found that Aboriginal offenders were more often sent to jail, even when controlling for prior record and type of offence. In particular, Aboriginal offenders were more often incarcerated for minor offences. Although Aboriginal offenders have been found to have fewer outstanding fines, studies consistently report a higher rate of fine-default admissions to correctional centres for Aboriginal offenders (e.g., Hamilton and Sinclair, 1991). Avio (1993) has reviewed the federal cabinet's clemency decisions in commuting death penalty sentences in Canada from 1926 to 1957. After taking into account aggravating and mitigating factors, the study found that decisions were also influenced by, among other factors, the ethnicity of the offender and the offender-victim racial configuration. La Prairie (1996) reported that the use of incarceration is greater for Aboriginal people when controlling for type of offence; Bala (2000) has documented instances where racist language is used in judgements, typically to justify harsher sentences for members of racialized groups; and Mosher (1998) has documented the courts role in the "racialization of crime" in Ontario.

4. *Racial discrimination in corrections.* La Prairie (1996) has reported that Aboriginal offenders are less likely than non-Aboriginal offenders to receive full parole. Harman and Hann (1986) found that race influenced

parole decisions within all offence types, even though more Aboriginal offenders were eligible for parole. This finding was confirmed by Linn (1992). It has been reported that Aboriginal people are more likely to waive their right to a parole hearing and, if granted parole, they are more likely to be readmitted to a correctional facility for a parole violation (Canadian Bar Association, 1988; Law Reform Commission, 1991).

Hamilton and Sinclair (1991) found that Aboriginal elders and religious persons were not accorded the same respect by correctional authorities as other religious leaders; and both Aboriginal and non-Aboriginal inmates in Manitoba correctional facilities reported that the justice system treats Aboriginal offenders differently and more negatively than non-Aboriginal offenders (McMahon, 1992).

The studies that have been referred to are a sampling of a much larger literature. Not all studies have shown that overt discrimination is occurring, and many others have been inconclusive. Nonetheless, there is a preponderance of evidence pointing to the importance of both systemic and overt discrimination in explaining justice system decisions. Moreover, even if the role of overt discrimination cannot be demonstrated in every instance, it is highly likely that the cumulative effects of many decisions, taken over time and at many stages of criminal justice system processing, produce a substantial overall disparity in treatment (McMahon, 1992).

Although research on overt discrimination is not without methodological flaws, there are other important sources of evidence pertaining to the existence of systemic and overt discrimination in the justice system. This includes the authoritative body of evidence produced by a significant number of public inquiries that have examined Aboriginal justice issues, as well as some recent decisions of Canadian lawmakers and courts.

OTHER EVIDENCE

During the past two decades, a number of major public inquiries and reviews have examined Aboriginal justice issues. Some of their findings have been referred to earlier. The conclusions reached by these commissions must be accorded a good deal of attention and must be regarded as highly authoritative for a number of reasons. Typically, these public inquiries:

· include a comprehensive synthesis and analysis of large bodies of relevant research;

- conduct significant additional research to fill gaps in information and understanding;
- go beyond the strict confines of scientific research to gather a much broader base of evidence. This allows for more authoritative findings and conclusions to be reached than would be possible with statistical studies alone. In particular, such inquiries and reviews often hear personal testimony, hold public hearings, and seek out the advice of experts in the field;
- are headed by individuals with reputations for objectivity, leadership, and judgement;
- are usually appointed by governments. Therefore, they typically are cautious in arriving at conclusions and recommendations.

While space does not permit a detailed discussion of the findings of these commission and review reports, overviews of the findings and commentaries may be found elsewhere (Hylton, 2000; McMahon, 1992; Royal Commission on Aboriginal Peoples, 1993). For present purposes, it will suffice to point out that the same findings and recommendations are repeated over and over again in these reports. For example, in summarizing over 30 such studies completed over three decades, the Royal Commission on Aboriginal Peoples (1993:16) stated: "All the inquiries concur that Aboriginal people who encounter the justice system are confronted with both *overt and systemic discrimination* and that this discrimination is one reason why many Aboriginal persons have not received due justice" (emphasis added). Similar observations have been made by others who have reviewed these reports (e.g., McMahon, 1992; Rudin, 1999).

A final source of evidence regarding widespread overt and systemic discrimination against Aboriginal people in the justice system comes from Canadian lawmakers and courts. Increasingly, they have also recognized that racism and discrimination against Aboriginal people are realities in Canada. For example, Parliament has acknowledged that the application of the same sentencing principles and practices in every case may lead to systemic discrimination against Aboriginal people. As a result, section 718.2(e) of the Criminal Code now explicitly requires judges to take cultural factors into consideration when sentencing Aboriginal offenders.

The importance of section 718.2(e) of the Criminal Code has recently been confirmed by the Supreme Court. In R. v. *Williams* (1998 S.C.J. No. 49 Q.L.), the Court unanimously ruled that prospective jurors could be questioned about their racial views in order to preserve the fairness of a trial. Following the Williams decision, two Saskatchewan courts found evidence of widespread discrimination towards Aboriginal people.[5] In one case, jurors were screened for racial bias and five prospective jurors openly admitted that they held racial biases towards Aboriginal people that they would be unable to set aside if they were called to serve on the jury. Finally, the declaration of principle in Canada's proposed new Youth Criminal Justice Act (Bill C-3) requires that young persons who commit offences be treated in a manner that respects gender, ethnic, cultural, and linguistic differences.

These and other laws and cases clearly indicate that Canadian lawmakers and courts have acknowledged the existence of widespread discrimination within Canadian society and within the operations of the justice system. Furthermore, Parliament and the courts have recognized that to achieve fairness in the administration of justice for Aboriginal people, and members of other racialized groups, the protection of extraordinary laws and criminal procedures is required.

Solutions: The Limits of Conventional Approaches

In response to the increasing recognition that discrimination against Aboriginal people is a reality in Canada's justice system, Aboriginal justice task forces and commissions, government agencies, human rights commissions, and many other individuals and organizations have developed a plethora of recommendations intended to decrease prejudice and discrimination and to encourage fairness. However, there is now a predictable repetitiveness to many of these findings and conclusions.

The Alberta Task Force (1991) examined some 22 Aboriginal justice task forces and inquiries. Over and over again the reports repeated recommendations from a 1975 national federal-provincial conference dealing with Aboriginal people and the justice system. Recurring recommendations included: the need for more Aboriginal involvement in planning and delivery of services, more Aboriginal community responsibility for programs, mandatory cross-cultural education for staff working in the system, increased numbers of Aboriginal staff, the use of Aboriginal paraprofessionals, the provision of special assistance to Aboriginal offenders, the establishment of more Aboriginal advisory groups at all levels, increased recognition of Aboriginal culture and law, and more latitude for Aboriginal self-determination.

The types of recommendations contained in Aboriginal justice task forces and commissions have generally led to a few common types of initiatives within the justice system. These have included such initiatives as:

- affirmative action hiring policies;
- the creation of specialized units within larger organizations staffed by Aboriginal people or members of other racialized groups;
- cultural awareness programs;
- "input" from racialized groups where, for example, elders or community leaders may be consulted about program or policy design issues, or even about individual decisions;
- "Indigenization" programs where some traditional practices are allowed within mainstream programs, for example, sweat lodges or sweet grass ceremonies may be held within correctional institutions, or program information is translated into Aboriginal languages.

While space will not permit a detailed discussion of the effectiveness of these types of initiatives, individual evaluations, as well as reviews of the literature, have generally concluded that they have met with limited success (e.g., Hylton, 1999b, 2000). Some research even suggests that these types of initiatives may sometimes lead to more negative attitudes and treatment of Aboriginal people.[6] While some exceptions do exist, they are few in number and, even in these cases, the gains reported have generally been quite modest or time-limited. The most stinging indictment of these reforms is that they have failed to reduce prejudice or discrimination. Indeed, the evidence reported earlier in this chapter about the increasingly disproportionate use of punitive sanctions against Aboriginal people suggests these problems are increasing, not decreasing.

While there are many reasons for the failure of these initiatives, one underlying weakness should be mentioned. There have been remarkably few efforts reported in the literature to significantly modify the social, economic, or political institutions of the dominant society to promote equality among racialized and non-racialized groups. Rather, the programs, policies, philosophies, and values of the dominant society are taken as a given. They are typically viewed by the authorities as the best possible approach to deal with everyone, including members of racialized groups. Available resources are then used to assist members of racialized groups to fit in, accept, or adjust to mainstream programs and values.

Understanding Discrimination
as a Symptom of Deeper Societal Ills

The causes of racism and discrimination directed at Aboriginal people in Canada are no different from the causes of racism and discrimination directed at other racialized groups, both here and in other countries. Moreover, racism and discrimination are inexorably linked to classism and sexism. The roots of these social ills may be found in the power relations that exist among dominant and subservient groups in societies characterized by social inequality. They grow out of a determination by the powerful to maintain their privileged position. To achieve this, they must justify why others should be prevented from accessing the power and resources they enjoy. Thus, racism, classism, and sexism are "produced and maintained by differential power between a dominant group and a subordinate group" (Bolaria and Li, 1988:22).

Since they are denied opportunities, for example, for education and employment, members of racialized groups often live in poverty, on the margins of society. Therefore, racialized groups disproportionately suffer from all the problems that poverty brings. Poverty leads to further labelling, isolation, and disenfranchisement, and provides further "ammunition" for those who seek to discriminate against members of racialized groups. A self-fulfilling prophecy is perpetuated and the status quo, that is, social inequality based on race, is maintained (Kallen, 1995).

These dynamics are clearly evident with regard to Aboriginal people in Canada. The discrimination against Aboriginal people that occurs in the justice system is but one dimension of the discrimination against Aboriginal people that occurs in Canadian society generally. In fact, it is no exaggeration to say that Aboriginal people constitute an "underclass" in Canada. For example, the Royal Commission on Aboriginal Peoples (1996) has pointed out that Aboriginal people have lower employment, education, and income compared to other Canadians, suffer from an extensive burden of ill health, and are disproportionately involved with child welfare and social services authorities. Moreover, Aboriginal women are disproportionately affected by many of these conditions, often as the heads of single-parent families. They also face a host of other barriers that discourage meaningful involvement in Canadian and Aboriginal social, economic and political institutions.

When the deep roots and multiple consequences of racism are more fully appreciated, the limitations of the types of affirmative action, cultural awareness, and "input" programs described earlier can be more fully appreciated. It is not that these programs are not worthwhile or that they should not be pursued. But, by themselves, they cannot address the race-based social inequality at the root of discrimination against Aboriginal people in this country. On their own, they must be regarded as very modest and limited attempts to dismantle the structural basis of institutional racism in Canada. Worse, they may deflect attention away from the need to examine more fundamental changes.

Towards Structural Analysis and Structural Solutions

Long-term, meaningful solutions to Aboriginal overrepresentation in the justice system, as well as many other problems that result from social inequality based on race, must be formulated in a broader context that addresses structural inequality in Canadian society. This type of analysis has been steadfastly avoided in most reviews of Aboriginal justice issues. Rather, most studies, including almost all of the Aboriginal justice inquiry and commission reports, have suffered from a number of common weaknesses. Typically, they examine current symptoms, viewing them as the result of social disorders besetting Aboriginal people; fail to take account of the long history of colonialist policies that have systematically undermined Aboriginal social, economic and political self-sufficiency; view "race" as a trait of Aboriginal people, rather than as the result of a long process of social construction involving the Canadian state; and assume that solutions to Aboriginal overrepresentation can be found within the justice system itself, by tinkering with various laws, policies, and programs. However, an exception may be mentioned. The review completed by the Royal Commission on Aboriginal Peoples (1995, 1996) involved a more fundamental analysis of the structural relations between the Aboriginal peoples and the Canadian state.[7] Not surprisingly, the Commission's analysis also called for much further reaching reforms to address race-based social inequality in Canada.

The *Report of the Royal Commission on Aboriginal Peoples* (1996) is a monumental work—the result of five years of study and an inquiry process more extensive than any other Royal Commission in Canadian history. The central thrust of the Commission's recommendations revolve around the strongly related concepts of: (1) a *renewed relationship* between Aboriginal and non-Aboriginal peoples in Canada; (2) *self-determination* expressed in new structures of self-government; (3) *self-reliance* through restoration of a land base and economic development; and (4) *healing* to achieve vibrant communities and healthy individuals equipped to fulfil the responsibilities of citizenship.

For the Commission, the principles of a renewed relationship would include: (1) *mutual recognition*—Aboriginal and non-Aboriginal people acknowledging and relating to one another as equals, coexisting side by side, and governing themselves according to their own laws and institutions; (2) *mutual respect*—"the quality of courtesy, consideration and esteem extended to people whose languages, cultures and ways differ from our own but who are valued fellow-members of the larger communities to which we all belong" (Royal Commission, 1996:682); (3) *sharing*—the reciprocity that characterized early relations between Aboriginal and non-Aboriginal people that has become unbalanced over time as Aboriginal people have been displaced from their traditional sources of wealth; and (4) *mutual responsibility*—Aboriginal peoples and Canada should seek to actualize a relationship as partners who have a duty to act responsibly towards one another and also towards the land they share.

One of the Commission's principal findings relates to the importance of Aboriginal self-government. The Commission concludes that Aboriginal nations have a unique legal and historical right to govern themselves within the Canadian federation. The Commission's analysis is most pertinent to the present discussion, since there is no reason to believe that effective solutions to address Aboriginal overrepresentation in the justice system can be imposed on Aboriginal people by the dominant society. Indeed, there is no reason to believe that such an approach would have any better results than the policies and programs that have been imposed on Aboriginal people over the past 125 years. This "doing for" approach has a long history in Canada. It is one fraught with high and growing expenditures, ineffective results, and resentment on the part of service-providers and the Aboriginal people who have been the supposed beneficiaries of the dominant society's largess. There is, however, a better way. It involves Aboriginal people designing and implementing their own solutions with the agreement and support of the Canadian state, in other words, self-government.

In countless studies completed over the past several decades, it has repeatedly been shown that the self-government approach to addressing Aboriginal community issues is far superior to the "doing for" approach long favoured by Canadian governments. In particular, it has been demonstrated that Aboriginal self-government programs are more successful than programs imposed by the dominant society in:

- incorporating principles, beliefs, and traditions that are a part of Aboriginal culture;
- attracting and retaining Aboriginal staff;
- involving the Aboriginal community in the design and delivery of programs;
- fostering greater acceptance by individual clients and Aboriginal communities;
- creating economic benefits for Aboriginal communities that address issues of social and economic inequality;
- extending services that were previously unavailable through non-Aboriginal programs;
- drawing attention to social issues in Aboriginal communities, and generating interest, involvement, and support for finding solutions;
- providing levels of services that approach or equal levels of services in non-Aboriginal communities;
- reducing the need for the intervention of the state in the lives of Aboriginal peoples and communities; and
- providing services at a cost that is no more, and sometimes far less, than the cost of imposed "solutions."

Many examples of self-government programs in the justice sector and in other sectors have been provided elsewhere (e.g., Hylton, 1999a; Royal Commission, 1996; Rudin, 1999). The findings to date clearly point to the positive potential of government that is operated by and for Aboriginal people. This approach has moved beyond isolated pilot projects, but, in most quarters, Aboriginal control of service delivery is still not accepted as a usual or proper approach for providing services to Aboriginal people. For this to occur, a much stronger commitment on the part of governments will be required. If there is a true desire to address social inequality and the problems it produces, it is clear that successful strategies will have to be based on an acceptance of the principles of Aboriginal self-government.

Conclusion

Overwhelming evidence has been presented to show that the justice system discriminates against Aboriginal people. The most persuasive evidence can be found in the increasingly disproportionate number of Aboriginal people who are incarcerated in Canadian prisons. However, the phenomenon of Aboriginal overrepresentation in Canadian correctional institutions is a symptom of a much deeper problem: systemic and overt discrimination against Aboriginal people pervades the justice system and Canadian society generally. As Hamilton and Sinclair (1991:96) have pointed out: "Aboriginal peoples have experienced the most entrenched racial discrimination of any group in Canada. Discrimination against Aboriginal people has been a central policy of Canadian governments since confederation."

Moreover, the disproportionate representation of Aboriginal people has been increasing and there are also new challenges on the horizon. Even without any systematic research showing that youth crime or youth gangs are increasing, sensational media portrayals and self-serving justice system accounts, sometimes aided and abetted by what Hagedorn (1990) has termed "courthouse criminology," portray violent and organized crime as being "out of control" in this country. Increasingly, these portrayals include subtle and not so subtle references to Aboriginal and other racialized youth (Dukes and Valentine, 1998; Schissel, 1997).[8] As a result, governments appear willing to continue to target attention and resources to apprehend and punish the very racialized young people who are already so disadvantaged in this country. Put more bluntly, this moral panic about crime and gangs is turning out to be a more "politically correct" and sanitized version of yesterday's more blatant forms of racism.

The symptoms of social inequality, whether poverty, crime, violence, or substance abuse, will continue unabated until there is a meaningful commitment to address race-based social inequality in Canada. Such a commitment will require a willingness to examine the racial biases that are an integral part of the dominant beliefs, values, rules, and practices of Canadian institutions. This type of analysis has been steadfastly resisted by most who have examined Aboriginal justice issues. Instead, the focus has been on appearances rather than real solutions. Recommendations involving such initiatives as affirmative action or cultural awareness programs can be easily accommodated within existing systems, but they cannot bring about the fundamental changes that are required in Canada's social structure. Alternative pathways have been proposed by the Royal Commission on Aboriginal Peoples and others, but they have yet to be embraced by Canadians, or by Canadian governments or institutions.

Notes

1. The term "racialized" refers to the process "by which societies construct races as real, different and unequal in ways that matter to economic, political, and social life" (Commission on Systemic Racism, 1995:40).

2. Personal correspondence from Manitoba Justice.

3. Personal correspondence from Saskatchewan Justice.

4. Personal correspondence from Saskatchewan Justice.

5. The author appeared as an expert witness in both of these trials.

6. Recently, for example, the author undertook a review of three evaluations of the cross-cultural training program of the Winnipeg Police Service. The results of the evaluations indicated that many police officers emerged from cross-cultural training with more negative attitudes than they had before entering the training (Hylton, 2000).

7. The discussion that follows draws on Brant (1999).

8. Bala (2000), for example, has reported that during the 1999 Ontario provincial election, in a high-profile ad campaign, the Toronto Police Association urged voters to support "law and order" candidates. One of the ads pictured five obviously Latino young men. It was subsequently determined that the subjects in the ad were from Los Angeles.

References

Alberta Task Force. 1991. *Report of the Task Force on the Criminal Justice System and Its Impact on Indian and Métis People of Alberta*. Edmonton.

Andrews v. Law Society of British Columbia (1989) 2 W.W.R. 299 and 307 at 3C8.

Avio, K. 1993. "Inequality in clemency decisions on murder cases," in J. Curtis, E. Grabb, and N. Guppy, eds., *Social Inequality in Canada: Patterns, Problems, Policies*. Scarborough: Prentice-Hall, 500-11.

Bala, N. 2000. *"Responding to youth crime in Canada,"* Queen's University Law School, unpublished manuscript.

Bolaria, B., and P. Li. 1988. *Racial Oppression in Canada*, 2nd ed. Toronto: Garamond Press.

Brant, M. 1999. "Renewing the relationship: A perspective on the impact of the Royal Commission on Aboriginal People," in J. Hylton (1999a:92-111).

Canadian Bar Association. 1988. *Locking Up Indians in Canada*. Ottawa: Canadian Bar Association.

Canadian Centre for Justice Statistics. 1998. "A one day snapshot of inmates in Canada's adult correctional facilities," *Juristat* 18, 8:1-15.

Commission on Systemic Racism in the Ontario Criminal Justice System. 1995. *Report of the Commission on Systemic Racism in the Ontario Criminal Justice System*. Toronto: Queen's Printer for Ontario.

Doob, A. 1994. *Race, Bail and Imprisonment: A Report to the Commission on Systemic Racism in the Ontario Criminal Justice System on the Data Collected by the Canadian Centre for Justice Statistics*. Toronto: Commission on Systemic Racism in the Ontario Criminal Justice System.

Dukes, R., and J. Valentine. 1998. "Gang membership and bias against young people who break the law," *Social Science Journal* 35, 3:347-60.

Ericson, R. 1982. *Reproducing Order: A Study of Police Patrol Work*. Toronto: University of Toronto Press.

Forcese, D. 1999. *Policing Canadian Society*, 2nd ed. Scarborough: Prentice-Hall Allyn and Bacon Canada.

Griffiths, C., and S. Verdun-Jones. 1994. *Canadian Criminal Justice*, 2nd ed. Toronto: Harcourt Brace.

Hagedorn, J. 1990. "Back in the field again: Gang research in the nineties," in C. Huff, ed., *Gangs in America* Newbury Park, CA: Sage, 240-59.

Hamilton, A., and C. Sinclair. 1991. *Report of the Aboriginal Justice Inquiry of Manitoba*, Winnipeg.

Harman, W., and R. Hann. 1986. *Release Risk Assessment: An Historical Descriptive Analysis*. Ottawa: Ministry of the Solicitor General.

Harding, J. 1985. "Public drunkenness in Regina," in P. Havemann, et al. (1985).

Havemann, P., K. Couse, L. Foster, and R. Matonovitch. 1985. *Law and Order for Canada's Indigenous People*. Regina: Prairie Justice Research, University of Regina, School of Human Justice.

Henry, F., C. Tater, W. Mattis, and T. Rees. 1995. *The Colour of Democracy: Racism in Canadian society*. Toronto: Harcourt Brace.

Hill, D., and M. Schiff. 1988. *Human Rights in Canada: A Focus on Racism* , 3rd ed. Ottawa: Canadian Labour Congress and the Human Rights Research and Education Centre.

Hylton, J. 1979. *Job Satisfaction in the Regina Police Department*. Regina: Regina Police Department.

—. 1981. *Admission to Saskatchewan Provincial Correctional Centres*. Regina: University of Regina, Prairie Justice Research Consortium.

—. 1994. "Financing Aboriginal justice," in R. Gosse, J. Youngblood Henderson, and R. Carter, eds, *Continuing Poundmaker and Riel's Quest: Presentations Made at a conference on Aboriginal Peoples and Justice*. Saskatoon: Purich Publishing.

—. 1999a. *Aboriginal Self-Government in Canada: Current Trends and Issues*, 2nd ed. Saskatoon: Purich Publishing.

—. 1999b. "The case for self-government: A social policy perspective," in Hylton (1999a:78-91).

—. 2000. "R. v. the Manitoba Warriors: A socio-legal analysis of racism in the Canada's criminal justice system," Winnipeg: Phillips Aiello Law Firm.

Kallen, E. 1995. *Ethnicity and Human Rights in Canada*, 2nd ed. Toronto: Oxford University Press.

Kaminski, L. 1991. "An historical survey of Aboriginal juvenile delinquency in Manitoba," unpublished manuscript, Winnipeg.

La Prairie, C. 1996. *Examining Aboriginal Corrections in Canada*. Ottawa: Aboriginal Corrections, Ministry of the Solicitor General.

Law Reform Commission of Canada. 1991. *Report on Aboriginal Peoples and Criminal Justice: Equality, Respect and the Search for Justice as Requested by the Minister of Justice under Subsection 12(2) of the 'Law Reform Commission Act'*. Ottawa: Law Reform Commission.

Linn, P. 1992. *Report of the Saskatchewan Indian Justice Review Committee*. Regina.

Lundman, R. 1980. *Police and Policing: An Introduction*. New York: Holt, Rinehart and Winston.

McMahon, T. 1992. "Aboriginal People and Discrimination in the Justice System: A Survey of Manitoba Inmates and Related Literature," LL.M. thesis, University of Ottawa.

Mosher, C. 1998. *Discrimination and Denial: Systemic Racism in Ontario's Legal and Criminal Justice Systems, 1892-1961*. Toronto: University of Toronto Press.

R. v. Williams (1998). S.C.J. No. 49 Q.L.

—. 1995. *Bridging the Cultural Divide: A Report on Aboriginal People and Criminal Justice*. Ottawa: RCAP.

—. 1996. *Report of the Royal Commission on Aboriginal Peoples*. Ottawa: RCAP.

Royal Commission on Aboriginal Peoples. 1993. *Aboriginal Peoples and the Justice System*. Ottawa: RCAP.

Rudin, J. 1999. "Aboriginal self-government and justice," in Hylton (1999a:205-27).

Schissel, B. 1997. "Youth crime, moral panics, and the news: The conspiracy against the marginalized in Canada," *Social Justice* 24, 2:165-84.

10

"Making Sense" of Moral Panics: Excavating the Cultural Foundations of the "Young, Black Mugger"

NOB DORAN

Recent critical criminology in North America has become increasingly concerned with "moral panics" about crime, especially "youth crime." In the United States, this has mainly concerned itself with the increasingly high levels of African-American imprisonment and their targeting by police in urban areas such as Washington (Chambliss, 1994; Platt, 1996).[1] In Canada the concept is most prominent in Schissel's (1997) recent work that argues that those young Canadians "who are marginalized and disadvantaged" (10), not just immigrant and Native youths,[2] are frequently portrayed by the media as "folk devils" (51-71) in "a coordinated and calculated attempt to nourish the ideology that supports a society stratified on the bases of race, class, and gender, and that the war on kids is part of the state-capital mechanism that continually reproduces an oppressive social and economic order" (10). Moreover, all these writers make a similar connection between the workings of the larger social structure and the demonizing of these vulnerable groups. Yet, as this chapter will argue, these analyses of the relationship between moral panics and "contemporary capitalism" are somewhat lacking because they fail to explain *how* this relationship operates. In other words, because they tend to ignore the problem of language (and moral panics are typically expressed linguistically), they are unable to demonstrate the process of "symbolic formation" (Hall, 1974:278) by which certain groups (but not others) "naturally" and "commonsensically" (albeit "ideologically") become constructed as folk devils. In contrast, I will argue that the theoretical work pioneered by Stuart Hall in the field of "cultural studies" can be helpful in this regard, and will allow us to go beyond the limitations of these critical criminologists.

Analysing "Moral Panics" within the North American Context

Chambliss (1994) begins his analysis from an ethnographic involvement with recent forms of police surveillance in the "urban ghetto" (177). From his initial observations of the ways in which the police selectively target "young, black males" (179), he goes on to portray the prison population as being disproportionately represented by "minorities, especially young African Americans and Latinos" (181) and how "the intensive surveillance of black neighborhoods, and the patterns of surveillance of white neighborhoods has the general consequence of institutionalizing racism by defining the problem of crime generally, and drug use in particular, as a problem of young black men" (183).

This has been coupled with a significant growth in the criminal justice system: "spending on corrections—prison building, maintenance and parole—has more than doubled in the last ten years ... the number of police officers doubled in the United States between 1980 and 1990" (184). Yet Chambliss contends that these increases are not in response to a rise in the crime rate. For him, "the notion of a crime increase is a perception, apparently created by the law enforcement establishment, the media, and politicians. But this is not supported by the facts" (184). Much of the rest of his paper is then concerned with suggesting how a moral panic over crime has been created since the 1960s via the efforts of these powerful groups (190-92). As a result,

> it is not surprising, but sociologically predictable, then, that doubling the number of police officers in the last 10 years has tripled the number of people in prison and jail, filled these institutions with minor offenders, exacerbated the disproportionate imprisonment of minorities, and institutionalised racist beliefs that make being a young black man synonymous with being criminal. (192)

Platt (1996) makes a similar argument, albeit from a different vantage point. His study begins from the heady world of national politics, not the everyday surveillance of the urban ghetto. Yet he, too, identifies a "moral panic about crime and lawlessness" (3) alongside the recent expansion of the U.S. criminal justice system. But from his perspective, issues at the structural level demand most attention. That is, he connects this moral panic with the "weakening political authority of the state" (4) and remarks on how structural unemployment, cuts in public spending, declining electoral participation, and the neglect of a growing racial divide "have ripped open the social fabric" (5) with the alarming result that "the whole political establishment has followed the lead of the New Right in successfully staking out the terrain of insecurity and couching its repressive measures in a popular moralism" (5). And this new discourse has been so successful that the "traditional liberal agenda on crime … [has] disappeared from official political discourse" (3). Furthermore, although Platt claims that "there is nothing particularly new about politicians and the media constructing moral panics to mobilize public opinion against illusory crime waves," (5) his complaint is that this particular one has been so convincing because there no longer exist "any competing interpretations that explain the demise of the American dream or provide a vision of a more compassionate society" (5). In other words, although Platt does not have the ethnographic footing that helped Chambliss ground his discussion, he goes well beyond Chambliss in pointing out that such a distorted portrayal of crime may "resonate widely with people who want solutions right now and are willing to concede democratic rights to a more authoritarian regime" (5).

Yet despite these differences in emphasis, Platt, like Chambliss, identifies similar folk devils:

> By 1979, African Americans comprised 46 per cent of all prisoners…. Similar racial disparities could be found for Latinos in the Southwest and for Native Americans in states like Alaska, Montana and North and South Dakota. African Americans bear the brunt of the law-and-order crackdown. Almost one in three arrests now involve an African American, typically male and young. (9)

Nevertheless, Chambliss and Platt are unable to give us a sense of exactly how these perceptions are symbolically formed by the media, politicians, etc., or of how such perceptions come to dominate public opinion at the expense of older liberal understandings of the crime and society relationship. Any analysis of the specific methods by which these powerful institutions "make sense" of crime is quite absent from their work. In contrast, Schissel's work does pay attention to certain aspects of this process, at least with regard to the media.

In making his argument, Schissel (1997) relies heavily on Cohen's (1980) original research on the mass media's involvement with moral panics and the creation of folk devils in Britain a generation ago. In that pioneering work, Cohen had carefully documented the mass media's "sense-making" procedures through which the "mods and rockers" became portrayed as folk devils to a wider English population. Moreover, he also traced the process by which that "framing" then acted as a model for the subsequent behaviour of youths, spectators, control agents, and others. Yet Schissel, like Platt and Chambliss, wants to locate his analysis at a deeper structural level than that of Cohen. Thus, he insists on going beyond Cohen's (1980:12-26, 177-204) mixture of "transactional" theorizing and American "subcultural" theory, in order to suggest a causal explanation much more reliant on the work of Hall et al. (1978). This latter analysis insisted that the moral panic over the emergence of the "young black mugger" in 1970s England could only be explained by combining Cohen's approach with a structural and theoretical understanding emanating from scholars such as Althusser and Gramsci.[3]

Although Schissel claims that he is drawing on Hall et al., his use of their work remains somewhat limited. For him, they are to be understood primarily as critical theorists of the media because they "illustrated how the raw materials of crime facts get filtered to the media and are produced as 'factual' stories that ultimately serve to reproduce the ideologies of powerful people" (1997:11). Thus, when Schissel attempts his own analysis he focuses mainly on how the Canadian press engages in what he sees as a similar process.[4] This includes an examination of both the form and content of recent media coverage of crime in Canada. For example, he identifies a number of journalistic strategies targeted against youth, including—the depiction of unusual youth crimes so as to imply specific connections between morality and social position, the depiction of youth crimes that neglect relevant socio-economic realities, the depiction of exceptional crimes as the norm, the depiction of crimes so as to suggest a crime wave, the sensationalist use of headlines and pictures, and the frequent use of "expert declarations" about the supposed "natural evil" of youth. In terms of the content of this coverage, Schissel identifies three prominent folk devil typifications discursively created by the media: "poor families (living in poor communities), racially based gangs and groups (made up of recent immigrants or Aboriginal Canadians), and both single mothers and mothers who work outside the home" (51).

Yet Schissel's analysis fails to do justice to the full sophistication of Hall et al.'s understanding of the "ideological" role of the media in creating contemporary folk devils. Unlike Schissel, Hall et al. go to great lengths to explicitly move beyond crude formulations of the media as intentionally biassed. Moreover, their work takes very seriously a number of issues ignored by Schissel. That is, they concern themselves with how the press first "encodes" events, how it also routinely aims to influence the "decodings" of those events, and then how it orchestrates public opinion around its "explanations." In addition, Hall et al. examine not only how readers and the lay public make sense of this news coverage, but also how a deeply rooted, cultural grammar, shared by both the press and the reading public alike, is able to produce one particularly powerful folk devil; because this image is the negation of all the positive social images which constitute that shared ideological culture. In other words, Hall's cultural studies approach moves us beyond media "textual strategies" and towards a deeper understanding of both the cultural foundations of "signification" and the media's ability to mobilize public opinion around its views.

Making Sense of Problematic Realities:
The Culture-Ideology-Media Connection

Like Schissel, Stuart Hall's early work was concerned with media strategies used to make sense of problematic realities. Yet, as he complained at that time, "the study of ideology as a specific social *praxis* lacks anything more than the most rudimentary conception of the processes of symbolic formation" (1974:278). And as we have seen in the North American studies cited above, they too suffer from a similar neglect. But Hall was determined to help rectify this situation—"we must insist that analysis of political signification through linguistic transaction in the public domain must give special weight to the linguistic mediation, and the process of symbolization itself" (1974:280). And he found the "method of semiological analysis" (1974:280) a convenient starting point. For example, he showed the ideological nature of the linguistic structure of "majorities/minorities" in his own preliminary analysis of how the English media, as well as more conventional social control agents, "signified" political deviance: "all the agents of signification when dealing with this type of political behaviours employ the minority/majority distinction. The world of political deviance is systematically 'classified out' in terms of this basic opposition" (1974:280-

81). Here, like Schissel, Hall is concerned with identifying the ideological strategies used by the media to classify out problematic reality.

But Hall realizes that the mere identification of this linguistic binary opposition is not enough. Although it is commonsensically used to redescribe problematic events (for example, student demonstrations) within a "normal" range, and is naturally used by politicians and agents of control, not just the media, Hall understands that this mundane, discursive "version of the ancient principle of 'divide and rule'" (1974:285) only gets its power because it can "tap sacred and symbolic values which are widely shared" (1974:289) by all classes. In other words, the power of this and other oppositions is deeply rooted, and thus analysis must move to that deeper, cultural level. More generally, Hall starts asking questions about the complex relationship between ideology and culture, and how that may manifest itself in the everyday practices of the media, politicians and people on the street.

Beginning with Marx's general materialist framework, Hall (1977) painstakingly articulates the connections between culture, ideology, and media at the different levels of the social formation. From the deepest linguistic level, the cultural, via the "dominant ideology" level, and then to the mundane functioning of "ideology," and finally to the everyday practices of newspapers, Hall demonstrates the exact nature of the ideological links between these levels. Moreover, he insists that ideology is not just the product of ruling class ideas but that it exists at the level of everyday experience as well. Consequently, his elaboration seeks to show the ideological nature of culture at both the level of "legal, political, economic, and philosophical discourses" (1977:324) and of everyday "common sense." Moreover, he realizes that although there may be one "dominant ideological field" in the social formation, this is constantly being challenged and thus work is involved in "containing" other subordinate value systems.

With regard to the working of ideology, he, like Poulantzas, highlights its function of separating classes and then uniting them again into a false unity, whether that be of "consumers," "the nation," or "a consensus." And it is within this last location that Hall places the media. For him, the media's ideological function is to separate class opinion and then to unite it into the false unity of "public opinion." In other words, Hall directs our attention towards the media's "consensus-shaping" work and its associated mechanisms for producing ideological encodings and preferred (audience) decodings.

Exemplifying The Thesis:
The "Young Black Mugger" as an Ideological Signification

According to Hall (1974), periods of crisis are extremely useful for studying the process of signification and that of ideology more generally:

> in crisis moments, when the *ad hoc* formulas which serve, 'for all practical purposes,' to classify the political world meaningfully and within the limits of legitimacy are rendered problematic, and new problems and new groupings emerge to threaten and challenge the ruling positions of power and their social hegemony, we are in a special position to observe the work of persuasive definition in the course of its formation. This is a privileged moment for the student of ideologies. (298)

Thus when the "mugging" moral panic emerged in Britain in the early 1970s, Hall and his colleagues (1978) took this opportunity to examine Hall's (1974, 1977) thesis. Starting from the premise that "ideological discourse is characterized by the rigidity of its structuring at the level of 'deep' interests, and by the relative 'openness'—the flexibility, the labile quality of its forms—at the 'surface' level" (Hall, 1974:291), their empirical aim in 'Policing the Crisis' (1978) was to go behind the myriad of surface forms (as displayed in the different newspapers' coverage and understanding of the problem of mugging) to the underlying "deep structure." As Hall had written:

> The borrowing of a Chomskyian metaphor of 'deep' and 'surface' structures for the study of ideological discourses is not fortuitous, since the study of ideologies as a specific level of a social formation requires precisely such a model by which quite unrestricted elements give rise, via 'rules' of transformation, and by way of specified forms of praxis (signification) and institutions (e.g. the mass media), to a heterodox variety of 'surface' forms. (1974:291)

Hall and his colleagues hoped to reach this deep structure by following (albeit in a reverse sequence) the theoretical model outlined by Hall (1977), by which one begins with a plethora of surface forms but one's primary aim is to move beyond this level to the underlying generative "grammar."

MEDIA ANALYSIS AND SURFACE INTERPRETATIONS

Beginning from a firm rejection of any conspiratorial notion of ideology, Hall and his colleagues begin with the mundane ideological mechanisms of the media (Hall, 1977:342-48). Specifically, they start with an examination of the everyday practices of encoding, unintentionally produced by the practical constraints on modern news-gathering. For example, the pressure of producing a newspaper every day often makes journalists dependent on a small number of "primary definers" (Hall et al., 1978:57) in powerful positions to help them make sense of the events around them (54). As a result, the media, despite their relative autonomy, still tend to reproduce the ideas of the powerful (59). That is not to say, however, that journalists reproduce one ideological position. Hall et al. go to great lengths to insist on the variety of ways that British newspapers encode events into their own peculiar "public idiom" (61),[5] while all the time remaining within certain ideological limits. And these limits are taken for granted, informed by the working assumptions that constitute the "professional ideology" (53) of journalism. For example, one tacit journalistic assumption is that "because we occupy the same society and belong to roughly the same 'culture' ... there is, basically, only *one* perspective on events" (55). Another tacit working assumption concerns "reasonableness," namely, that all the newspapers' "publics, however distinct, are assumed to fall within that very broad spectrum of 'reasonable' men and readers are addressed broadly in those terms" (61).

Yet Hall et al. are not content simply to discuss the media's encoding function. They also seek to display the media's second ideological function, that of reflecting on this plurality of social knowledge and then classifying and ranking it within existing "normative and evaluative classifications" (Hall, 1977:341). This requires enormous ideological labour, much of it carried out by newspaper editorials and feature articles. Moreover, by examining the "work" done by these press editorials and features, Hall et al. are able to uncover the "implicit theories of human nature and society" (89) tacitly assumed by the different newspapers in their making sense of stories as "newsworthy" ones to their own particular audiences. This is because each news story involves "the presentation of the item to its *assumed* audience, in terms which, as far as the presenters of the item can judge, will make it comprehensible to that audience" (54). This newspaper concern with trying to get its audience to decode in one way rather than another comes out more clearly in the editorials and features. For example, almost all the editorials of the papers studied supported the harsh sentences for the youths (89). Generally, editorial writers abandoned any "liberal" interpretation of the crime and instead adopted a "traditional viewpoint" (89) in which human nature "is faced perennially with the same stark choice—between good and evil" (91) and where the law is seen as the "ultimate protector of all 'our' interests" (92). Similarly, with regard to the features, each newspaper sought to embed the problem within the assumed "cultural map" of its specific audience. In other words, each story was (hopefully) "made to mean" within the cultural framework of interpretation typically employed by that newspaper's readership. Thus, a critical examination of these feature articles is illuminating because, here, the connection "between media processes and more widely distributed lay ideologies of crime becomes most visible" (96). For example, at the national press level, certain themes emerged as typical explanations of this mugging incident, themes such as "social disorganization," "race," "environment," "ghetto," and "the city in decline" (100-03), were all presented as explanations of this new problem of "anti-social, black youth" (102). At the local press level, the primary explanations that emerged were those of the "environment" (109)—albeit of one specific part of the city only—"leisure opportunities" (111), and the changing "family" (113).[6]

Yet, despite this wide range of competing explanations, as Hall et al. point out, none of the papers went beyond a tacit but well-defined limit in pursuing the underlying causes of this crime. No newspaper asked hard questions about, for example, "what determines the environment" (118). Instead, all the papers invoked, what Hall et al. refer to as "public images" (118) in order to resolve these problems ideologically. These rather ambiguous "public images," such as "youth," "family," and "ghetto," work by not only being "graphically compelling, but by stopping short of serious searching analysis" (118). As a result, crucial questions about "fundamental structural characteristics of society: the unequal distribution of housing; the low levels of pay in particular industries; the nature of welfare benefits; the lack of educational resources; racial discrimination" (118) are not even brought into the debate. And for Hall and his collaborators, this unintentional short-circuiting of the analysis is one of the most important ways by which the media operate ideologically.

They then proceed to examine the third ideological function of the media, namely, to "organize, orchestrate and bring together that which it has selectively represented and selectively classified" (Hall, 1977:342). In other words, newspapers engage in an elaborate process by which they help shape an apparent consensus over news issues. This is most frequently represented in those occasional editorials in which a newspaper "takes the public voice" (Hall et al., 1978:63). Here, the newspaper is not so much concerned with giving its own viewpoint as with proposing that it is giving the public's viewpoint. But if such editorials claim to be speaking on behalf of the public, they must have some minimal basis in public opinion. And, typically, it is through the letter columns that public opinion seeks expression in the press. Consequently, Hall et al.'s case study then concerns itself with how such public opinion is "orchestrated," by examining in detail the letters written by the public concerning one specific mugging incident.[7] First, they notice that although the publication of letters itself is a structured exchange (not everyone who writes gets his or her letter selected for publication), often, room is found in the letter columns for contrary views and minority opinions. In fact, many people believe that the job of such columns is to "stimulate controversy, provoke public response, lead to lively debate … sustain the claim that the mind of the press is not closed, and that its pages are open to views it does not necessarily approve" (121). Nevertheless, Hall et al. remind us that because of the prior structuring process, these letters

> are in no sense an accurate representation of public opinion … [instead] their principal function is to help the press organize and orchestrate the debate about public questions. They are therefore a central link in the shaping of public opinion — a shaping process the more powerful because it appears to be in the reader's keeping and done with his or her consent and participation. (121)

For example, the sample of letters that they studied mostly "took off from the points of newsworthiness first identified in the *news* treatment" (122), thus suggesting one of the most basic ways in which public opinion is shaped.[8] More generally, however, the letter columns were marked by a sense of "scrupulous balance" (128), illustrating another of the media's ideological functions, that of allowing a balanced, but limited, number of views to be published—rather than of siding with one specific viewpoint over another.[9] In this case, that balance was between letters from either the traditionalist or the liberal perspective, while the limit was that other views on the subject were not heard.

These published letters made sense of the crime in almost diametrically opposite fashions. "*Society* was at the heart of the 'liberal' case against the sentence, the question of *morality* was at the centre of the traditionalist case" (124). Thus, liberal writers tended to blame the social environment for this criminal activity, while the traditionalists opposed this model via their appeal to moral discipline—for them, "morality *overcomes* environmental disadvantage" (127). In fact, this concern with discipline was at "the heart of the traditionalist case on crime" (128).

In addition, the forms of these two types of argument were also quite different. A consistent deep structure in these letters was the traditionalists' reliance on "ordinary personal experience," in contrast to the liberal writers' more "abstract and theoretical attitude" (126). Furthermore, the traditionalist writer used common-sense arguments, which "seemed to rest on the *felt legitimacy* of popular long-standing 'folk-wisdoms'" (125), or what "everyone knows" about the truth of crime. In contrast, the liberal letters "had to *argue* their way by a much longer, less assertive, more rational route to less popular conclusions" (125).

Yet Hall et al. are very sensitive to the fact that public opinion is not totally orchestrated and dominated by the media via mechanisms like the selective publication of letters.

> The idea that the mass media, because of their massive coverage, their linking of different publics, their unilateral power in the communications situation, therefore wholly absorb and obliterate all other, more informal and face-to-face levels of social discourse, is not tenable. (129)

Thus they then examined a collection of private letters to discover those forms of lay public opinion that exist outside the realms of media discourse to see whether or not the attitudes expressed within these private letters shared the same "systems of meaning" (129) as the public ones.

Interestingly, the vast majority of them did fit, albeit in a displaced fashion, within the "traditionalist" viewpoint. Here Hall and his colleagues found some rather extreme displacements of views already expressed, especially concerning the racial background of the muggers and the need for harsh punishments against them. In these letters, crime not only appeared as a manifestation of "evil human nature" (133) but also as something necessitating sadistic and brutal punishment. In fact, these letters' linking of the "race, sexuality and sadism" (133) triad formed a deep structure that "also underpins the more displaced (and therefore publicly acceptable) themes and images of *other* letters we have seen" (133). In other words, there was a "transmutation from this triadic basis to its 'more acceptable' expression in the call for discipline" (133) when one moved from these private letters' concerns with sadism, etc., to the published (traditionalist) letters' concern with discipline. Finally, Hall et al. point out certain bedrock sentiments that inform all these letters (134), namely, the fundamental root concept of the family, and its child-rearing ability.[10] "This theme constantly recurs in terms of its centrality in the bringing up of the child—the 'normal' family produces 'normal' children; therefore it must have taken an abnormal family to produce the 'monster'" (134).

The letters' significant differences also serve to highlight the "shaping process" by which that public opinion that manifests itself at the most local levels of gossip, rumour, and private letters becomes increasingly constrained as it moves into the realm of the media:

> 'Public opinion' about crime does not simply form at random. It exhibits a shape and structure. It follows a sequence. It is a social process, not a mystery ... the more a crime issues on to the public stage, the more constrained by the available frameworks of understanding and interpretation, the more socially validated feelings, emotion and attitudes are mobilised around it. (136)

Yet, they don't want to lose sight of the importance of the public opinion they found in these private letters, because it gives insights into the common sense ideologies of people who are totally removed from the formal channels of the media.

Thus, they finish this part of their analysis by reflecting back on the entire range of insights they have uncovered. Most importantly, they discovered that despite the vast differences between the highly orchestrated articulations of the press (as expressed in the news stories, editorials, features, and letters) and the relatively unstructured informal expressions of lay public opinion (expressed most clearly in the private letters):

if we look again, below the variety of surface forms, to the more generative level, we discover the presence of ideological structures, which might hitherto have escaped our attention. At each stage—in the courts, in the news, in the editorial judgments, in the letters, in the abusives—despite their many and significant differences, a familiar lexicon appears to be at work, informing the discourse. The same, very limited *repertoire* of premises, frameworks, and interpretations appear to be drawn upon whenever the topic of crime and punishment has to be deployed. (137)

In other words, it is now time to leave this field of media analysis in order to get to that "generative structure" that is able to produce all of these different surface interpretations.

CULTURAL ANALYSIS AND GENERATIVE 'DEEP STRUCTURE'

At this deeper level, Hall et al. begin by identifying a number of themes (discovered through their empirical analysis) that tacitly constitute this traditionalist world view because it (along with the liberal world view) *"organised and formed the limits of* the public discussion of crime" (139). More importantly, they want to show how these images contribute to this traditionalist world view's power to "generalise itself across social and class divisions" (140) and constitute itself as the dominant ideological field, rather then the liberal world view, at this time.

"Respectability" is one such theme that helps in this regard, in part because both the working class and the middle class adhere to it, albeit in very different ways. Moreover, it has a very specific relationship to crime especially because for the working class, crime (and moral misconduct more generally) constitutes one possible route downwards from the respectable and into the rough working class. "Work" itself is another central image. And here Hall et al. point out the tacit "moral calculus" that is so important for the everyday understanding of crime. Whereas it is through work that most people obtain their "leisure, pleasure, security, free activity, play" (142), crime, according to this understanding, "is set off against work in the public mind, because it is an attempt to acquire by speed, stealth, fraudulent or shorthand methods what the great majority of law-abiding citizens can only come by through arduous toil" (142). A third social image is that of "discipline" and of England as a disciplined society (seen most obviously in times of war). Once again it has very different meanings for different classes, yet its power rests in this ability to general- ize itself throughout society. Not surprisingly, youth are seen as potential threats to this sense of discipline, along with others who do not appropri- ately respond to the emotional controls, the sexual repression, the regula- tion of feelings, the taboos on pleasure (144), bound up with this discipline.

A fourth image, the "family," is also intimately connected with the first three discussed. And the problem of youth takes a more central position within this complex institution:

> the alignment of the sexual and the social—a fundamental task of the family—is just the homology of structures which creates inside us those *repertoires* of self-discipline and self- control for which, later, the wider world is to be so thankful. It is little wonder then, that fears and panics about the break- down of social discipline—of which crime is one of the most powerful indices—centre on the indiscipline of 'youth', 'the young.' (145)

A fifth image is that of the "city," and here Hall et al. stress the cross-class unity created through nineteenth-century attempts at fostering "civic pride" and related conquests of threats to the city, such as disease, unsanitary con- ditions, and the like. Yet for these writers crime is experienced as a threat by the working class in the city, at this particular historical moment, because it coincides with other, more serious urban dislocations (most importantly, the breakup of the traditional working-class neighbourhood).

However, all these images can only make complete sense, they argue, if one understands them as fitting within one all-encompassing image. "Overarching these social images and holding them together is the only image of the totality which sometimes seems to have achieved anything like universal currency: that of England" (146). But as this sense of Englishness has two distinct aspects to it, the second aspect sets up a defi- nite problem for people from the Caribbean, or of West Indian ancestry. On the one hand there is the sense of the English as being, beneath it all, basically decent. On the other hand, there is another powerful sense, the "imperialist" notion of Englishness. "It is present in the Englishman's divine right to conquer 'barbaric' peoples, a right which is then redefined not as an aggressive economic imperialism, but as a 'civilising burden'"

(147). The final image is that of the "law." And perhaps the most interesting aspect of their discussion is their realization that the working class exhibits a quite contradictory relationship to it, best exhibited in "the paradox of the two images of the police—the appeal of the image of the 'bobby on the beat' and the strong sense that 'all coppers are bastards'" (148). Yet, with any rise in crime, because the working class probably suffers the most (as 'street crime' will probably take place in their neighbourhoods), they, too, have a material stake in this support for the law.

Now that the deep structure of the traditionalist world view has become more visible,[11] we can see why the moral panic generated in the 1970s naturally and commonsensically organized itself around the young black mugger as its representative folk devil. This figure was "the reverse image, the alternative to all we know: the negation ... he was a sort of personification of all the positive social images—only *in reverse*: black on white" (161-62). In other words, this particular folk devil image was so powerful because it was the opposite of so many of the positive social images, which, as we have just discovered, formed the deep structure of the traditionalist world view. Moreover, the traditionalist world view, itself, was so powerful because, as we have also seen, it was able to unite all classes within its viewpoint and thus command the ideological field, at the expense of the liberal alternative.

Conclusion

It has only been possible here to illuminate a small portion of the contribution that Stuart Hall's work makes. Moreover, the analysis outlined here has had to be ruthless in its presentation of just the bare essentials of (only) half the argument. Other issues central to the work of Hall et al. on signification, most notably its roots in common sense, the origins of the liberal and traditionalist world views themselves, etc., have had to be placed to one side. In addition, the second half of their analysis, concerned with the "spiraling of signification" at times of crisis, has not even been touched. Nevertheless, from this brief sketch, I hope to have suggested the potential utility of this approach to the study of moral panics.

Despite its obvious sophistication, I must finish by pointing out a couple of disquieting features of Hall's work. First, there is the quite straightforward issue of culture. The methodological rigour of Hall et al's analysis came from their stubborn insistence on starting from the interpretations of muggings in 1970s England and working backwards to the deeper structure. Although North American cultures share many similarities with England's, it is essential that any analysis of moral panics begin with those themes, images, etc. that are prevalent on this continent. The other problem is a more serious one and concerns itself with the specific analysis carried out by Hall et al. The essence of their study was the uncovering of the ideological methods used by the media to make sense of the mugging moral panic. Unfortunately, recent research indicates that they too are ideological. That is, just as the press acted ideologically, via their tacit methods of news collection, explanation, orchestration etc., Hall et al. tacitly replicate those same (ideological) methods in their own analysis of this moral panic.[12] Such a realization presents future research in this area with a number of theoretical difficulties. Fortunately, current critical scholarship is beginning to address these and related problems.[13]

Notes

1. Of course, this reaction emerges from a widespread and long-standing assertion in the U.S. uniform crime reports, and in certain areas of U.S. criminology, that African-Americans commit a disproportionate amount of crime. For example, see Comer (1985), Georges-Abeyie (1984), Laub et al. (1987), Sample and Philip (1984), Tonry, (1995).

2. The question of overrepresentation of ethnic minorities in crime has become a lively debate in recent years in Canada. The following give some indication of its contours: Hatt (1994), Johnston (1994), Mosher (1996), Roberts (1994), Rushton (1988), Roberts and Gabor (1990), Wortley (1996). Neugebauer-Visano (1996) reported on recent ethnographic work that tackles certain aspects of this issue.

3. For attempts at introducing these scholars' insights into Canadian criminology, one might consult Ratner and McMullan (1985), Samuelson (1985) for Gramsci's influence, and Smandych (1986) for Althusser's (via Poulantzas's) influence.

4. Although it should be pointed out that critical analyses of the media with specific reference to crime can be found in a number of other Canadian authors' work, see, for example, Ericson et al. (1987, 1991), McCormick (1995).

5. For example, the popular national newspaper *The Daily Mirror* translated an annual report of the Chief Inspector of the Constabulary into the succinct headline "AGGRO BRITAIN," suggesting a connection between present-day crime and the *Mirror's* own prior news coverage of "aggro football hooligans and skinheads" (Hall et al., 1978:62).

6. Although outside the scope of this analysis, it should be noted that a number of 'criminological theories' have recently constituted themselves (or reconstituted themselves) around one or another of these images. For example, the lifestyle/exposure theory of Hindelang et al. (1978) focuses on individuals' lifestyles and their resulting exposure to crime, while the early 'environmental' concerns of the Chicago school have been revitalized since the 1970s (Bottoms and Wiles, 1997). Hirschi's 'social control' theory (1969) has also developed in ways that increasingly focus on the 'family' and its role in forming the self (Gottfredson and Hirschi, 1990; Sampson and Laub, 1993).

7. For a contrasting analysis of the ideological nature of letters to the press, see Smith (1990: ch. 5).

8. Hall (1977) points out that "hegemonic codes provide precisely those necessary *spaces* in the discourse where corporate and subordinate classes insert themselves" (345). As can be seen here, most letter writers 'inserted themselves' within the dominant frames of meaning established by the media's own reporting of the news.

9. As Hall (1977) clarifies the point,

> the media, then, like other state complexes in the modern stage of capitalist development, absolutely depend on their 'relative autonomy' from ruling-class power in the narrow sense. These are enshrined in the operational principles of broadcasting—'objectivity,' 'neutrality,' 'impartiality' and 'balance'.... Balance, for example, ensures that there will always be a two-sided dialogue, and thus always more than one definition of the situation available to the audience. (345)

10. This concern with child-rearing practices is now becoming prevalent in the criminological literature as well. For example, Gottfredson and Hirschi (1990) argue that ineffective child-rearing practices lead to poor self-control, which is, in turn, related to later criminal (and other harmful) activities.

11. Unfortunately, it is not possible here to articulate the other half of this deep structure—its roots in everyday 'common sense.' Such foundations, of course, provided the grounds for many of the (traditionalist) letters published and also accounted for much of their rhetorical power.

12. See Doran (2000) for an analysis of the recursive loop that Hall et al. get entangled in when they fail to pay attention to their own ideological methods.

13. Foucault (1977, 1980), of course, initiated this type of work with his insistence on the examination of the close relationship between institutional forms of knowledge and state power. Donzelot's (untranslated) work (1984) also promises much with its explicit attention to power/knowledge 'crises' and its much stronger emphasis on politics.

References

Bottoms, A. and P. Wiles. 1997. "Environmental criminology," in M. Maguire, R. Morgan, and R. Reiner eds., *The Oxford Handbook of Criminology*, 2nd ed. Oxford: Clarendon Press, 305-59.

Chambliss, W. 1994. "Policing the ghetto underclass: The politics of law and enforcement," *Social Problems* 41, 2:177-94.

Cohen, S. 1980. *Folk Devils and Moral Panics*, 2nd ed. Oxford: Martin Robertson.

Comer, J. 1985. "Black violence and public policy," in L. Curtis, ed., *American Violence and Public Policy*. New Haven: Yale University Press, 63-86.

Donzelot, J. 1984. *L'invention du social*. Paris: Fayard. (Republished by Seuil in 1994.)

Doran, N. 2000. "Don't believe the hype: muggings, moral panics and the Marxist paradigm," paper presented at the British Sociological Association annual meeting, York, England, April.

Ericson, R., P. Baranek, and J. Chan. 1987. *Visualizing Deviance: A Study of News Organization*. Toronto: University of Toronto Press.

—. 1991. *Representing Order: Crime, Law and Justice in the News Media*. Milton Keynes: Open University Press.

Foucault, M. 1977. *Discipline and Punish*. London: Allen Lane.

—. 1980. *Power/Knowledge: Selected Interviews and Other Writings, 1972-1977.* New York: Pantheon.

Georges-Abeyie, D. 1984. "Definitional issues: Race, ethnicity and official crime/victimization rates," in Georges-Abeyie, ed., *The Criminal Justice System and Blacks.* New York: Clark Boardman.

Gottfredson, M., and T. Hirschi. 1990. *A General Theory of Crime.* Stanford, CA: Stanford University Press.

Hall, S. 1974. "Deviance, politics and the media," in P. Rock and M. McIntosh, eds., *Deviance and Social Control.* London: Tavistock, 261-305.

—. 1977. "Culture, media and the 'ideological effect'," in J. Curran, M. Gurevitch, and J. Woollacott, eds., *Mass Communication and Society.* Milton Keynes: Open University Press in association with Edward Arnold. (Republished by Sage in 1979.)

Hall, S., C. Critcher, T. Jefferson, J. Clarke, and B. Roberts. 1978. *Policing the Crisis: Mugging, the State and Law and Order.* London: Macmillan.

Hatt, K. 1994. "Reservations about race and crime statistics," *Canadian Journal of Criminology* 36:164-65.

Hindelang, M.J., M.R. Gottfredson, and J. Garofalo. 1978. *Victims of Personal Crime: An Empirical Foundation for a Theory of Personal Victimization.* Cambridge, MA: Ballinger.

Hirschi, T. 1969. *Causes of Delinquency.* Berkeley: University of California Press.

Johnston, P. 1994. "Academic approaches to race-crime statistics do not justify their collection," *Canadian Journal of Criminology* 36, 2:166-73.

Laub, J., D. Clark, L. Siegel, and J. Garofalo. 1987. *Trends in Juvenile Crime in the United States: 1973-1983.* Albany, NY: Hindelang Research Center.

McCormick, C. 1995. *Constructing Danger: The Mis/representation of Crime in the News.* Halifax: Fernwood.

Mosher, C. 1996. "Minorities and misdemeanors: The treatment of black public order offenders in Ontario's criminal justice system, 1892-1930," *Canadian Journal of Criminology* 38:413-38.

Neugebauer-Visano, R. 1996. "Kids, cops and colour: The social organization of police-minority youth relations," in G. O'Bireck, ed., *Not a Kid Anymore: Canadian Youth, Crime and Subculture.* Scarborough: Nelson.

Platt, A. 1996. "The politics of law and order," *Social Justice* 21, 3:3-13.

Ratner, R.S., and J. McMullan. 1985. "Social control and the rise of the 'exceptional state' in Britain, the United States, and Canada," in T. Fleming, ed., *The New Criminologies in Canada: State, Crime and Control.* Toronto: Oxford University Press, 185-205.

Roberts, J. 1994. "Crime and race statistics: Toward a Canadian solution," *Canadian Journal of Criminology* 36:175-85.

Roberts, J., and T. Gabor. 1990. "Lombrosian wine in a new bottle: Research on crime and race," *Canadian Journal of Criminology* 32:291-305.

Rushton, P. 1988. "Race differences in sexuality and their correlates," *Journal of Research in Personality* 23:35-54.

Sample, B., and M. Phillip. 1984. "Perspectives on race and crime in research and planning," in D. Georges-Abeyie, ed., *The Criminal Justice System and Blacks.* New York: Clark Boardman, 21-36.

Sampson, R., and J. Laub. 1993. *Crime in the Making: Pathways and Turning Points through Life.* Cambridge, MA: Harvard University Press.

Samuelson, L. 1985. "New parallels between Marxist and Non-Marxist theories of law and the state," in T. Fleming, ed., *The New Criminologies in Canada: State, Crime and Control.* Toronto: Oxford University Press, 270-84.

Schissel, B. 1997. *Blaming Victims: Youth Crime, Moral Panics and the Politics of Hate.* Halifax: Fernwood.

Smandych, R. 1986. "The origins of Canadian Anti-Combines Legislation, 1890-1910," in S. Brickey and E. Comack, eds., *The Social Basis of Law: Critical Readings in the Sociology of Law*. Toronto: Garamond, 53-65.

Smith, D. 1990. *Texts, Facts and Femininity*. London: Routledge.

Tonry, M. 1995. *Malign Neglect: Race, Crime and Punishment in America*. New York: Oxford University Press.

Wortley, S. 1996. "Justice for all? Race and perceptions of bias in the Ontario criminal justice system—a Toronto survey," *Canadian Journal of Criminology* 38:439-67.

11

The Social and Legal Banishment of Anti-racism: A Black Perspective

AKUA BENJAMIN

The Toronto Star article headlined "The Raw Nerve of Racism," dated 21 August 1988, reported on the shooting death of Lester Donaldson by Metropolitan Toronto Police. In this report it was noted that Donaldson "was a paranoid schizophrenic" (Donovan, 1988:B1). In a subsequent report by the *Toronto Star* (18 Sept. 1988) focused on "Why we are putting the mentally ill behind bars," it was stated that "neighbors reported that he [Donaldson] had taken hostages, was alone in his room when killed and had a history of psychiatric problems" (Crawford, 1988:B1). As late as 8 July 1994, in an article entitled "Donaldson Panel Seeks Special Response Unit," the *Toronto Sun* characterized this victim as "Jamaican-born Donaldson, 44, a paranoid schizophrenic with a history of violence against police" (Payne, 1994:27). This focus on Donaldson's psychiatric history demonized him as someone mentally unstable. Donaldson was also criminalized. According to the *Toronto Star* (21 Aug. 1988) Donaldson "was once convicted of assaulting police officers who went to investigate a complaint that Donaldson was sexually assaulting his niece" (Donovan, 1988:B1).

Michael Wade Lawson, who was shot in the back of his head by Metropolitan Toronto Police in December 1988 was also criminalized in the media. Unlike Donaldson, Lawson was mentally stable; he had no criminal records; he lived in a middle-class suburban neighbourhood. The media, however, reported that he was shot in a stolen car (Cox and Donovan, 1989:A1) and "Police Cite Self Defence in Killing of Driver 17" (*Globe and Mail*, 10 Dec. 1988).

The past psychiatric history, criminal record, and seemingly negative behaviours of the victims were often emphasized in these media reports.

These portrayals fit historic and existing negative racial stereotypical imagery of Blacks as criminals. James (1997:315) notes that "the criminal images of Blacks, particularly males, have persisted over the years. These images help to reinforce police stereotypes, particularly those of young Black males."

By emphasizing the past behaviours and criminal records of those shot by police, the media gave a one-sided and racist view of the victim. For instance, there was little positive background information given as to the character of the victim: Wade Lawson was a successful student at his high school. Also, media reports showed very little favourable and normal actions of the victim at the time of the shooting, such as emphasizing that Donaldson was sitting having supper when police intervened and shot him. Above all, the incursions between the victims and police prior to the shooting and the attempts by the victim to gain redress were overshadowed. For example, Albert Johnson was shot and killed by police in 1979. Prior to his death, he lodged complaints of police harassment with the Ontario Human Rights Commission. Thus, a negative portrayal of these individuals and an eclipsing of their positive experiences and behaviour is in evidence. Moreover, these reports show how Black subjects with their positive and generally human qualities disappear and the related legitimate issues and concerns are rendered invisible or are banished.

This chapter examines media reports by the *Toronto Star*, the *Globe and Mail*, and the *Toronto Sun* to show how cultural and systemic racism makes inevitable the social and legal banishment of Blacks. Within this framework, I explore the discourses and material consequences where Blacks, and leaders of Black organizations in particular, have been discredited and criminalized as part of a process of banishment. The process of banishment was also extended to antiracism policies, programs and other initiatives by the present Ontario government. The chapter concludes with a discussion of the challenges in addressing and overcoming social and legal banishment of the Black community.

The mass media are tremendously influential in shaping thoughts, ideas, beliefs, and behaviours through their promulgation of cultural racism. In defining cultural racism, Henry et al. (1995:46) draw attention to everyday language in which "whiteness" is overwhelmingly positive while "blackness" has distinctly negative synonyms. Also, they note that it is "reflected in the images generated by the mass media (racial minorities are often portrayed as problems) and it is also manifested in … ideologies and practices."

In discussing the powerful role of the media, Kellner (1995:24) states:

> Radio, television, film and the other products of media cul-
> ture provide materials out of which we forge our very identi-
> ties, our sense of self-hood, our notion of what it means to be
> male or female, our sense of class, of ethnicity and race, of
> nationality, of sexuality of "us" and "them." Media images
> help shape our view of the world and our deepest values, what
> we consider good or bad, positive or negative, moral or evil.
> Media stories provide the symbols, myths and resources
> through which we constitute a common culture. Media spec-
> tacles demonstrate who has power and who is powerless, who
> is allowed to exercise force and violence and who is not. They
> dramatize and legitimate the power of the forces that be and
> show the powerless that they must stay in their places or be
> destroyed.

Hence, the extent to which the media present stereotypical imagery of
Blacks as criminals (Henry et al., 1999), contributes to the overproduction
of this imagery, which in turn has influenced and shaped a societal ideology that invites a response to this "lawless" and "heinous" group of individuals. The belief or ideology promulgated is that these are individuals,
or the group, to be feared, to be shunned, and by extension to be isolated
or banished from civil society. According to Henry et al. (1995:14) "racist
ideology provides the conceptual framework for the political, social and
cultural structures of inequality and systems of dominance based on race,
as well as the processes of exclusion and marginalization of people of
colour that characterize Canadian society." Thus it can also be stated that
ideologies promoted by cultural racism undergird the systematic practices
of systemic racism or systemic discrimination. Henry et al. define systemic
racism broadly as "laws, rules and norms woven into the social system that
result in an unequal distribution of economic, political and social
resources and rewards among various racial groups" (48). There is, therefore, an interrelationship between cultural and systemic racism and, by
extension, between social and legal banishment. Henry et al. (1999:97)
explain that "although the various forms of racism can be isolated for discussion purposes, in reality, they form a complex dynamic of interrelated
attitudes, feelings and behaviours that are linked to the collective belief
system and are expressed in institutional policies and practices.

This ideology has powerful impacts and influences the actions of individuals and institutions. An essential step in countering racism, therefore, is to examine critically the media's role in producing and reproducing racisms, and the ways in which these racisms materialize and impact on Blacks.

"Black/s" is a self-definitional term used by individuals and organizations within the Black community in Metropolitan Toronto and beyond. The term "Black" also connotes a political recognition of all peoples of African heritage. Hence, it is used as a term to build unity among the diversity of people of African heritage. Also, while many Black community organizations are located in the Metropolitan Toronto area, many Blacks understand the community to extend beyond geographical boundaries. Thus, the Black community is recognized as a community of people of African heritage with similar concerns regarding issues of racism, education, employment, and so on.

Not Just Social or Racial Exclusion, but Banishment

The notion of banishment is another way of coming to understand the racist exclusion of Blacks who have long resided in Canadian society. According to Goldberg (1995:100):

> Racist exclusion involves relative lack of access to, or absence from the distribution of, or lack of availability of goods or services, opportunities or privileges, rights and powers, even social responsibilities and burdens. These absences, lacks, and impediments by means of which exclusions are instituted must be explicitly or implicitly manifest in racially significant terms…. The proper yardstick against which to assess the degree of racist exclusion, the depth of the condition, is not simply the level of inclusion and access to social resources. It is rather the fuller measures of incorporation into and influence upon the body politic, whether economically, politically, legally, or culturally.

When this yardstick is related to the position overall of the Black community, "banishment" is quite apt. According to *The Concise Oxford Dictionary*, "banishment" means "to dismiss from one's presence or mind."

This definition captures the way in which members of Toronto's Black community feel that they have been positioned within the wider society. Beginning with the rescinding of the employment equity legislation by the Ontario Conservative government in 1995, many Black community members note that since then there has been a lack of public policy discussion or government programs on issues of anti-racism and equity. Others note the general lack of knowledge of the contributions of Blacks to Canadian society, both in the past and today, and the lack of a social voice on the structural issues and concerns that impact the different segments of the Black and other racialized communities. The removal of anti-racism from the public policy agenda and the failure by government to initiate programs aiming to reverse the effects of racism towards Blacks reflect the negation, or more precisely, the banishment of Blacks. In this regard, many within the Black community feel demoralized by these erasures or invisibilities. They register their concerns through expressions such as "We are out of sight and out of mind"; "It is as though we are not part and parcel of this society"; "We are in no man's land";[1] "We are indeed the children of Ham.... We are banished."[2] Thus the concept of "banishment" calls attention to the repositioning of Blacks in the body politic and in civil society. Moreover, I have selected the term "banishment" as it conceptually and symbolically expresses the qualitative essence of being outside the borders of marginality. (The Black community has often been ascribed the position of marginality in relation to mainstream Canadian society.)

Social Banishment

Social banishment refers to an insidious silence or shunning, the absence and negation of concerns or issues from the point of view of the racialized groups, beneath the pre-eminence or homogenizing of dominant norms, values, and perspectives that flourish within the public domain. Brought on by the racism of the media, this absence and negation of racialized groups have become normative practices within other institutions and in society generally. These practices often begin with acquiescence to the racialized imagery or discourse in the media. The behaviour or actions that follow this imagery, discourse, and indeed ideology are reflective of the "acceptance" of the media's promulgation of cultural racism. This dynamic is captured by Butler (1993:18) in her reference to Fanon's recitation of the racist interpellation. She notes:

the black body is circumscribed as dangerous, prior to any gesture, any raising of the hand, and the infantilized white reader is positioned in the scene as one who is helpless in relation to that black body, as one definitionally in need of protection by her/his mother or, perhaps, the police. The fear is that some physical distance will be crossed, and the virgin sanctity of whiteness will be endangered by that proximity.

Accepting such imagery or discourse is to accept a definitional position in relation to that racialized body or knowledge. Such a position denotes an objectification and separation or "othering" of the black body between the reader and the black body. Henry et al. (1999:29) specify that this concept of "other" indicates "we/they" groups,

> "We" are the white dominant culture or culture of the organization (police, school, workplace); "they" are the communities who are the "others" possessing "different" (undesirable) values, beliefs and norms. "We" are law-abiding, hardworking, decent and homogeneous. We are the "Canadian-Canadians."

Intrinsic to the status of "we" is ascribed power and to the status of "they" the antithesis of power, that is, powerlessness. Therefore, "acceptance" of the racialized person or knowledge is to accept a relational divide in which the dominant "We" are ascribed rewards, entitlements, and other privileges and the racialized body or group is virtually denied such privileges.

As Butler (1993) indicates, the interpellatory nature of knowledge about the Black person or racialized group forces or demands a response or action. This response may be explicit or implicit, at a conscious or an unconscious level. When the response or action is biased towards the "we" or dominant group, it may serve the function of protecting or preserving the dominant group and dialectically rejecting or negating the perspectives, issues, and concerns of the racialized group. Furthermore, such actions can have real material effects: benefits or gains for the "we" and consequences of deprivation for the racialized group.

The sum of all such gains can be ascertained by assessing the preponderance of hegemonic concerns, perspectives, and issues promoted by the media. The dialectical consequences of such gains is the absence or negation of the concerns, issues, and perspectives of the racialized group.

When these gains and consequences are enacted within institutions and/or organizations they amount to systemic racism or systemic discrimination. Consequently, it can be inferred that the society's perpetuation of social banishment rests on practices of systemic racism in its institutions. Such attitudes set the stage for legal banishment.

Legal Banishment

Legal banishment can occur on two interrelated levels: (1) the physical banishment of individuals through removal of the person by such acts as incarceration or deportation, and (2) the withdrawal of democratic rights, legal entitlements, and civic responsibilities of individuals, groups, and communities. The implementation of these two processes usually falls within the structures of agencies and institutions. These agencies and institutions have the authority, mandate, policies, laws, traditional practices, and power to legally exclude, remove, and banish in order that the status quo of the dominant society remains undisturbed.

In the shootings described above, race was declared inadmissible as a factor in legal inquiries into these shootings. Glasbeek (1994:94) explains that "a coroner's inquest is a mechanism which serves to reassure the public that its institutions are working well. It has a legitimating function." He further adds that: "one explanation for the avoidance of the wider issue of racism is that the coroners do not believe that there are problems of systemic racism which require investigations and that to give standing and credence to such allegations is to render a disservice." Thus, these inquiries reinforced systemic racism in the criminal justice system and led to the banishment of the legal, democratic rights of the Black community for a fair and impartial hearing with the necessary evidence *including* giving consideration to issues of race.

Importantly, what was banished was not simply the issue but also, and conversely, the legitimacy of the Black subject. This means that by disallowing legitimate claims to recognize and address issues of racism that impact the daily lives of Blacks and other racialized groups, an important and essential aspect of Black humanity and existence was also banished. Above all, this phenomenon was rationalized and presented as a normative procedure and practice under the jurisdiction of the state and with the tacit agreement of the overall society.

It can also be stated that the outcome or consequence of the legal banishment of racism in the criminal justice system has contributed to the exoneration of all police officers charged in the shooting of Black victims. This is indicated in the statement of the Commission of Inquiry into the Criminal Justice System (1995:377): "Since 1978, on duty police officers have shot at least 16 Black people in Ontario, ten of them fatally. In nine cases criminal charges were laid against the officers. Not one was convicted." Again Butler (1993:18) states:

> The police are thus structurally placed to protect whiteness against violence, where violence is the imminent action of that black male body. And because within this imaginary schema, the police protect whiteness, their own violence cannot be read as violence because the black male body prior to any video is the site and source of danger, a threat, the police effort to subdue (and in this case remove) this body, even if in advance, is justified regardless of the circumstances.

The discussion above suggests the interconnectedness of social and legal banishment. It is often insufficient simply to banish an issue from the social agenda by negation or dismissal. The issue has to be excoriated by legal means or by legal banishment. Thus, where the media perform social banishment, the public inquiry completes the circle by "legally" formalizing that banishment. The combined processes of social and legal banishment reflect a deepening and strengthening of racism in which Blacks and other racialized subjects are negated, effaced in the overall society. The discussion below attends to this recognition.

Discrediting and Criminalizing Black Organizational Leadership

Social and legal banishment were the outcome or consequences for Black leaders who advocated against police shootings and for systemic changes to the criminal justice system. Black Action Defense Committee (BADC) was formed in 1988 after the shooting of Lester Donaldson. Members of this organization had given leadership to the organizations involved in seeking justice for victims of previous police shootings, such as Buddy Evans in 1978 and Albert Johnson in 1979.

The BADC worked with a coalition of Black-community groups and organizations, such as the Jamaica Canadian Association, the Congress of Black Women, the Black Secretariat, Harriet Tubman Organization, The All African People's Revolutionary Party, Black Business and Professional Association, and others. The advocacy and social action undertaken by this coalition were supported by many individuals and organizations in other ethnic and equity-seeking organizations, including members of the First Nations community in Toronto. The demands of this coalition centred on justice for the victims, their families, and the community traumatized by police shootings. The focal point of this advocacy advanced the issue of racism in policing and the need for effective anti-racism action, including addressing changes in policing and systemic discrimination in the criminal justice system as well as in other institutions such as employment and education. Considerable lobbying was directed towards civic and government officials, including members of the opposition political parties, regarding the responsibilities related to policing.

Onto this discursive field the Black leadership was increasingly presented to television viewers and/or newspaper readers. The *Toronto Sun*, 6 May 1992, captioned an article "Coalition of Extremists" and negatively portrayed the work and character of many of these leaders (Harvey, 1992:72). On 5 July 1992, the same newspaper carried a large photograph of a Black leader lying on the ground being restrained by police. This was accompanied by a report with the headline "They gave peace no chance." The report also stated that the tone of the rally at which this leader had to be restrained and arrested was "incendiary" (Blatchford, 1992:27). Often, the sound-bite and headline presented to television viewers and readers would be decontextualized and could be interpreted as inflammatory and anti-Canadian. For instance, the *Toronto Star* dated 21 August 1988, noted that a Black leader stated that "Canada is a racist state, if you have a racist state then you have a racist police" (Donovan, 1988:B1). One of the media's tactics was to promote the leadership as a small band of rabble-rousers who did not speak for the majority of members of the Black community. There were radio talk shows and letters to the newspaper editors suggesting that the BADC, particularly its leadership, was not to be given serious consideration as those individuals were not credible and by no means represented the general Black population (Donovan, 1988; Drummie, 1994).

Efforts were made by law enforcement to discredit the leadership of the BADC through legal means. This extended to criminalizing several members of the organization or those associated with it in a variety of ways, such as entrapment and allegations of sexual harassment. This led to criminal charges against one of the leaders. The outcome of the trial was this leader's conviction. The *Toronto Sun*, 15 March 1994, carried a large headline of the conviction, stating "9-Month Jail term for ..." There was also a photograph of the leader with his name and a caption entitled "Dark Side." The incivility of the leader was conveyed in the article as "Not one shred of remorse" (Drummie, 1994:20).

In attempting to discredit and criminalize Black leaders, cultural racism and systemic racism were strongly interrelated and concurrently were social and legal banishment. The media's attempts to decimate the character and actions of the leadership of the BADC positioned the issues for fair policing and anti-racism measures in the criminal justice system, raised by these leaders, as invalid, illegitimate, and anti-Canadian. Moreover, in characterizing the Black leaders as anti-Canadian, the media encouraged in its readers a "patriotic" response—i.e., the state and police were under attack and had to be defended. However, the attempts to banish the Black leadership literally and legally were resisted with some success. The critical issues for fair policing however were banished as there was little public discussion that broadened the issues of policing to other communities and the overall society.

The tide of cultural and systemic racism moved beyond the Black leadership and Black community to advocates or initiators of anti-racism measures by the New Democratic Party, then government of Ontario.

Discrediting of Anti-Racism and Banishment by the Government

In 1990 the New Democratic Party was elected as the government of Ontario. Harney (1996) noted anti-racism was in ascendancy after this election. Stephen Lewis, a past leader of the provincial NDP, was appointed to head an inquiry into experiences of racism by members of the Black community. This initiative was instituted after street disturbances in downtown Toronto following a demonstration organized by the Black Action Defense Committee against police violence. The Stephen Lewis Report (June, 1992) concurred with the historic concerns of a wide range of Black members, youth, and community leaders. This report recognized systemic racism and it noted that "*at root was anti-black racism.*" Lewis made a number of recommendations that called for systemic redress. One of his key recommendations was for a Commission on Systemic Racism In The Criminal Justice System. When the NDP government announced that it would institute such a Commission, a well-known *Toronto Sun* reporter wrote: "This is no neutral commission of inquiry, but a commission of confirmation, and what it is to confirm is the New Democratic Party's view of things which is that there is no more pressing problem in the world than racism." The reporter further noted that "four of the six members including the two co-chairmen are visible minorities and professional activists who have made at least some part of their living and reputations looking for racism" (Blatchford, 1992:32).

As anti-racism initiatives developed, a backlash became increasingly evident and the media stepped up its attack on these initiatives and on the government itself. The *Toronto Sun*, well known for its racist reporting (Ginzberg, 1985), decried the anti-racist policies and actions of the government. In an editorial on 7 May 1992, the *Sun* attacked the Ontario Premier for his remarks about the "disturbing pattern of police shootings of Black suspects" by stating that "our 'leaders' [are figuring] out new ways to suck up to the latest and loudest special interest group."

As mentioned above, this attack on anti-racism initiatives extended to the Employment Equity Act, a law that targeted four disadvantaged groups: women, people with disabilities, First Nations peoples, and racial minorities. Its goal was to ensure equitable hiring and promotion of those disadvantaged groups. In its report of 11 November 1993, the *Toronto Star* attacked this legislation as a special measure that reversely discriminated against White men. This legislation became the death knell for the NDP government. As Harney (1996:38) states, "by 1992, both government anti-racism and employment equity were just beginning to fall under the shadow of the rightist press's big guns. They were in the end to become the central targets of the Right's crypto-racist election campaign in 1995." The knowledge produced by the media and served to its readers and viewers was that anti-racism and employment equity were special-interest issues. "Special interest" became the code word for issues associated mainly with Black and other racialized groups. The use of this term in relation to other knowledge implied that these issues were antithetical to the dominant values of society and, above all, that they posed a threat to the maintenance of power and dominance of White, able-bodied males.

While many factors and issues influence an electorate, it would appear that the Ontario electorate was influenced by this view of anti-racism promulgated by the media. This was reflected in the election of the Ontario Conservative Party in 1995. Soon after the government was sworn into office, it fulfilled a key electoral promise of rescinding the Employment Equity Act. This was the first Act to be repealed by the present government. The government followed this action by cancelling all anti-racist policies, initiatives, and structures. Since then there has been both social and legal banishment of anti-racism from the body politic of this province and this has strengthened systemic racism in the province.

Conclusion

This paper highlighted the ways in which inaction and acceptance of cultural racism can lead to consequences of social and legal banishment of antiracism measures. For Blacks, racialized groups and communities, and the wider society, these consequences must be identified and resisted if the community and wider society are to advance equitably and justly.

The processes of social and legal banishment have, however, placed severe limitations on community- and agency-building within the Black community. Today much of the Black community-organizing that focused on policing, the criminal justice system, and other anti-racism initiatives has been quelled, as energies were sapped and debilitated by the present Conservative government's actions. This has contributed in large measure to organizational inertia. A key factor that has historically challenged Black community-building is the lack of resources needed to undertake a rebuilding process. There are also issues of building agency within a generation of Canadians with changing identities, perspectives, and a world view influenced and shaped to a large extent by the media.

Many serious challenges are yet to be addressed if the community is to renounce and struggle against processes of social and legal banishment and gain a sense of selfhood as a viable and valuable part of Canadian society. Nevertheless, there are those in the Black community who give hope and encouragement as they continue to pursue the struggle for social justice.

Notes

1. This phrase was coined by an activist in the Toronto Black community and was understood by many as an apt expression of the feeling that Blacks were in a society without heart and that showed little care or concern for issues of equity or social justice.

2. Ham was a biblical figure who was said to have been banished from God. It has often been mythologized that Blacks are the children of Ham.

References

Blatchford, C. 1992. "They Gave Peace No Chance," *Toronto Sun*, 5 July 1992, 5.

—. 1992. "The Fix Is In at Racism Inquiry," *Toronto Sun*, 10 Jan. 1992, 32.

—. 1994. "Dudley Speaks ... For Whom?" *Toronto Sun*, 15 March 1994, 5.

Butler, J. 1993. "Endangered/endangering: Schematic racism and white paranoia," in R. Gooding-Willims, ed., *Reading Rodney King, Reading Urban Uprising*. London: Routledge, 15-27.

Cox, X., and K. Donovan. 1988. "Police Cite Self Defence in Killing of Driver 17," *Globe and Mail*, 10 Dec. 1988, A1.

Crawford, T. 1988. "Why We are Putting Mentally Ill Behind Bars," *Toronto Star*, 18 Sept. 1988, B1.

Donovan, K. 1988. "The Raw Nerve of Racism," *Toronto Star*, 21 Aug. 1988, B1.

Drummie, G. 1994. "9-Month Jail Term for Laws," *Toronto Sun*, 15 March 1994, 5.

Ginzberg, E. 1985. *Power Without Responsibility: The Press We Don't Deserve*. A content analysis of the *Toronto Sun* for Urban Alliance on Race Relations. Toronto: Urban Alliance on Race Relations.

Glasbeek, H. 1994. "A Report on Attorney-General's Files, Prosecutions and Coroners' Inquests Arising out of Police Shootings in Ontario to the Commission on Systemic Racism in the Ontario Criminal Justice System." Toronto: Commission on Systemic Racism in the Ontario Criminal Justice System.

Goldberg, T. 1993. *Racist Culture, Philosophy and the Politics of Meaning*. Cambridge, MA: Blackwell.

Harney, S. 1996. "Anti-racism, Ontario Style," *Race and Class* 37:3.

Harvey, I. 1992. "Coalition of Extremists," *Toronto Sun*, 6 May 1992, 72.

Henry, F., C. Tator, W. Mattis, and T. Rees. 1995. *The Colour of Democracy: Racism in Canadian Society*. Toronto: Harcourt Brace.

—. 1999. *The Colour of Democracy: Racism in Canadian Society*, 2nd ed. Toronto: Harcourt Brace.

James, C. 1997. "The distorted images of African-Canadians: Impact, implications and responses," in C. Green, ed., *Globalization and Survival in the Black Diaspora: The New Urban Challenge*. Albany: State University of New York Press, 307-27.

Kellner, D. 1995. "Cultural Studies, Multiculturalism and Media Culture," in G. Dines and J.M. Humez, eds., *Gender, Race, and Class in Media: A Text Reader*. Thousand Oaks, CA: Sage.

Lewis, S. 1992, June. "Report on Race Relations to Premier Bob Rae." Toronto: Queen's Printer.

"Numbers Games." 1992. *Toronto Sun*, 6 May 1992, 10.

Payne, S. 1994. "Donaldson Panel Seeks Special Response Unit," *Toronto Sun*, 8 July 1994, 27.

Report of the Commission on Systemic Racism in the Ontario Criminal Justice System. l995. Toronto.

"White Men Need Not Apply." 1993. *Toronto Star*, 11 Nov. 1993, A22.

Wortley, S., R. MacMillan, and J. Hagan. 1997. "The racial polarization of perceptions of criminal injustice," *Law and Society Review* 31 (4):637-76.

12

Dangerous Duality:
The "Net Effect" of Immigration and
Deportation on Jamaicans in Canada

ANNMARIE BARNES

Research that examines the relationship between crime and race continues to occupy a space riddled with contention, ambivalence, and the constant threat of marginalization. At issue are concerns about the risks
attached to the collection and publication of race-based data and a lack of
consensus concerning racial definitions. Both Tonry (1997) and Wortley
(1999) provide informative overviews of many of the widely discussed
issues in this debate. Noting that many countries do not keep official
records of offenders' racial background due to "political and ethical sensitivities," Tonry suggests that the collection of such data directly impacts the
ability of governments to improve the negative experience of some minority groups who come into contact with the justice system (Tonry, 1997:26).
While cognizant of the potentially damaging use of race-crime statistics,
Wortley argues against a ban on the collection of such data in Canada and
proposes, instead, a "special study approach" that would be done by
"trained, objective researchers" (Wortley, 1999:270).

Although Tonry and Wortley express concerns about the issue of over-
aggregated categories like Black/White, they follow the trend of most
discussions of race that, even while accepting racial categorizations as
socially constructed, treat them nonetheless as given categories. But the
idea of race is neither uncontested nor value-free, and cannot be reduced
to mere phenotypical observation. Fanon (1963) describes the psycho-
logical impact of being racially inscribed as Negro in *The Wretched of the
Earth*.[1] The construction of racial identity, in a very real sense, traps and
imprisons people who are variously designated as visible minorities or
racial "Other." The term "black," for example, is not a neutral descriptor,
but carries, instead, pejorative connotations that attempt to infuse the

individual with essentialized traits that are almost entirely negative. To be Black is to be considered the opposite, and the inferior, of White. The fact that such connotations are not explicit in most contemporary discussions of race does not negate their presence in either coded language or the real-life experiences of racialized peoples. Furthermore, discussions about race become inescapably political since they embody particular assumptions about power and perpetuate discourses that challenge and/or support specific power relations. To speak about race is, in this sense, as essentially political as not to speak. As political, in fact, as who speaks. Wortley's advocacy on behalf of "objective" researchers begs an important question concerning what defines objective research on race and who is considered capable of doing such research.[2]

Notwithstanding the acknowledged limitations of any discussion premised on the notion of race, this chapter examines how popular notions of the racialized Other intersect with the criminalization and subsequent deportation of a particular group of immigrants, broadly categorized as Jamaicans,[3] in Canada. In recent years, the idea of the dangerous outsider has informed widespread immigration reform in both Canada and the United States, resulting in the increased deportation of illegal immigrants and legal immigrants who have been defined as criminal. Recent trends in Canadian deportation practices have led to the conclusion that some racial/ethnic groups are vastly overrepresented in the deportee population, and have prompted calls for closer scrutiny of the administration of the Immigration Act. It would be misleading, however, to suggest that the racialization of crime, or the criminalization of racialized immigrants, is a recent phenomenon in Canada. To the contrary, the historical record reveals that various immigrant groups have been labelled as criminal outsider at different historical intervals.[4] Perhaps one of the most documented examples of racialized criminalization in Canada can be found in the origins of early narcotics legislation and its link to the Chinese in British Columbia. A brief look at the events surrounding the introduction of the Opium Act provides a useful comparative framework for the discussion of current deportation policies.

The criminalization of the use of opium in Canada developed out of an environment of anti-Asiatic sentiment, most specifically directed against the Chinese in British Columbia. Some 15,000 Chinese males had been brought to Canada during the 1880s to help build the Canadian Pacific Railway. But when many of them stayed after completion of their contract, primarily because they did not receive the promised return fare

(Baureiss, 1985), resentment towards the Chinese prompted calls for a restriction of further Chinese immigration. The government's initial response was articulated by Prime Minister John A. Macdonald: "It will be all very well to exclude Chinese labour, when we can replace it with white labour, but until that is done, it is better to have Chinese labour than no labour at all" (Li, 1988:29). The Chinese immigrant was regarded as little more than a commodity necessary to the construction of Canada's railway, and the government lost little time in passing its first anti-Chinese bill upon the completion of the railway in 1885.[5] Macdonald expressed the views of many white Canadians when he referred to the Chinese as a mere sojourner who "is valuable, the same as a threshing machine or any other agricultural implement which we may borrow from the United States or hire and return to its owner" (Knowles, 1997:51).

Widespread resentment against the Chinese erupted in riots in 1887 and again in 1907, when a protest organized by the Vancouver-based Asiatic Exclusion League turned into major destruction of Chinese and Japanese property in Vancouver. The federal government formed a commission headed by Mackenzie King to investigate losses from the riot. Cook (1969) suggests that King became aware of the Chinese opium connection when he received two claims from Chinese opium-manufacturers whose stock had been destroyed in the riot. King's recommendations to the government resulted in the swift passage of the Opium Act in 1908. What is of significance here is the irony that an investigation into an anti-Chinese riot actually brought about a punitive state sanction that added to the Chinese status of racial undesirable, a label of criminalized Other. The dual impact of narcotics legislation and restrictive immigration policies on the Chinese finds a modern counterpart in the intersection between current drug laws and deportation practices and their impact on foreign nationals. This will become evident in the discussion of the experience of Jamaican immigrants that follows.

"Danger to the Public"

In 1995, the Immigration Act of Canada was amended to include a "danger to the public" provision. Introduced as Bill C-44, subsection 70(5) of the Act now provides for the arrest and deportation, without the right to appeal, of permanent residents living in Canada, when "the Minister is of the opinion that the person constitutes a danger to the public in Canada."

A "danger to the public" ruling is contingent on the determination that the individual has been convicted of an offence for which a term of imprisonment of 10 years or more may be imposed. The Act was introduced against the background of two interracial criminal events in late 1994 that received overwhelming media attention and led to calls for changes in immigration policies. The first was the Just Desserts case in which four Black males attempted to rob a café and a young white woman, Vivi Lemonios, was killed in the process. The second case was the shooting of white police officer, Todd Baylis, by a young black Jamaican male who was living in Canada illegally and had been previously ordered deported. Jamaicans were also, but not solely, involved in the Lemonios shooting. Jakubowski relates some of the frenzy that followed the Baylis shooting, noting that a joint RCMP-Immigration Canada task force was immediately created, and resulted, by September 1995, in the deportation of 497 foreign-born criminals (Jakubowski, 1997). She posed some interesting questions about the potential impact of Bill C-44: "But who would be classified as a dangerous offender? Who would be considered a threat to Canadian society? Will 'race' factor into the determination process? Will any one group of immigrants (for example, Jamaicans) be more prone to deportation?" (Jakubowski, 1997:96). The answers to Jakubowski's questions can be summarized rather briefly: Jamaicans have borne the brunt of the punitive effects of Bill C-44, and since 1995 they represent an overwhelming majority of persons declared a danger to Canadian society and subsequently deported from Canada.

Between July 1995 and December 1997, almost 40 per cent of all persons declared a "danger to the public" and deported from Ontario under the new amendment have been Jamaican nationals (Falconer and Ellis, 1998). Of some 355 persons deported to a total of 48 countries, Jamaica received 138 deportees. This represents more than five times the number deported to the next highest recipient country, Trinidad, which had 6 per cent of deportations from Ontario. Jamaica received more deportees declared a danger than the combined number to the United States, Europe, and South America. Falconer and Ellis cite these statistics as proof that the Canadian government developed the legislation to "target a specific racial group with the specific aim of cleansing the community of those perceived as a 'danger to the public' " (24). There have been other reactions from legal practitioners who also suggest that Jamaicans have been targeted for deportation since the advent of Bill C-44. For example, one lawyer recently accused immigration officials of being involved in an apparent "frenzy to deport Jamaicans," and suggested that the "hype" to deport Jamaicans is linked to a "genuine fear that if a Jamaican is allowed to stay one extra day, they will commit crimes and embarrass the Department" (Barnes, 1999b). Generally, there has been a significant increase in total deportations from Canada since 1995, as the numbers in Table 1 reveal:

Table 1: *Total Deportations From Canada*

Year	Total Deported	Criminal Deportees	% of Total
1995	4,798	1,756	36
1997	7,968	1,446	18

A comparison of the years 1995 and 1997 shows an increase of over 60 per cent in total deportations from Canada. In effect, although the number of deportations increased so dramatically for this period, the actual number of criminal deportees fell in 1997 and reflected 50 per cent less of the total than in 1995. That is, whereas in 1995 criminal deportees represented 36 per cent of total deportations, they amounted to just 18 per cent of the total in 1997, when the vast majority of people were deported from Canada for non-criminal reasons. In the category of those deported on criminal grounds, a significant number were for drug-related charges. In fact, drug charges represent an overwhelming percentage of all criminal cases for deportation, which is seen as a direct consequence of the War on Drugs during the last two decades. The Jamaican situation provides a clear example of this relationship between drugs and deportation.

Deportation to Jamaica

Between 1990 and 1997 Jamaica received a total of 9,993 deportees, with the majority coming from the United States, closely followed by Canada and the United Kingdom.

> More than 55 per cent of total deportations to Jamaica, that is, 5,578 persons, were deported on drug-related charges, including 4,597 from the U.S., and 582 from Canada.

> In 1997, 62 per cent of all persons deported from the U.S. to Jamaica were for drugs; the comparable percentage for Canada was 35 per cent.

> To put these numbers in perspective, in 1990, Jamaica received a total of 691 deportees (from all countries). Of these, 48 were from Canada. In 1997, Jamaica received 1,699 deportees, with 277 coming from Canada.

This increased deportation of Jamaican nationals has created serious security issues within Jamaica and has prompted international concerns about the impact of deportation on developing nations. The Jamaican Prime Minister has reportedly publicly denounced Canadian deportation practices, noting that "pointing a finger in the wrong direction may only serve to [increase] social tension or allow racism to rear its ugly head. No country can hope to dispose of its social problems by dumping them at the doorsteps of its neighbours" (Foster, 1996). Similarly, in a personal interview, K.D. Knight, Jamaica's Minister of National Security and Justice, questioned the ethical implications of deporting individuals who have long severed their connections with their country of birth and who are, in effect, products of the society to which they migrated (Barnes, 1999a).

The deportation issue has also led to recent tensions between Guyana and Canada after the Canadian government chartered two private jets in December 1999 and flew seven Guyanese men to Guyana. The men were left stranded at the airport without any documentation. Canada defended its actions by pointing a finger at the failure of Guyanese officials in Canada to provide travel documents for the men and by citing the lengthy delay in processing them for deportation. Guyana protested Canada's invasion of its airspace as a provocative disregard for Guyana's sovereignty, and warned that the government would not tolerate future displays of such "big power arrogance." The Canadian High Commissioner to Guyana was quoted as saying Canada would be ready to do it again to "preserve the integrity of the immigration system and to ensure the safety and security of Canadian citizens" (Maharaj 2000:1).

Jamaica's Minister of National Security and Justice, K.D. Knight, criticized the insularity of such views in a statement to the Caribbean's Third Joint Meeting of Ministers Responsible for National Security and the Inter-Governmental Task Force on Drugs in May 2000. Knight called for a joint resolution in negotiating with developed countries, stating that such countries must be made to understand that "in solving crime in their countries, the deportation of hardened criminals to our shores stretch our crime-fighting capacity to the outer limits" (CANA, 2000:3). And in a country where the homicide rate was 21 times greater than that of Canada in 1997, Jamaica already has more than its fair share of crime-related problems.

Double Jeopardy?

In a recent move to address the crime-related effects of deportation on the country, the Jamaican government amended the Criminal Justice (Administration) Act to allow for the monitoring of deported individuals charged with certain crimes. Under normal circumstances, unless an individual deported for criminal reasons is also wanted on a criminal charge in Jamaica, that person is a free citizen. But the amended Act now allows for deportees convicted of specified offences, including murder, to be classified as a "restricted Person" when his/her "conduct and activities have been of such a nature that he may be reasonably regarded as constituting a threat to the public safety or public order of Jamaica" (Criminal Justice (Administration) Act, section 54B(1) at paragraph C). Subsection 4 of the Act provides that the Minister may impose "restrictions as to residence, reporting to the police, registration, the use or possession of firearms or other weapons, or otherwise as the minister may deem to be necessary in the interest of public order and public safety."

The monitoring of deportees was rationalized in a letter from the police high command to the Attorney General of Jamaica last July, which stated that deportees were responsible for "staggering new dimensions in the commission of crimes." The letter referred to several categories of criminal activity as North American-style crimes that have become noticeable in Jamaica only since the onset of massive deportations from North America. The report claimed that between June 1997 and June 1999, deportees were responsible for 700 murders, which represents 34 per cent of the homicide figures for that period (Barnes, 1999c). The fact that only 45 deported individuals had actually been charged with murder was cited as proof of the sophistication of these criminals and the degree of fear they incite in the general population.

Deportation seems to have become the modern equivalent of transportation and banishment as a solution for the problem of crime in North

America. And the deported criminal offender experiences double jeopardy as someone who is considered a menace to society in both the deporting and the receiving country. While the full impact of deportation on receiving countries is difficult to measure,[6] it is clearly becoming a cause for concern in many developing nations. Conversely, deportation continues to be used as a successful response to criminal activity involving foreign-born nationals in both Canada and the United States. This response, Roberts (1988:9) suggests, has been historically grounded in a desire "to keep the stream of immigration pure, but, more to the point, to keep profits high and problems few." The objective of keeping Canada White is no longer openly discussed, as it was during the round of anti-Chinese legislation, but the issue of cost still holds widespread appeal to many Canadians.[7]

Women and Social Cost

Indeed, arguments about economic costs seem to constitute a basic difference in discussions about men and women who are prospective candidates for deportation. An analysis of danger to the public cases that have been litigated in Canadian courts reveals a general tendency to focus on the criminality of men, but more on the potential economic costs of women to the society. Images of women as "welfare queens" who give birth to "passport babies" and become dependent on Canada's welfare system are not uncommon portrayals in recommendations for deportation. The precedent-setting *Baker* case, though not a criminal case, provides an excellent example of the kind of language used by immigration officials to describe the undesirable female immigrant:

> The PC is a paranoid schizophrenic and on welfare. She has no qualifications other than as a domestic. She has FOUR CHILDREN IN JAMAICA AND ANOTHER FOUR BORN HERE. She will, of course, be a tremendous strain on our social welfare systems for (probably) the rest of her life. There are no H&C (Humanitarian and Compassionate) factors other than her FOUR CANADIAN-BORN CHILDREN. Do we let her stay because of that? I am of the opinion that Canada can no longer afford this kind of generosity. (*Baker v. Canada*, [1999] S.C.J. No. 99, emphases in original)

The Supreme Court disagreed with the immigration officer's assessment and consequently ruled that the interests of Canadian-born children should be treated as a primary concern in the assessment of applications on humanitarian and compassionate grounds. The impact that this ruling will have on the deportation of female criminal offenders who have Canadian-born children remains to be seen.

Net Effect: Whose Responsibility?

The connection between get-tough crime policies and the political realities that drive immigration law and policy leaves little hope for meaningful reform in the days ahead. Notwithstanding the recognition by some Canadian judges that individuals who arrive in Canada as children, and who later become involved in criminal activity, are more products of the Canadian environment than of their country of birth (*Bhagwandass v. Canada*, [1999] F.C.J. No. 1905), deportation of such individuals remains high on the Immigration Minister's agenda. In describing a new bill that will radically change Canada's current immigration laws,[8] Citizenship and Immigration Minister Elinor Caplan defended her proposal to enact even tougher deportation rules:

> Closing the back door to those who would abuse the system will allow us to open the front door even wider, both to genuine refugees and the immigrants Canada will need to grow.... Our priority is the safety and national security interests of Canada. Criminals are inadmissible (Thompson, 2000:A1).

The minister makes a moot point. Criminals have always been inadmissible to Canada. The question is, what is the extent of Canada's responsibility to immigrants who become criminal subsequent to their admission to Canada?

The legal and ethical implications that arise from the immigration and deportation exercise can be illustrated by way of a fishing analogy that likens North American governments to fishermen, immigration to a net, and immigrants to fish who are swept up by the net. Imagine for a moment that fishermen are allowed to fish, at will, in the unpatrolled waters of the developing island nations of the Caribbean. It would be reasonable to argue that if, in spite of the fishermen's best efforts to catch good fish, that is, only people without criminal records, they somehow landed fish that were already beginning to rot, they should be free to cast them promptly from their boats. But what if the fish became maimed during the process of fishing, perhaps because of the conditions inflicted by the net experience, would the fishermen have a responsibility to tend to the wounded? And what if they caught good fish that survived for years, and then became ill? Should the fishermen be absolved from responsibility and be allowed to return the fish to the sea, regardless of the threat of pollution to others?

Governments of neighbouring regions are beginning to feel the effects of deportation on their shores and are asking Canada and the United States to become sensitive to their moral, if not legal, obligation to think about the global consequences of the net experience. Global thinking is scarcely a challenge for either Canada or the United States. Indeed, the United States prepares an annual International Narcotics Strategy Report, in which it rates countries on the basis of their co-operation in the anti-drug fight. The U.S. Foreign Assistance Act also requires that the President annually certify or decertify countries based on their performance in the drug wars. The 1999 Report certified Jamaica for its co-operation, but gave directives for the Jamaican government to act more aggressively in finding and punishing drug lords and other major criminals. Ironically, the US government apparently fails to see the dissonance between its requirement that poorer countries in the region should spend millions in fighting the U.S. drug wars, at the same time that the United States is dumping unwanted criminals on these countries' doorsteps. Many of these drug lords that the U.S. returns to Jamaica are the same people the Report now expects Jamaica to find and punish! The irony is especially acute when we recall that deported individuals, unless wanted on criminal charges in their country of birth, are free to roam the streets and engage in all sorts of criminal behaviour, until caught. As Knight reports: "On return they sometimes end up as street people but often times, are rescued by their criminal cronies who provide shelter and the wherewithal for their involvement in criminal activities. At this stage, they become influential in organised crime, spreading their network to the very countries from which they have come." (CANA, 2000). Knight argues that de facto citizenship must be considered when decisions are being made regarding whether to punish and/or rehabilitate, or to deport criminal offenders who have severed ties with their country of birth.

Conclusion

This discussion of the experience of early Chinese immigrants to British Columbia and the recent increase in the deportation of Jamaican nationals illustrate some of the connections between immigration and criminal laws and how both intersect to marginalize particular racial groups. With the new immigration proposals that will create even more punitive sanctions for immigrants who become criminal offenders, Canada continues to affirm its disregard for the social problems that are direct or indirect consequences of its immigration policies. It does not require in-depth analysis to make the connection between immigration policies that give preference to railroad or domestic workers and the potential impact on the family structures of such workers, or the implications for family reunification. One might question, for example, to what extent the social dysfunctions that cause criminal offending among young immigrants are an unintended consequence of earlier immigration "labour" policies that separated youths from their parents. Research that seeks to explore such connections will provide a clearer sense of how apparently neutral policies can produce discriminatory impacts on particular groups.

The idea of the dangerous outsider continues to capture the imagination of policy-makers and the Canadian public. And as developing countries begin to feel the effects of deportation on their economically fragile social systems, their reactions result in the development of policies that will make life even more challenging for the unwanted deportee. Confronted with dislocation from the adopted homeland, the deportee is frequently left to struggle without social support or hope for gainful employment in the "home" to which he/she is returned. Homi Bhabba (1997:445) writes: "In a feverish stillness, the intimate recesses of the domestic space become sites for history's most intricate invasions. In that displacement, the border between home and world becomes confused." It is in this moment of displacement that the 'foreign-born criminal/deportee' discovers the unhomeliness of the alienating space to which he/she is banished. The net effect of the immigration/deportation exercise has produced a chasm that makes it impossible for the deportee to find a way home.

Notes

1. Fanon (1963:112-13) relates his reaction when a young boy singles him out for attention:

   'Look at the Nigger!'... My body was given back to me sprawled out, distorted, recolored, clad in mourning that winter day. The Negro is an animal, the Negro is bad.... I was responsible at the same time for my body, for my race, for my ancestors. I subjected myself to an objective examination, I discovered my blackness, my ethnic characteristics.... On that day, completely dislocated, unable to be abroad with the other, the white man, who unmercifully imprisoned me, I took myself far off from my own presence, far indeed, and made myself an object. What else could it be but an amputation, an excision, a hemorrhage that splattered my whole body with black blood? But I did not want this revision, this thematization. All I wanted was to be a man among other men.

2. Delgado (1995:51-53) argues that a scholarly tradition attempts to limit discourse by excluding minority writings on issues of race. He dismisses the notion that such scholars fear that minority writers cannot be objective about racial issues by pointing to the fact that White writers are not above self-interest and may well have vested interests in maintaining the status quo. On the other hand, Lopez (1996) suggests that the silence of White scholars in race-based scholarship could well be perceived as an attempt to relegate minority voices to the margins and, by ignoring them, to maintain control over discourses on race.

3. The use of "Jamaican" as a homogeneous group is an example of over-aggregation that stems from stereotyping people on the basis of shared nationality. Jamaicans living in Canada hail from various socio-economic circumstances and diverse "racial" backgrounds.

4. Roberts and Doob (1997) suggest that the media have, over time, focused on the problem of "immigrant" crime, including "gangs" from China and Vietnam operating in Toronto and Vancouver, and more recently, Somali refugees in Toronto and Ottawa. A recent *Globe and Mail* article focuses again on the Chinese in a report headlined: "China set up crime web in Canada, report says" (29 April 2000, A1).

5. This took the form of a head tax of $50 imposed on Chinese entering Canada. The head tax was raised to $100 in 1900 and to $500 in 1903. Chinese were also denied the franchise in several provinces, including British Columbia (Li, 1988).

6. I am currently conducting research on the impact of deportation on crime rates in Jamaica, but while the study will provide useful information about the actual numbers of crimes for which deportees have been convicted, it will be constrained in its ability to assess the overall impact of deportation on unreported or unsolved crimes. The influence that deportees may have on the commission of crimes by other persons will also remain unknown.

7. An elected member of Parliament, himself an immigrant to Canada, bluntly told this author that if non-citizens become a cost to Canada, regardless of their length of residence, they should be kicked out of this country.

8. Bill C-31 was tabled in Parliament on 6 April 2000, and includes provisions that would speed up deportations of landed immigrants classified as serious criminals, require landed immigrants already in Canada to renew their status every five years, and make it impossible for people on welfare to sponsor family members as immigrants to Canada.

References

Baker v. Canada, [1999] S.C.J. no. 99

Barnes, A. 1999a. Personal Interview with K.D. Knight, Aug.

—. 1999b. "Jamaicans said being targeted for deportation," *The Lawyers Weekly*, 19 Nov. 13.

—. 1999c. "Immigration, deportation, and the social construction of the criminal other," Paper presented at the 4th International Metropolis Conference, Washington, D.C., Nov. 1999.

Baureiss, G. 1985. "Discrimination and response: The Chinese in Canada," in R. Bienvenue and J. Goldstein, eds., *Ethnicity and Ethnic Relations in Canada*. Toronto: Butterworths.

Bhabba, H. 1997. "The world and the home," in A. McClintock et al., eds., *Dangerous Liaisons: Gender, Nation, and Postcolonial Perspectives*. Minneapolis: University of Minnesota Press.

Bhagwandass v. Canada, [1999] F.C.J. no. 1905.

CANA Report. 2000. "Rising crime rate in region linked to deportation," *The Weekly Gleaner*, 11-17 May 2000.

Cook, S. 1969. "Canadian Narcotics Legislation, 1908-1923: A conflict model interpretation," *Canadian Review of Sociology and Anthropology* 6, 1:36-46.

Criminal Justice Administration Act (The) of Jamaica (1973), amended in 1996.

Delgado, R. 1995. "The imperial scholar: Reflections on a review of civil rights literature," in K. Crenshaw et al., eds., *Critical Race Theory: The Key Writings that Formed the Movement*. New York: New Press.

Falconer, J., and C. Ellis. 1998. "Colour profiling: The ultimate 'Just-Desserts'," unpublished Paper.

Fanon, F. 1963. *The Wretched of the Earth*. New York: Grove Press.

Foster, C. 1996. *A Place Called Heaven: The Meaning of Being Black in Canada*. Toronto: HarperCollins.

Jakubowski, L. 1997. *Immigration and the Legalization of Racism*. Halifax: Fernwood.

Knowles, V. 1997. *Strangers at Our Gates: Canadian Immigration and Immigration Policy, 1540-199*, rev. ed. Toronto: Dundurn Press.

Li, P. 1988. *The Chinese in Canada*. Toronto: Oxford University Press.

Lopez, H. 1996. *White By Law: The Legal Construction of Race*. New York: New York University Press.

Maharaj, R. 2000. "Landmark ruling could affect deportations," *Caribbean Camera*, 6 Jan. 2000.

Marshall, I. ed. 1997. *Minorities, Migrants, and Crime: Diversity and Similarity across Europe and the United States*. Thousand Oaks, CA: Sage.

Roberts, B. 1988. *Whence They Came: Deportation from Canada 1900-1935*. Ottawa: University of Ottawa Press.

Roberts, J. and A. Doob. 1997. "Race, ethnicity, and criminal justice in Canada," in M. Tonry ed., *Ethnicity, Crime, and Immigration: Comparative and Cross-national Perspectives*. Chicago: University of Chicago Press.

Thompson, A. 2000. "Immigrant smuggling: Ottawa gets tough," *Toronto Star*, 7 April 2000.

Tonry, M. 1997. "Ethnicity, crime, and immigration," in M. Tonry ed., *Ethnicity, Crime, and Immigration: Comparative and Cross-National Perspectives*. Chicago: University of Chicago Press.

Wortley, S. 1999. "A northern taboo: Research on race, crime and criminal justice in Canada," *Canadian Journal of Criminology* 41, 2:261-74.

Appendix

The following is a select list of government reports and legal cases highlighted in the text and made available here for quick reference.

Government Reports

Manitoba Public Inquiry into the Administration of Justice and Aboriginal People. 1991. *Report of the Aboriginal Justice Inquiry of Manitoba.* Winnipeg: Public Inquiry into the Administration of Justice and Aboriginal People.

This is a two-volume report examining a range of issues concerning Aboriginal peoples and the criminal justice system in Manitoba. The first volume gives consideration to all aspects of criminal justice and includes numerous recommendations. The second volume deals specifically with the deaths of Helen Betty Osborne and John Joseph Harper.

~

Ontario Commission on Systemic Racism. 1995. *Final Report.* Toronto: Queen's Printer.

This report examines the problem of systemic racism in the Ontario criminal justice system. Recommendations to facilitate change are provided, based on the conclusion that racial discrimination exists and the perception of discrimination is high, particularly among minority racial and ethnic groups.

~

Royal Commission on Aboriginal Peoples. 1996. *Final Report*, 5 vols. Ottawa: RCAP.
Website: http://www.indigenous.bc.ca/rcap.htm

This five-volume report examines the situation of Aboriginal peoples in Canada. The report covers a broad range of issues such as education, land claims, governance, justice, family life, health and housing, the arts, gender issues, and regional issues. Included is a list of recommendations on how to improve the condition of Aboriginal people. This report represents the most comprehensive examination of Aboriginal issues to date.

~

Royal Commission on Aboriginal Peoples. 1996. *Bridging the Cultural Divide: A Report on Aboriginal People and Criminal Justice*. Ottawa: RCAP.

This report of the Royal Commission focuses on Aboriginal justice issues. It sets out a new national agenda for Aboriginal justice, seeking improvements within the justice system, but also explores the prospects for new developments of justice such as Aboriginal systems of justice.

Legal Cases

R. v. Gladue, [1999] 1 S.C.R. 688.
The accused appealed her three-year prison sentence for manslaughter, arguing that background circumstances of the accused as an Aboriginal person should be considered. The Court denied the accused's appeal for a new sentencing hearing, holding that the current sentence is not unreasonable and is in accordance with the general principles of s. 718.2(e).

R. v. Hibbert, [1995] 2 S.C.R. 973.
The accused appealed his conviction on a charge of attempted murder, alleging errors in the judge's charge to the jury on the law of duress. The Court allowed the appeal and ordered a new trial on the grounds that three errors were made to the jury in relation to common intention, *mens rea*, and whether duress can operate to excuse the accused's conduct.

R. v. Hill (1985), 51 C.R. (3d) 97 (S.C.C.).
The accused, charged with second-degree murder, appealed his conviction, claiming that in raising the defence of provocation, the trial judge failed to instruct the jury that the age and sex of the accused is to be taken into account in determining whether or not the accused has met the criteria for the "ordinary person" test. In determining whether an "ordinary person" would be provoked, the Court claimed that the "ordinary person" has similar characteristics to the accused–a hypothetical 16-year-old male subject to homosexual advances.

R. v. Ly (1987), 33 C.C.C. (3d) 31 (B.C.C.A.).
This case is similar to the issues in *Hill*, where the accused claimed that the ethnicity of the accused should be taken into account in determining who the hypothetical "ordinary person" is for the test of provocation. Ly, a Vietnamese male subject to loss of face or honour as a result of his common-law wife's infidelity, argued that the reasonableness of his response can only be understood in the context of his ethnicity. The Court rejected Ly's argument, claiming that an "ordinary person" for the purposes of provocation is "the ordinary married man who, because of a history of the relationship between the spouses, had a belief that his wife was not being faithful to him."

R. v. Williams, [1998] 1 S.C.R. 1128.
The accused appealed his conviction, alleging that the trial judge erred in not providing sufficient warning to the jury to be aware of or disregard biases or prejudices they may hold towards the accused as an Aboriginal person. The Court allowed the appeal on the grounds that there is widespread prejudice against Aboriginal people in the community and such views can give rise to problems of partiality with the jury.

Contributors

ANNMARIE BARNES is completing a Ph.D. in Criminology at the University of Toronto with a primary focus on issues of race within the criminal justice system. She is currently engaged in a study of the interconnections between North American drug laws and immigration laws and policies and their combined impact on racialized groups from/within the Caribbean. Address for correspondence: Centre of Criminology, University of Toronto, Room 8001, 130 St. George Street, Toronto, Ontario, M5S 3H1. E-mail: annmarie.barnes@utoronto.ca

AKUA BENJAMIN is a Professor in the School of Social Work at Ryerson Polytechnic University. She is presently completing her doctoral work in the Department of Sociology and Equity Studies at OISE/University of Toronto. Her doctoral thesis is entitled "Criminalizing Jamaican/Black: The Working of Ideology." Akua is also an activist on issues of criminal justice, anti-racism, immigrant and women's issues, and issues of social justice. Address for correspondence: School of Social Work, Ryerson Polytechnic University, 350 Victoria Street, Toronto, Ontario, M5B 2K3. E-mail: abenjam@acs.ryerson.ca

WENDY CHAN is Assistant Professor of Criminology at the School of Criminology, Simon Fraser University. Her research interests are in the areas of feminist criminology, feminist legal theory, and critical criminology. Her publications include a monograph titled *Women, Murder and Justice*. Address for correspondence: Wendy Chan, School of Criminology, Simon Fraser University. 8888 University Drive, Burnaby, BC, V5A 1S6. E-mail: wchane@sfu.ca

COLLEEN ANNE DELL is an Assistant Professor in the Department of Sociology at Carleton University, and is the National Research Adviser for the Canadian Community Epidemiological Network on Drug Use and the Health and Enforcement in Partnership network, with the Canadian Centre on Substance Abuse. Her primary areas of research are women in the criminal justice system and Aboriginal issues. She has worked with women in conflict with the law for nearly a decade at the Elizabeth Fry Society of Manitoba. Address for correspondence: Carleton University, Department of Sociology, 1125 Colonel By Drive, Ottawa, Ontario K1S 5B6. E-mail: cadell@ccs.carleton.ca

CHRIS 'NOB' DORAN is an Associate Professor in the Department of Social Science and is associated with the Centre for Criminal Justice Studies at the University of New Brunswick, Saint John. His work has appeared in a variety of edited books and scholarly journals. Currently, he is working on the development of a formal theory of "incorporation." Address for correspondence: Chris Doran, Department of Sociology, PO Box 5050, Saint John, NB, E2L 4L5. E-mail: doran@unb.ca

JOHN H. HYLTON is Executive Director of the Canadian Mental Health Association in Saskatchewan and an Adjunct Professor at the University of Regina. His publications include books on young offenders, impaired driving, community corrections, Aboriginal human services, and Aboriginal self-government. He has been a senior adviser to a number of commissions dealing with Aboriginal policy issues, including the Manitoba Aboriginal Justice Inquiry and the Royal Commission on Aboriginal Peoples. Address for correspondence: 1010 Wascana Highlands, Regina, Sask. S4V 2J5. E-mail: jhylton@cableregina.com

YASMIN JIWANI is the principal researcher at the FREDA Centre for Research on Violence Against Women and Children. Her doctorate in Communication Studies examined race and representation in the Canadian news media. Her recent work includes a study on *Rural Women and Violence in BC* (Department of Justice Canada) and *Violence Prevention and the Girl Child* (Status of Women Canada). She has recently been appointed to the Department of Communication Studies, Concordia University. Address for correspondence: Department of Communication Studies, Concordia University, Loyola Campus, 7141 rue Sherbrooke ouest, Montréal, Québec H4B 1R6. E-mail: yjiwani@sfu.ca

AUDREY MACKLIN was formerly Associate Professor of Law at Dalhousie Law School and is currently with the Faculty of Law, University of Toronto. Her research interests focus on issues of migration, culture, and gender. She formerly served as a member of the Canadian Immigration and Refugee Board, where she adjudicated refugee claims. Address for correspondence: Faculty of Law, University of Toronto, 78 Queen's Park, Toronto, Ontario, M5S 2C5. E-mail: a.macklin@dal.ca

ANDREA MCCALLA is completing a Master's degree in Sociology at McMaster University. Her main interests are in race and ethnic relations, social stratification and mobility, racialization, and the administration of justice. Address for correspondence: Department of Sociology, McMaster University, Hamilton, Ontario, L8S 4L8. E-mail: mccallad@mcmaster.ca or amccalla1@home.com

KIRAN MIRCHANDANI is Assistant Professor in the Department of Adult Education, Community Development and Counselling Psychology at the Ontario Institute for Studies in Education of the University of Toronto. She completed her Ph.D. at McGill University and her current research focuses on how race, ethnicity, and gender structure the experiences of home-based workers in Canada. Address for correspondence: OISE/ University of Toronto, 252 Bloor Street West, 7-111, Toronto, Ontario, M5S 1V6. E-mail: kiran@oise.utoronto.ca

JULIAN ROBERTS is a Professor of Criminology at the University of Ottawa. He is currently the editor of the *Canadian Journal of Criminology*. Recent publications include: *Public Opinion, Crime and Criminal Justice* (with L. Stalans, 2000) and *Making Sense of Sentencing* (with D. Cole, 1999). Address for correspondence: Department of Criminology, University of Ottawa, 550 Cumberland, PO Box 450, Station A, Ottawa, Ontario, K1N 6N5. E-mail: jroberts@uottawa.ca

JOAN SANGSTER teaches history and is Director of the Frost Centre for Canadian Studies and Native Studies at Trent University. Her publications include *Dreams of Equality: Women on the Canadian Left, 1920-1950* (1989) and *Regulating Girls and Women: Sexuality, Family, and the Law in Ontario, 1920-1960* (2001). Address for correspondence: Trent University, History Department, Lady Eaton College, South 101.3, Peterborough, Ontario, K9J 7B8. E-mail:jsangster@trentu.ca

VIC SATZEWICH is Professor and Chair of the Department of Sociology at McMaster University. His research interests are in the areas of racism, migration, First Nations studies, and the Ukrainian diaspora. He is the author of *Racism and the Incorporation of Foreign Labour* (1991) and co-author (with Terry Wotherspoon) of *First Nations: Race, Class and Gender Relations* (2000). Address for correspondence: Department of Sociology, McMaster University, Hamilton, Ontario, L8S 4L8. E-mail: satzewic@ mcmaster.ca

GLADYS SYMONS is a Professor at the École nationale d'administration publique in Montreal, where she teaches epistemology, research methodology, and organizational sociology. She is currently studying emotional space in public organizations, comparing hierarchy, gender, and ethnic group affiliation. Address for correspondence: École nationale d'administration publique, 4750 Henri-Julien, 5e étage, Montréal, Québec, H2T 3E5. E-mail: gladys_symons@enap.uquebec.ca

Index